Falling AWAKE

FR. MARK BURGER

Copyright © 2015 Fr. Mark Burger.

All rights reserved. No part of this book may be reproduced, stored, or transmitted by any means—whether auditory, graphic, mechanical, or electronic—without written permission of both publisher and author, except in the case of brief excerpts used in critical articles and reviews. Unauthorized reproduction of any part of this work is illegal and is punishable by law.

ISBN: 978-1-4834-4099-6 (sc)
ISBN: 978-1-4834-4098-9 (e)

Library of Congress Control Number: 2015918208

Because of the dynamic nature of the Internet, any web addresses or links contained in this book may have changed since publication and may no longer be valid. The views expressed in this work are solely those of the author and do not necessarily reflect the views of the publisher, and the publisher hereby disclaims any responsibility for them.

Any people depicted in stock imagery provided by Thinkstock are models, and such images are being used for illustrative purposes only. Certain stock imagery © Thinkstock.

Lulu Publishing Services rev. date: 11/9/2015

Contents

January 1
1 The Importance of Being New 1
2 Stormy Weather 2
3 One Tick at a Time 2
4 Weather Forecast 4
5 Sixty-Five Thousand Miles 4
6 Resisting the Tribe 5
7 Grandma's View 6
8 A Window into the Future 7
9 Stop Hibernating! 8
10 Are You in the Middle? 9
11 The Eyes Have It 10
12 Know the River 11
13 I Am So Thankful in Front of You 12
14 It's Good for You 14
15 Digging a Hole to China 14
16 A Cockroach 15
17 Thoreau's Question 16
18 Did You Hear Me? 17
19 Making a Decision 18
20 Guess Who's Coming for Dinner 19
21 Taking Care 19
22 When Life Takes Its Toll 20
23 Milestones 22
24 Stop Running! 23
25 Heaven's Gate 24
26 It's Not the Fall That Will Kill You 25

27	Where's Your Bible?	25
28	The Right Way	26
29	A Safe Harbor	27
30	Take a Look in the Mirror	28
31	As You Fall Asleep Tonight	29

February 31

1	A Row of Medicine Bottles	31
2	High-Speed Good Intentions	32
3	Set Free	33
4	Salt	34
5	Planting Good Old Seed	35
6	The Treasure of Good People	36
7	Looking at the Stars	37
8	Trying to Read the Book	38
9	Make This Day Really Count	39
10	Take Good Care of Your Teeth	39
11	Like Someone Was Watching Me	40
12	A Life Sentence	41
13	Endangered	43
14	What Happens When We Ignore Our Faults?	44
15	Considering Life's Dragons	45
16	Every Day a Gift	46
17	Solomon's Bees	47
18	Pearls	48
19	Precious	49
20	A Costly Bowl of Stew	50
21	Writing a Masterpiece	51
22	Think	52
23	Watch Your Language!	53
24	Holding Hands	55
25	Odd Birds	56
26	Mending	56
27	Buddha Responds	57
28	Remembering the Ring of Gyges	58
29	God Just May Be Getting Started	59

March 61
1 Look to the Night Sky 61
2 Arriving 62
3 Doing What He Could 63
4 Heart Fires 63
5 Levi's Jeans 64
6 Gathered Up 65
7 Take It When It Comes 66
8 Stirring Up Your Spiritual Life 67
9 They Feared a Great Fear 68
10 Leave Your Expectations Behind 69
11 A Nudge Toward Our Blessings 71
12 What Would Old Diogenes Think? 72
13 How About Taking a Break? 73
14 Thanking God for Sophia 74
15 Just Like That! 75
16 Grounded! 76
17 Learning How to See 77
18 Feathers 78
19 Being Awake Enough 79
20 Better or Worse? 80
21 Fun with Math 81
22 Which Is It? 81
23 A Sheltering Tree 82
24 Discovering Your Coaches 83
25 Morning Stillness 84
26 Rabid People 84
27 What Treasure? 86
28 God Behind the Scenes 87
29 Opening a Restaurant 88
30 God and Your Cat 88
31 How Far Away Are You? 90

April 91
1 Loose Cannons 91
2 He Has Work 92

3	Old Pictures	93
4	Introducing a Failure	94
5	Can You Remember Why?	95
6	The Law of the Echo	96
7	Without Wax	97
8	Do You See Now?	98
9	Go Off Schedule	98
10	Knock, Knock, Knocking	99
11	He Is Risen! Now What?	100
12	Time to Glow	102
13	Show Me the Way	103
14	What Will It Take?	104
15	Fretting About the Future	105
16	A Sheltering Shade	106
17	Hey, Listen Up!	107
18	Stupid Thoughts	108
19	Right Side Up	109
20	The Years of Your Life	110
21	A Wonderful Place to Be	111
22	Rounding the Bases	112
23	Be Careful of How You Treat Your Camel!	113
24	A Special Blue Pennant	114
25	It Was that Kiss	116
26	Hands or Feet?	117
27	Which Bucket?	118
28	Out of the Box	118
29	Asking for a Gift from the Holy Spirit	119
30	The Next Best Time	121

May 122

1	Ever Feel Like a Loser?	122
2	Clock Watching	123
3	Funny Things	124
4	Hissing	124
5	Hang On to Your Serenity	126
6	It's Very Near	126

7	Restoration	127
8	Burning the Ships	128
9	Finding Peace in his Footsteps	129
10	Saving the Scene	130
11	Is Your Parrot Coughing?	131
12	Polished By Experience	132
13	Ambassadors for World Peace	133
14	Real Love	134
15	The Right Direction	134
16	Sunday School Lesson	136
17	Are You An Intellectual?	137
18	Good-bye	137
19	What Are You Saying?	138
20	Finding a Reason	139
21	Who Will Know?	140
22	When the Sun Shines	141
23	Maybe You Can Show Me	142
24	Do You Want to Be Rich?	142
25	Stubborn as a Donkey	143
26	Masterpiece	144
27	A Way to Healing	145
28	Flying Right	146
29	Lunch with God	147
30	The Gift You Have Received	148
31	The First Day of the Week	149

June 151
1	Are You Immunized?	151
2	Island Shell	152
3	Make Something Good	153
4	Learn to Whisper	154
5	Summer Time is God's Time	155
6	The Sound of Music	156
7	Learning on the Job	157
8	What Might God Be Up To?	158
9	Take a Break	159

10	Emmanuel	160
11	Thirsty	161
12	A "Paying" Audience	162
13	The Keys of the Kingdom	163
14	Seeing God	164
15	Hitched Together	164
16	The Most Dangerous Animal	165
17	Being Wise	166
18	Wasting Time	167
19	Keep Your Family Out of Jail	168
20	Weather Reports	170
21	Try Something New	171
22	A Change of Focus	172
23	Calling Forth a Masterpiece	173
24	Finding a Bit of Peace and Quiet	174
25	Headed for Home	175
26	Are You Awake?	176
27	Hooked	177
28	Continually Blessed	178
29	Drop by Drop	179
30	What Do You "Know"?	180

July 182

1	Invisible People	182
2	Free	183
3	Wounded Hearts	183
4	A Second Look	185
5	Feeling Pain	185
6	What Difference?	186
7	Now What?	187
8	Around the Corner	188
9	Among the Ruins	188
10	Your Choice	189
11	The Gift of Days	190
12	Check Your Commas	191
13	Heat or Light?	192

14	Grass	193
15	Good Neighbors	193
16	Drying Wells	195
17	Squeeze Play	196
18	Do You Know Someone Who Needs a Sandwich?	197
19	The Long Race	198
20	Don't Forget to Remember	199
21	Mind Your Manners	200
22	Tissue Paper Horses	201
23	Granted	202
24	Organic Christianity	203
25	Eyes Wide Open	203
26	There's No Better Time	205
27	Taking Time to Check In	205
28	What Are You Doing with Them?	206
29	Peaceful Waters	207
30	How Big Is Your Fear?	208
31	Widening the Borders	209

August 211

1	The Next Step Closer	211
2	Take a Hike!	212
3	The One Who Lives	213
4	A Life Worth Living	214
5	A Few Ruined Trees	214
6	New Worlds	216
7	That Kind of Attention	217
8	Too Heavy	218
9	Remembering Teddy's Words	219
10	Unexpected Irritations	219
11	Cut Flowers	220
12	No Time Like Now	221
13	Need a Monk?	222
14	A Walk Through the Day	223
15	It Will Come	224
16	New Oceans	225

17	The Deepest Loneliness	226
18	A New World Coming	227
19	A Deep Pool	228
20	Throwing Stones	228
21	What is God Doing?	229
22	Before the Alarm	231
23	Clay in the Potter's Hands	231
24	Do You Need a Grandma?	232
25	Undone	233
26	A God Diet	234
27	Are You Able?	235
28	Newton's Vision	235
29	Heading Back Home	237
30	The Way of Love	238
31	Learning to Savor	239

September 241

1	The Main Thing	241
2	Feeling God's Presence	242
3	Letting It Go	243
4	The "Eyes" Have It!	244
5	God Close By	245
6	No Pipe Dreams	246
7	Shortsighted	247
8	A Unique Perspective	248
9	Time	249
10	Today	250
11	A Purposeful Pause	250
12	What Do You Say?	252
13	The Wisdom that Comes from Experience	252
14	A Door to New Worlds	254
15	Craving Air	255
16	Someday	256
17	Truly Blessed	257
18	I'm Worried about You	257
19	The Trouble with Comfort Inns	258

20	He Hears	259
21	How Some Blessings Find Us	260
22	A Terrible Sadness	262
23	A New Direction	263
24	The Way We Are Made	263
25	Living Trust	264
26	Blinded	265
27	Wounded Healers	266
28	A Tale from the Fourth Grade	267
29	An Angry Letter	268
30	Spiders	269

October 270

1	Tending Your Fire	270
2	Reassuring Words	271
3	Steady!	271
4	Unmoved	273
5	Unaware	273
6	Where Are You Headed?	274
7	An Inner Room	275
8	Kindling Compassion	276
9	Test Flights	278
10	From a Tiny Seed	279
11	Something Greater	280
12	Out in the Cold	281
13	How Would You Answer?	282
14	Pray for Clemency	283
15	Inner Peace and Calmness	284
16	God Abides	285
17	Garbage Trucks	286
18	The Two Kinds of Reality	287
19	A Funny Bridge	288
20	Take Note	289
21	Are You?	290
22	Echo	291
23	His Good Friend	292

24	Fighting the Good Fight	293
25	Awake	294
26	When Tears Speak for Us	295
27	The Shape We Are In	296
28	Just Be Good	296
29	How Good?	297
30	Under the Influence	298
31	Fading	298

November 300

1	Checking In	300
2	Thank You Notes	301
3	Have You Missed It?	302
4	A Wind-born Blessing	304
5	A Voice on the Other Side of the Door	304
6	Living Up to Our Name	305
7	Declaring Your Freedom	306
8	When in Doubt	307
9	Finding Your Diet	308
10	God and Braided Hair	309
11	Flowing Freely	310
12	What Spirit Fills Your Home?	311
13	Fudge	312
14	Have a Seat!	313
15	Looking	314
16	From the Ground Up	315
17	Are You the One?	316
18	A New Awareness	317
19	Don't Forget the Little Things	318
20	For the Storms That Are Coming	319
21	Change the World	320
22	Oops!	321
23	Christians Without Borders	321
24	Finding What We Need	323
25	The Love that Feeds Us	324
26	Roadblocks	325
27	Da Vinci's View	326

28	Which Is It?	327
29	A More Profound Experience	328
30	Stand in Awe	329

December 330
1	Is It Time?	330
2	Now More Than Ever	331
3	Your Amazing Journey	332
4	Salt Water Taffy	333
5	Included	334
6	How Do You Serve?	335
7	Can't Remember?	335
8	Devotions	336
9	Your John the Baptist	338
10	Saints in Your Life	339
11	Winter Gloves	340
12	Masterpiece	341
13	Chores	342
14	What Service Is All About	342
15	The Gospel Again, for the First Time	344
16	A More Beautiful Place	345
17	Lifting Your Spyglass	345
18	Those Who Serve	346
19	Look Again	347
20	The Whole Nine Yards	348
21	Because of Jesus	348
22	The Best Gift This Christmas	349
23	Safely Home	350
24	Heavenly Peace	351
25	Artists Who Work in Living Flesh and Blood	352
26	Believing Is Seeing	353
27	A Light For Them	354
28	What God Will Make of Us	355
29	A Hole in the Bucket	356
30	When at Sea	357
31	All The World has Changed	358

There's a story about a dad who took his small son with him to town one day to run some errands. When lunchtime arrived, the two of them went to a familiar restaurant for a sandwich. They ordered their food, and when it was brought to the table the little boy asked his dad, "Are we going to pray out loud here like we do at home before we eat? Thinking the boy was too embarrassed to pray out loud in public the father said, "Son, we'll just have a silent prayer." They both closed their eyes and bowed their heads.

Dad got through praying first and waited for the boy to finish his prayer, but he just sat with his head bowed for an unusually long time. When he finally looked up, his father asked him, "What in the world were you praying about all that time?" With the innocence and honesty of a child, he replied, "How do I know? It was a silent prayer."

Wondering what prayer was like for one so young as his son his dad then asked, "tell me what was going on inside you when you had your eyes closed?" The boy replied, "Well, first I could hear everybody eating and talking. Next I stopped hearing people but started feeling all calm; then God came. It was like right before you fall asleep except you fall awake. I liked it. Can we get ice cream when we're done?"

I love that little boy's answer. He describes very well what the many spiritual masters have said about deep prayer, that it is a kind of awakening. When was the last time you took a few moments to close your eyes and "fall awake"?

It is my prayer that this book be a means by which you may "fall awake" every day and find yourself feeling calm as God's presence dawns on you. May your "falling awake" lead you to hear God's voice and know his peace. If you can't have that, well, then have some ice cream. Maybe that will help you be awake!

January

January 1
The Importance of Being New

Can you believe it? Here we are at the start of another January!

As this year begins I have been reading some of the writings of Chaim Potock. In his autobiographical novel *In the Beginning*, he writes, "All beginnings are hard." He goes on to say that it's hard to be a new baby. It's hard to start a new school. It's hard to move to a new home, a new neighborhood. It's hard to be a new teenager. It's hard to be a new husband or a new wife. It's hard to be a new parent. It's hard to be newly retired, and it's hard to be new at getting older. It's hard to be a new widow or widower. It's hard to be a new anything.

Although it may be difficult to be a new anything, being new is one of the most important things any of us can ever be. Being new gives us the chance to start over, to begin again, to write on a blank page, to be creative. When we are new at something, we get a chance to make new mistakes and to discover new things because of those very mistakes. Being new may be difficult, but it is vital.

Being new is vital because being new is the future. It is what God calls each of us to be. Think about it for a moment. Doesn't every major religion have as one of its goals the continual renewal of its members? Being continually renewed is the process that takes us deeper into the mystery of God. When we are forced to stretch and to grow beyond our comfort zones, there is new life in us.

As you stand at the doorway of this New Year, why not resolve to make this year a special year? Why not make it a year of renewal for yourself?

January 2
Stormy Weather

One of my favorite passages from the Gospel of Mark is from the fourth chapter, which tells the story of Jesus asleep in a boat as a storm blows in. You recall, I'm sure, that according to the story, the storm is very intense and the apostles are terrified. They begin to panic, and immediately wake Jesus up.

The gospel doesn't say that the apostles thought Jesus could do anything about the storm. One commentator suggests they may have awakened him simply to allow him to join in the panic and help bail out the water. Whatever their reason, we know that while the apostles were panicking, Jesus was the only one in the boat who was completely calm in the face of the storm. He simply stood up and yelled at the wind, told it to be quiet, then spoke to the sea and told it to be still. And so there followed a great calm. Finally, he looked at his friends and reassured them, telling them not to be terrified. The calm one brought calmness to everything and everyone around him.

That part of Mark's Gospel is meant to show us what happens for those who "awaken" Jesus with their prayers. Do you know why we call the main part of our church the nave? The word "nave" comes from the Latin word for "ship." When we come to church for Mass we are in reality boarding a ship on which Jesus is present, ready and willing to calm any storm that may be brewing in and around any one of us.

If you are experiencing some rather stormy weather in your life right now, why not board the Lord's ship and awaken him with your prayers? He is ready and willing to stand up against any storm that may threaten you.

January 3
One Tick at a Time

The other day, as our students were finding their places in the gym before we celebrated Mass together, I got into an interesting conversation with one of our second graders. I asked him how he liked school. He thought for a moment and said, "I kinda like it, but I'm not glad about it." I asked him what he meant. "Well, I sort of like school, being with my friends, but you know it's just too long a time that I have to go to school!" "How long do you have to go to school?" I asked. "Well it's nearly forever before I'll get out." "So you think you have to go to school for too many years, is that it?" I asked. "No, I mean it's like hours and hours before I get to go back home again. I just can't stand it being here that long!"

Have you ever felt like that young student? Have you ever had a day that felt like the day ahead of you was just too long, and the work you had to do was just sheer drudgery? I think that's a common experience. It reminds me of a story that I sometimes use with people when they are at the start of some new reform or change in their life.

According to the story, a master clock maker was getting ready to repair the pendulum of a clock when the strangest thing happened. Just as he picked up the pendulum it began to speak to him.

"Please, sir," it begged, "leave me alone. It would be a great kindness you would do me if you would just leave me be. Now look at it from my point of view. Just think of the number of times I will have to tick day and night, night and day. So many times, sixty times a minute, sixty minutes each hour, twenty-four hours a day, three hundred sixty-five days a year! It will go on, year after year, with millions of ticks piling up on millions more ticks. I can never do all of that; it's just too much to ask, too much to contemplate, too much to do!"

The master clock maker was a master because he was truly wise. The master spoke gently to the pendulum: "Put all of that out of your mind. Stop and take a deep breath. The only thing that is required of you is one tick at a time. Just take one tick, and enjoy it. Then you will spend each hour and each day in the joy of each tick. Just taking one tick at a time and enjoying every one is all you need to do." And that is exactly what the pendulum did.

If you are feeling overwhelmed by the day's responsibilities, perhaps the master clock maker has some wisdom there that may be of help.

January 4
Weather Forecast

As I was praying one day this week an old story came to mind, which I then used for the rest of the week in my daily meditation. I found it to be very helpful; maybe you will find it to be of use, too.

A priest was taking a walk one cold, crisp winter afternoon when he met some of his parishioners. To make conversation with the old pastor, one of the parishioners asked, "Father, what kind of weather are we going to have tomorrow, have you heard?" "We are going to have the kind of weather that I really like," the priest replied. "Well, how do you know we'll have the kind of weather you really like?" another parishioner asked him. The priest paused and thought for a moment. "Now let me explain," the old priest began. "Having discovered years ago that I cannot always get what I like, I have since learned to always like what I get. So, you see, I am quite certain that we will have the kind of weather I like." The old priest paused again and said, "Wise folks know that happiness and unhappiness are found in the way we meet events as they come, not in the nature of events themselves. Choose happiness."

January 5
Sixty-Five Thousand Miles

I have a question for you. How many miles do you think you have walked in your life so far? I recently learned, by flipping through the channels yesterday and landing on an old "Mister Rogers" program, that the average person walks about sixty-five thousand miles in their lifetime! If Mister Rogers is right, I also learned that's like walking two and a half times around the world! Now that's a lot of walking.

As I thought about all of that walking, I began to ask myself where my feet have taken me so far in life. I was amazed at all of the places my feet – and me – have been. In my travels around the world, I've been in about thirty-one countries and almost as many states. In ministry roles I have been in uncounted homes, hospital rooms, nursing homes, hospices, missionary schools, dispensaries, parishes, retreat centers, jails, homeless shelters, and rehab centers. Once I was even out to a tiny hermitage in the desert. I've been to a lot more places than mentioned here, but I began headache thinking about all of this, so I stopped.

I wonder: if you were to take a few moments to consider all of the places your feet have carried you in your walk through life, what would your travelogue look like? In your love for your family, where have your feet taken you? Try to recall just how many places you have walked to in support of those you love. Consider how far you've walked in your journey to pursue an education, to secure a job or find a home. All of that constitutes a whole lot of walking!

As my headache faded and I began once again to consider those sixty-five thousand miles Mister Rogers had talked about, my inner voice asked me another question: "How far have you walked in your search for God?" That question got me thinking not only about the past but also about the future. It led me to a time of deep prayer as it began to dawn on me just how many miles God has walked in pursuit of me.

So, let me ask you to consider those very same questions: How far have you walked in your search for God? How far has God walked in searching for you?

January 6
Resisting the Tribe

As Rudyard Kipling grew older, he began to return more often to the English countryside to, as he put it, "live quietly." He said that when he was quiet he became more and more aware of the wisdom he had gathered throughout his life, and he liked to reflect on those bits of insight.

On one occasion a young, aspiring writer came to visit with Kipling. After some polite conversation, the young writer asked Kipling this question: "Sir, what advice would you want to give me as I go off to make my way in the world?"

Rudyard Kipling thought for a moment, then said: "I have found that in my life one thing has been true, and I am sure it is true and will be true in your life as well. This is what I have learned: The individual always has to struggle to keep from being overwhelmed by the tribe. To be your own man, to be your own person is a very hard business. If you try it, you will be lonely often and sometimes frightened. But no price is too high to pay for the privilege of owning yourself."

Jesus said something similar to this when he reminded his apostles, "What profit is there for one to gain the whole world, but lose his soul in the process? What could one really give that could be worth his life?" (Mark 8:36)

Rudyard Kipling was well aware of the influence others had on him. He knew that if he was not willing to live what he believed, he would end up being what "the tribe" told him to be.

You and I are also at the mercy of the tribe. We too have to be well aware of the influence others have over us. We too have to hold on to our beliefs, and live up to what Jesus has called us to be. The tribe often promises us the world; but, as Jesus reminded us, at what cost?

January 7
Grandma's View

I recently read about an eighty-seven-year-old woman who is one of those people we all know, someone who is just full of very practical, down-to-earth wisdom. According to the article, this elderly woman was being interviewed after a hurricane had blasted the East Coast. She spoke of how devastated she was when she watched the hurricane destroy the huge pine trees that had been her pride and joy. "Those beautiful trees have been there for most of my life," she said. "I could look out my front window and just give God thanks for them. I always felt like they were guarding and protecting me. I guess that's literally what they did for me during the storm. Oh my, now they just lay in a pile of total destruction."

There was a rather long period of silence after she had made those comments. Finally, the reporter asked her, "I see this has really shaken your faith. Just how will you ever go on living without those pine trees? Will you plant new ones?

"Absolutely not!" exclaimed the old woman. "You can't for one minute think that after all these years I'd let a little old hurricane take my faith away, do you?"

A little shaken, the reporter tried backtracking a bit, but before he could form another question, the old woman spoke up.

"Come here and look out my window! Do you see what's over there? Those are the great Green Mountains of New Hampshire. I haven't been able to see those beauties from here for over fifty years! Now isn't God so good that he would repair my loss by giving me those mountains to look at? You see, God wouldn't let a little storm ruin my faith. First he gave me pine trees, now look – mountains!"

Later on, his colleagues asked the reporter what the old woman was like. His response was simple: "She's the kind of grandma everyone needs!"

Do you need a grandma like that? Have the storms of life that have come your way made you lose your bearings? Perhaps grandma in the story above has something to offer you. When you experience loss, maybe a new perspective on things is what is needed. Is there a grandma in your life you can turn to for that new perspective? It would certainly be worth the effort to speak to someone like her.

January 8
A Window into the Future

There is a Zen story I like that reminds us, as the moral suggests, to pay attention to how we look at things. According to the story, a small snail feeling a bit hungry began to climb a cherry tree. It was a rather cold, windy day in late spring. Some birds were watching as the snail began to make its way up the tree. "What are you doing?" one of the birds said to the snail. "Why, I'm climbing up this tree to get a cherry. I'm famished!" said the snail. The birds all had a good laugh at the snail's expense. "You're an idiot!" said one of the birds. "Don't you see there are no cherries on that tree? Just how dumb are you?"

The snail did not stop, however, and continued up the tree. When the birds had finally finished laughing, the snail spoke. "As we can all see, there are no cherries up there in this tree," said the snail. "You must understand this: I take the long view and know well that by the time I get up there, why, there will be a veritable feast of cherries. Perhaps your view is too short," he concluded.

That story is one of my favorites. I often think of it when I speak with parents who are worried about a child who might be going through a difficult period. They often have tremendous fears and are quite overcome. I usually remind them that when it comes to their child's potential, they need to take the long view. It may not be apparent right now, but the future may see a whole feast of good things taking place in their children.

Learning to take the long view is good advice when it comes to children, and it is good advice when it comes to us. Just because we are unable to see ourselves as worth much right now doesn't mean that there isn't much good to come. It's important for each of us to remember that God is at work in us, and that God is not yet finished with us. The best is still to come; the long view may well be a window into our future.

January 9
Stop Hibernating!

I read recently about a young man who went to talk with his grandfather. "Grandpa," he said, "my doctor keeps telling me that I need to take these pills to keep my depression from destroying my life." "So, why don't you take the medicine?" asked grandpa.

"I'm afraid that it will damage my liver and shorten my life," the young man replied.

"Well, would you rather have a healthy liver or a good, happy mood? My advice is to risk a bad liver, then go ahead and enjoy the years you have in front of you. I wouldn't continue living the way you have been, hiding in hibernation. You can't hide from life; you have to live it!"

Then grandpa slapped him on the back and said, "Let me tell you about what happened to me when I was in college. Back then, my buddies and I thought the world owed us. Furthermore, we thought we knew better than anyone about everything. We were full of ourselves, and yet we were always unhappy.

"One day we got it into our heads that the beer they served us in the local pub was inferior to our tastes. We complained to everyone we could, demanding that it be changed. (Even though we thought it inferior, we still continued to drink the stuff!) We thought that since we paid tuition we should get what we wanted. We convinced ourselves that we were really abused. So, one day we decided to take a sample of the beer and pour it into a specimen bottle and submitted it to the campus clinic for analysis. The following day, the doctor at the campus clinic called us into his office to give us the results of the analysis. He read from the report, 'I'm sorry to have to tell you this, but the results of our tests confirm conclusively that your horse is suffering from jaundice.'

"Well, we were shocked. We did not know what to do. Then the doctor closed his file folder and looked us in the eye and said. 'It must be nice to live your life hiding behind your petty complaints. You guys have got to open your eyes and see that there is so much more to your life than what you want. There is so much you have to offer and to give for others, and all you do is complain about the rotgut beer. Wake up and start living your life like you mean for it to have some meaning. Stop hibernating!'"

Grandpa concluded by telling his grandson, "It's time for you to take your medicine and get on with your life. Stop hiding from life and worrying about what might happen to you, and start living with a purpose!"

Are you hiding behind complaints, worries, or anxieties that keep you hibernating and stop you from being fully alive?

January 10
Are You in the Middle?

I was part of a discussion with a group of men at breakfast a few weeks ago, where the topic was the proper way to guide young men and women in their religious formation. There were about ten to fourteen men there, of varying ages. All the men present were fathers, and all expressed real concern about how to help their children come to know God and be good people.

As you can imagine, there was a wide variety of opinions and approaches put forth, and it soon became apparent that these men really cared about their children's relationship with God. Eventually, it became my turn to offer an opinion or insight. One man asked me, "So, if you were to give us your opinion of what we ought to be doing to encourage our kids in the faith, what would you tell us?"

I told them what had come to my mind as I was listening to them express their concerns and worries about their kids, and shared something I had read about the Buddha, of all people. When the Buddha first set out on his own spiritual quest, he practiced many very difficult religious practices and austerities. Then one day, as he was sitting in the shade of a tree meditating, he heard a conversation between two musicians who were passing by. One said to the other, "Do not tighten the strings of your sitar too much or they will surely snap. Do not keep them too loose either or they will produce no music. Keep to the middle path."

These words hit Buddha right in his heart, and they revolutionized his whole approach to spirituality. From that time forward he advised his followers to seek moderation so as to find the "middle path" – not too strict, not too lenient.

What kind of path are you taking in your spiritual life right now? In training your children, what is your practice? Is your practice one of strict austerity, or is it one of leniency? Perhaps you might want to practice a middle way that keeps the "strings" from snapping and allows the music of the soul to still flow beautifully

January 11
The Eyes Have It

Recently I've been doing research for some talks I am going to give. In the course of that research I came across an expression from an African language called Xhosa. The phrase I found intriguing is the African equivalent to what we mean when we say, "I didn't sleep a wink." In Xhosa, that expression gets translated like this: "When dawn broke, I was looking through yesterday's eyes."

Isn't that a great expression? I came to love that expression, especially after it's meaning was explained. According to what I read, the expression illustrates how that African community looks at the power of sleep. They believe that by sleeping an individual is given the gift of "new eyes" for the new day. From their point of view, a new day requires new eyes, and a good night's sleep provides a new set of eyes for an entirely new day. If a person doesn't sleep well, from their point of view, they are left with yesterday's old eyes. This is an undesirable situation.

That is a great image for us when we are trying to make decisions about our lives and loved ones. We have an expression in English that comes close to that African one. Do you recall a time in your life when you were faced with a major decision, and you may have been talking it over with family, your spouse, or with a good friend, and after a rather lengthy discussion someone sums it all up by saying, "Why don't we sleep on it, and decide tomorrow what we ought to do?" Our idea of "sleeping on it" is another way of saying perhaps we need a new set of eyes to look at what we are considering before we make our final decision.

During the season of Lent, the Church gives its members an account from the Gospel of John that tells the story of the man born blind. In this story, Jesus reaches out and gives the man the gift of healing he needs: his eyesight. Jesus can also reach out to you and to me and give us the gift of healing we need – new eyes.

Can you imagine how different your life would be if you suddenly had a new set of eyes that would enable you to take a fresh look at your life? How different your relationships with family, friends, and others would be if you looked at them with new eyes? This is exactly what Jesus wants for each one of us. Take some time right now to ask God to grant you the gift of a new set of eyes.

JANUARY 12
Know the River

One of my goals in life is to travel down the Amazon River; when I retire that's one of the first things I'll do. This desire arose after a trip I took on the Nile River some years ago, when I was on sabbatical. That was an extraordinary trip, and I'm sure a similar excursion on the Amazon will be even better.

I bring all of this up because of a story I came across this past week. According to the story, an explorer had returned to his village in South America after a trip down the Amazon River. The people of the village were eager to hear about his adventures. "Tell us," they begged him. "What is the Amazon River like?" But how could he put into words what he had seen and felt and heard? How could he explain just how exhilarating it was to sense the danger of the wildlife he encountered as he paddled his little boat over treacherous rapids? He thought about it for a long time, and finally concluded that his own words could not do the Amazon justice. So the explorer told the people, "You must go and see and experience, and find out for yourselves! Here, I will draw you a map so you can make you way there; then you will know what the Amazon is really like."

The explorer did exactly as he had said, and drew a very detailed map of the Amazon River. It showed every bend and turn in the river. It showed the deepest points as well as its shallowest points, and it showed the narrowest and widest points of the river, too. The people of the village pounced on that map. They loved it so much they framed it and hung it in their town hall. They made copies of the map, and each one took a copy home with them. And because it was such a detailed map, all who had a copy felt they were truly experts on the Amazon River – even though no one ever actually made the journey there.

The explorer was quite sad when he saw what the people had done with his map. He couldn't believe it when he realized that none of the people had any intention of going to the Amazon to experience for themselves what it was like. They were content to stay home with the map and know a few facts about the river. No one in the village had any idea what a great gift the explorer had offered them, and no one was willing to truly accept it. They had allowed knowing about the river to be a substitute for really knowing the river.

January 13
I Am So Thankful in Front of You

When you first wake up each morning, and your mind begins to clear away the fog of sleep, what are the very first words that come to your mind? Have you ever thought about it?

For some people, the first words that come to mind upon waking may not be words that could be repeated in Church! Believe it or not, morning is not an easy time for some; rather, it is a long process of forcing oneself to wake up and face the day that has come far too soon. I have discovered over the years of knowing such people that it's probably best to leave well enough alone; these kind of people can be a bit touchy until about noon or so.

I began thinking about this recently after a seminarian asked me to teach him some ways to overcome some feelings of depression. As I formulated a response, it occurred to me that one thing the seminarian could do was to look at his morning prayer. Let me explain.

A few years ago I was invited to be part of a retreat team. When I asked what topic they wanted me to address, I was told to talk about the importance of Morning Prayer. Now that seemed to be a dumb topic for a retreat talk, but the people who invited me seemed to think it was very important. So I went to work thinking and praying about this. I even researched the history of formal prayer, and Morning Prayer in particular. A lot of what I learned was not very interesting, but one thing I did learn was more than interesting: it was profound.

I discovered that rabbis in ancient times put some Hebrew words into their formal early morning prayers. Those Hebrew words, *Modeh ani*, first appeared over two thousand years ago in a beautiful morning prayer that is translated like this:

"My God, the soul you placed in me is pure. You created it, You fashioned it, You breathed it into me, You safeguard it within me. Eventually you will take it back again in the Time to Come. As long as the soul is within me, I am so very thankful in front of You."

Very holy men added those final words, "so very thankful in front of You" to the prayer. Why? The holy men taught that the words were added so their students would be able to properly frame the new day and find many things for which to say to the Almighty: "I am so thankful in front of You."

Those holy men of old certainly knew human nature. They knew that when we take the time to frame our day around gratitude, we would find life worth living, because it is filled with so many things that are pure gifts to us from above.

So what are the first words you say as you wake up in the morning? I want to encourage you to pay attention to those first words because they can have the power to make or break your day. Hopefully your words won't be like those that cannot be repeated in Church; rather, I hope your first words of the day will be more like prayer. Like those holy rabbis from ancient days, perhaps your heart will be so full of gratitude that their first words of the day might become yours: "I am so thankful in front of You, O God".

January 14
It's Good for You

Here's a little story for you to use in your meditation. A friend gave it to me, and I find it useful in my own prayer. Perhaps you will too.

A man was told that if he mixed the juice of two particular fruits together and gave it to his dog, the dog would be stronger, healthier, more alert and agile. The man thought it was a great idea, so immediately he set about getting the fruit, mixing the juices, and preparing the solution for his dog. For about six months he would hold the head of his protesting German shepherd between his knees, force its jaws open, and pour the liquid down the dog's throat. As he forced the juice down his dog's throat, the man would mutter, "Come on, you stupid dog, stop fighting me. It's good for you!" The dog would gag, sputter and shake, and finally swallow the concoction.

At the beginning of the seventh month of this procedure, the dog managed to break away from the man and run around the room. When the dog broke loose from his master, the jar containing the juice fell to the ground and shattered, spilling its contents all over the floor. To the man's surprise, the dog stopped running and began to lick up the juice. This is when the man finally discovered that what his dog had been fighting was not the juice, but the method he had been using to give the juice to the dog.

This story ends with a simple question: "Are the people in your life fighting the gift you want to give them or the method you have been using to give it?"

January 15
Digging a Hole to China

Every one of us finds ourselves rushing from one place to another in our day-to-day activities. But have you ever stopped to look around at what you might be missing in your rush to get to your next destination? Let me explain.

At the library earlier this week, I came upon this bit of wisdom: "It's in the traveling, in making the trip itself, not in the destination, that life is truly lived." As I began thinking about it, I recalled a little story someone had shared with me just last week. According to the story, two small boys were digging a deep hole behind their house. Several older boys stopped to find out what the boys were up to, and asked the younger ones what they were doing.

"We are going to dig a hole clear through the earth," one of them said. "We plan to come out on the other end, just about in the middle of China!"

The older boys began laughing, "You can't dig all that way through the earth. That's impossible!"

There was a long period of silence, after which one of the smaller boys picked up a jar that was next to the hole. It was filled to the brim with spiders, worms, and other curious looking insects and slugs. He removed the lid, showed the older boys the wonderful creatures swarming around in the jar. "Even if we don't get there," the younger boy said, "look at all the great stuff we found already in this hole. Just think what other gross stuff we'll find!"

Even though we may not be thrilled to have a jar filled with spiders, worms, slugs, and other "gross stuff," that young boy made a great point. Some of the most wonderful things in life are often discovered and enjoyed while we are on our way to some other place.

As we are digging our own holes to China, we may see things we may never have discovered had we not paused as we made the trip. We can miss out on some of the best parts of life if we are in too much of a hurry to get where we are going. Some purposeful pausing can do wonders for us. Why not take some time this week to slow down enough to discover some really great stuff along your way?

January 16
A Cockroach

Have you ever read the story "Metamorphosis," by Franz Kafka? It is the story of a man who wakes up one morning to discover that somehow through the night he has been changed into a cockroach! He hadn't just had a bad dream; he really had been transformed into a cockroach. The story goes on to tell of all of the difficulties and troubles he endures as a result of becoming a cockroach. The most difficult thing for the man to endure is that, even though he can see he has indeed become a cockroach, in his heart he knows that this is not what he is supposed to be. He knows he is supposed to be a person, a really good person, and yet he sees that he is not. He tries over and over again to be what he knows he really is, yet he continually fails. Eventually he is killed, still a roach. (How's that for an uplifting story!)

As creepy as the story is, I have always found it a good starting point for meditation. Do you ever feel like the man in the story, knowing who you really are, yet seeing yourself being someone or something you are not? Life can be that way when we let the circumstances of our life or other people's opinions dictate who we are and how we are to behave. Many people find that their career and the work environment in which they find themselves cause them to become a person they never intended to be. Sometimes young people in high school or college find that peer pressure has cost them dearly when they discover they don't really like who are when they are with certain friends.

One of the great spiritual principles of faith is that God has called us to be the person he has created us to be, and if we allow external circumstances or the undue influence of others to change that, we will never be truly happy. Perhaps this would be a good time for us to take a good look at ourselves. Are we living the life God intended for us so that we might become the person God intended us to be?

January 17
Thoreau's Question

I read an interesting thing recently about the famous writer Henry David Thoreau. As he grew older he became aware that there was a voice in him that kept questioning what was happening in the world around him. He was strongly opposed to slavery, and so during the Mexican War he began to speak openly against the war because he saw the war as an attempt to expand slavery. He realized that the taxes he was paying were being used to fund the war, so he refused to pay his taxes. The government took notice, and Thoreau ended up in jail rather than pay his tax bill.

One day a friend of his came to visit him in prison. The friend, Ralph Waldo Emerson, was also strongly opposed to the war and to slavery as well. After a few pleasantries were exchanged, Emerson asked Thoreau, "Henry, just why are you here in prison?" Thoreau looked him straight in the eye and quickly said, "Waldo, tell me, just why are you *not* here in prison?"

Emerson later commented on the exchange by saying, "My convictions are in my head and in my thinking, Thoreau's on in his mind and heart and lived out in his life and practice."

Thoreau asked a very important question, one that all of us would do well to answer when it comes to our professed beliefs. If you think about your own convictions, or moral beliefs, are they just in your head? Or are they in your mind and heart, and lived out in your life and practice?

January 18
Did You Hear Me?

I recently came across an interesting parable. According to the story, a village blacksmith was asked to take on a new apprentice. The good news was that the young man was eager to learn, and he was willing to work hard for low pay. The not-so-good news was that the young man wasn't particularly bright. It would take the blacksmith a longer period of time to train this apprentice than what would have been necessary if the young man had been a bit smarter. Because the blacksmith didn't believe in wasting time, he immediately began instructing his new student. "Now listen to me," he said, "when I take the metal out of the fire, I'll lay it on the anvil. Then when I nod my head, you hit it with that big hammer."

The apprentice did precisely what he thought he was told. The result was that when the blacksmith finally regained consciousness two weeks later in the ICU at the local hospital, he realized that in the future he would have to be much more careful about how he explained things to the new apprentice!

The parable is meant to gently remind us that very often in our relationships with one another we fail to realize that what we think we are communicating may not actually be what those around us are hearing.

Saint Anthony the Great, one of the Desert Fathers, used to teach his disciples that a great spiritual practice is to check your words to see that they say what you think they do. If you do this, he would say, you will save the whole world a lot of unnecessary pain.

January 19
Making a Decision

The other day I was trying to make a decision about an important matter. I was in church praying about what course of action I should take when I remembered something from a conference I had attended a few years ago. Although it was not a particularly good conference, I do remember that a video was played there of an interview with the well-known TV evangelist, Robert Schuller. During the interview he was asked how he as a pastor went about making important decisions.

Dr. Schuller answered by telling a story from his childhood, of a time when he and his dad went out to gather firewood. As they walked along his dad spied a dead tree, which he immediately sawed down. Both father and son gathered the wood and took it home. In the spring of that year, to his father's dismay, he found that new shoots had sprouted from the trunk of the tree that the two of them had cut down.

Schuller went on to describe how his father immediately turned to him and said, "Bob, let's sit down right here and talk about what I have done." Schuller was shocked but sat down and listened to what his father had to say. His father said, "Bob, I thought for sure this tree was dead; the leaves had dropped, the twigs snapped, it seemed to me that there was no life there. But now I see that I was wrong. Now I see that there is still life at the taproot of this old tree. Bob, this is an important lesson. Never cut down a tree in wintertime. Never make an important decision, especially a negative one, in a low time. Don't ever make your important decisions when you are in your worst mood. Just take some time; just wait and be patient. The spring will come. Then you may see more clearly where life is."

Isn't that great advice? I was glad that I had written that story down, and that I could use it as I went about making several difficult decisions this past week. Perhaps you too are sometimes faced with making difficult decisions. It's my hope that maybe you, like me, will find this advice helpful.

JANUARY 20
Guess Who's Coming for Dinner

Someone recently gave me a book about marine biology. I have no idea why they thought I would like it, but I spent about forty-five minutes reading through some of it, and found some rather fascinating facts. One concerns the waters of the Bay of Naples and the Medusa jellyfish, which makes its home there and consumes lots of other life forms, including a particular snail.

The jellyfish eats the snail, which then enters the jellyfish's digestive tract. But the snail is protected from the digestive process by its shell and other mechanisms, and it cannot be digested. The snail takes advantage of its predicament by fastening itself to the jellyfish, where it begins to feed on its host. In fact, by the time the snail is full grown, it will have consumed the entire Medusa jellyfish!

The story of the snail and the Medusa jellyfish is a great parable for us when it comes to the things in our lives that we allow to get into our minds and hearts. We may have hurt feelings or resentments or grudges or maybe even some minor slights that can work their way into us. Before long, they are eating us alive. Jesus came to show us the way out of such tragedies. He encourages us to forgive each other from our hearts so there is no room for resentful feelings. He often reminded his disciples to go the extra mile in loving one another.

Are you letting the "snails" of past hurts or perceived mistreatment eat at you so that you have no peace? Why not take some time right now to ask God to give you the grace to let go of the past?

JANUARY 21
Taking Care

An elderly woman to whom I took communion when I was at Holy Family parish likes to send me little items she finds as she goes through her newspapers and magazines. Some are better than others, but I like this one:

A little city girl was visiting her grandfather's farm for the first time, and she stopped at the barn. "Oh, what a funny looking cow!" she cried out. "But where are its horns? Why doesn't it have any horns?"

Grandpa patiently replied, "Well, honey, you see, some cows are born without horns and never grow any at all. Other cows shed their horns. Some other cows we actually de-horn. And there are some breeds that simply don't have horns. There are lots of reasons why some cows have horns and others do not. But the reason that cow doesn't have horns is because she isn't a cow – she's a horse! And guess what? The reason you and I don't have horns is because we aren't cows. We aren't horses either. We are human beings, and God gave us something more important than horns."

"What did God give us humans, grandpa?" the little girl asked.

"Are you telling me you don't know?" grandpa asked.

"Grandpa, how am I supposed to know what God gave us? I'm not old enough to have been around when he was here, like you were!"

Grandpa replied, "God gave human beings a special job to do. The job he gave all people is to be caretakers of God's good earth. Everything on the earth is a precious gift from God and he expects that we will take real good care of it. That's why we don't have horns. Instead we have hands, so that we can lovingly take care of all God's good gifts."

I really like that little story because it sums up rather nicely what we are about when we consider all that has been given to us. We have been called to take care, to look after and truly appreciate all that has been given us. By taking good care of God's earth, we pass on to others what we, ourselves, have received from God through other folks who have been conscientiously caring for what had been entrusted to them.

Are you taking care of all that God has put into your hands?

January 22
When Life Takes Its Toll

I've been thinking about something I noticed when I was on vacation with friends last year. Part of our travels together involved driving on a toll road, which required us to stop from time to time to pay the toll. What struck me most about that experience were the people who worked the tollbooths.

In fact, I remember one of my friends saying, "How'd you like to have that terrible job? Can you imagine sitting there for eight hours a day just making change? That has to just deaden your spirits."

My friend's choice of words has stayed with me since that time. From the looks on the faces of each of the tollbooth workers I noticed, it certainly did seem true that their rather boring job might have in fact killed their spirits – they did look bored to death!

That image of the bored tollbooth workers is what came to mind the other day as I was reading about a man by the name of Kjell Magne Bondevik, an interesting fellow who has twice served as prime minister to Norway and now serves as an envoy for the United Nations.

Bondevik did something rather remarkable for a politician. During his first term in office he came to the realization that the pressures of his work, as well as some pressures at home and within himself, had brought on a deep depression. He felt dead inside, and announced that he would take a leave of absence to seek restoration. The pressures of life had taken a toll on him, and he had to do something about it. He did not want to cover up his difficulties because he knew that many people suffer in the same way, and he wanted them to know that there is hope.

Like those bored folks working the tollbooths, Bondevik was living in a kind of vertical coffin. He found his way out of his depression by seeking professional help, by taking many long walks with his wife, and by playing with his children. And because he is a Lutheran minister, he also knew that true restoration involves getting into an even deeper relationship with God. Eventually he did recover, and continues to do the things he needs to do to maintain a balanced, wholesome life.

Have you ever felt that life is taking an unbearable toll on you? Do you ever feel like you merely exist in a kind of vertical coffin? What do you need to do to find restoration? As Bondevik discovered, restoration requires some effort, including time with family and friends, and maybe professional help. Certainly it calls for deeper union with God. You can be certain of this: if you are feeling overburdened, overwhelmed, and worn out, there is good reason for hope. We don't have to end up bored to death in some old tollbooth!

January 23
Milestones

The ancient Romans were very well organized. One thing they did well was using trained slaves to walk a thousand paces at a time to mark the distance between the stone obelisks the Romans set by the side of the road. They called those obelisks "milestones." Although a thousand paces is estimated to be between 4,800 and 4,900 feet and a bit short of our present day mile, our use of the word "mile" may well have come from those early roadway markers.

As a student of history I always find it interesting when things from so many centuries ago find their way into our times. It's usually the little things we take for granted that are so ancient. Drive down just about any highway and you will see mile markers. Who would have thought that there were such things in ancient Rome? It just goes to show that the past, both recent and ancient, has much to teach us.

One of history's great spiritual masters, Saint Ignatius of Loyola, spoke often of the importance of examining our past. He did not mean that we should brood over the past, but rather that we should do an "examen" of our life to look for the milestones, or important times in our lives. We can then reflect on how God was active in our lives during these times, and whether or not we responded well to those activities of God. Ignatius said this would lead us into a deeper and richer experience of God's presence in our lives.

If you were to take some time to look at your past as a kind of examen, what milestones would mark God's movement in your life? When did you first come to know God and become a believer? Were there milestones that mark a time when God seemed distant and maybe even angry? Are there milestones in your past that represent your happiest days? Have you ever stopped to consider just how close to you God has always been?

Milestones, whether they mark ancient Roman roadways or the significant days of our spiritual journeys, are truly helpful in finding our way.

January 24
Stop Running!

I read an article the other day that I thought was funny, but also rather interesting. It was about Sir Arthur Conan Doyle, the man who created the famous detective, Sherlock Holmes. According to that article, Doyle loved to play practical jokes on his friends.

The article further noted that Doyle once made up a list of twelve of his best friends, many of whom were the most famous and respected people of his day. He sent each of them the same telegram: "You must get out of town at once; all has been discovered." Within twenty-four hours each of those twelve men had left town. Several of them were gone for at least a month. Afterwards, Doyle contacted his twelve friends and invited them for dinner. As they gathered together, he explained that he had sent the telegrams as a joke to see which of his friends might be scared enough of their past to take the warning seriously. He concluded that probably every one of us, in some way or other, is running from something.

As I read that story, I began to think about the people I counsel, and how many of them are, like Doyle's friends, running from something in their past. One important message Jesus came to give us is that we don't have to spend our lives running from the past. In fact, Jesus came to tell us that, because of the Father's great love for us, we could stop running. We don't have to be afraid, ashamed, or destroyed by the past.

Around this time of the year, the Church invites her members into the great Season of Lent. Traditionally Christians have had the practice of giving up something for Lent. Perhaps this year would be a good time to give up running; by that I mean giving up a frenetic pace of life that doesn't leave any quality time with loved ones, or any quiet time with God, or time for prayer and thinking. Then too this might be a great time to give up running from the past. If you are one of those people who find the past to be a burden, perhaps this is the year to let it go and move on.

Sir Arthur Conan Doyle was right, I think, when he said that probably every one of us is running from something. Maybe this Lent is the perfect time to stop.

January 25
Heaven's Gate

There was a man who, every morning as he was shaving, would turn on the news and listen to everything that had happened in the city and in the world throughout the night. When he finished shaving, he would turn off the radio and say to himself, "The world is one dark, ugly place and I'll be glad to be out of it when my time comes." In a very similar way, each night before he went to bed, that same man would turn on the TV and watch the news. By the time the news was over, he was shaking his head saying, "What an awful world we live in!"

After years of this, the man finally died. He was met at Heaven's gate by a very beautiful angel who walked with him and invited him to come along and see the wondrous sights. First they came to a beautiful sandy beach, filled with wonderfully happy families enjoying the sea and the sun. Next, they came to a wonderful mountain range, valleys filled with beautiful flowers, and gentle breezes blowing. As they walked along a bit further, they came upon a family enjoying a picnic, and they were invited to join in the meal. Finally, after they had enjoyed a tasty picnic lunch, they walked on. "Heaven is a wonderful place!" the man exclaimed. "I never dreamed that I would ever find such beauty, peace, joy, and happiness!"

The angel replied, "Oh, this isn't Heaven. You might call it Heaven's gate. This is just part of the world you actually lived in, but never saw or experienced. You were so full of bad news, there wasn't room for all of the goodness, beauty, and peace that surrounded you."

We live in a world today that is obsessed with bad news. Jesus came to give us good news and to show us how to see all of the beauty and goodness that surrounds us each day. Look around you: look at your loved ones, look at nature, look all around and open your eyes. God has packed his creation with one blessing after another.

Why not take some time this week to clear out all of the bad news and make room in your life for all of the goodness God truly wants you to have?

JANUARY 26
It's Not the Fall That Will Kill You

One of the Desert Fathers was asked for some wisdom about sin. The holy man thought about this for a moment, then replied. "The most important thing I have ever learned about sin I learned from my own father many years ago. We went out to a local river to fish. As we sat along the banks of the river fishing, I began to be filled with many questions. As I asked each question my father would give me some very stupid answers as well as some very wise answers. One of his wise answers comes to mind now as you ask me for a teaching about sin.

"My question and his answer will tell you all you need to known about dealing with sin. Here is the question I asked my father: 'Father, if I fall off this river bank, will I drown?' My father's reply was quite wise: 'No, son,' said my father. 'It isn't falling in that causes you to drown: it's staying in that causes you to drown.'"

The Desert Father concluded his remarks about sin by saying, "Falling into sin will not kill your soul, but staying in it will. Falling in is one thing; staying in is quite another. I suggest that you be aware of this fact as you make your choices in life."

That's pretty good advice, don't you think?

JANUARY 27
Where's Your Bible?

How important is the Bible to you? Do you have one that you keep in sacred place in your home, or is it stuffed among other books on a bookshelf in your basement? I ask this question because of an ancient story I came across this week, told by one of the Desert Fathers.

According to the story, a couple of very curious travelers making a pilgrimage to a holy shrine came across a desert hermit, who invited these curious travelers into his little hut. Now this hermit was reputed to be a very holy soul, and the travelers were delighted at the way he tried to make them feel at home in his humble dwelling. He shared a simple meal with them, which they enjoyed. Then they shared some conversation. During the course of their conversation, the travelers asked the hermit, "We have noticed how sparsely this place is furnished, and it appears you have next to no possessions whatsoever. How do you live with so little?"

The hermit thought about this and replied, "If you look around you will notice that I have ample floor space on which to sit and eat my meals and pray my prayers. In addition, I have these two piles of palm branches that make a nice bed for sleeping. I have food. What more could I ever need?"

The two travelers looked around the little hut, and one of them was scandalized that he couldn't see a Bible anywhere in the place. Finally the traveler said, "Brother, how could you ever be or claim to be a holy monk if you have no Bible in this place? You certainly appear to be a fraud to me."

The holy monk's reply was rather simple and to the point. He said, "That very book that told me in no uncertain terms to go and sell everything I had and give the money to the poor, I sold and gave the money from that sale to the poor. There is not much value in having the Holy Book enthroned in my hut, or even in carrying it around with me, if I will not take what it teaches to heart. Keeping the book is not the same as living its teachings."

That little story invites each of us to consider our attitude about the role that Scripture plays in our lives. Keeping a Bible in our homes is not the same thing as keeping its teachings.

January 28
The Right Way

I was in a local store the other day when I noticed a young man being pulled aside by store security for shoplifting. The young man did not protest or claim he was innocent; he knew he had been caught in the act of stealing. As I watched this take place I was reminded of a time years ago when I was asked to speak to an eighth grade class who, as a group, had been caught cheating on a final exam. They too, did not protest or claim innocence because they knew they had been caught in the act.

The cheating had been so extensive and so disheartening to their teacher that she actually thought about resigning from teaching altogether. Fortunately, she did not as she was an excellent teacher. She dealt with her cheating students in a forthright way so that they indeed, as she put it, "learned their lesson." After she had settled with her wayward students, she asked me to come into her class to teach a lesson on ethics and integrity.

I began my class by asking the students to explain this passage from Mark's Gospel, where Jesus asks: "For what will it profit them to gain the whole world and forfeit their life?" (8:36). After what seemed like a tremendously long period of silence, the students began to respond. One said, "I think it means, what good is it to have a lot of money or power if you don't get anyone's respect or you don't even respect yourself?" Another student thought it meant that evil would consume you until you become a really bad person. Other students said similar things.

My favorite response was a bit different. A quiet young man said, "When my dad found out I had cheated, he was really mad at me. He made me tell him everything I did, and then he told me that he was disappointed in me. Even when I told him that everybody was cheating and that nobody got hurt, he was still mad at me. He told me that no one likes a liar or a cheat. Then he made me memorize a saying: 'There is no right way to do a wrong thing.'"

Isn't that a great line? I liked it so much at the time that I scrapped everything I had prepared for the class, and used that saying as the centerpiece for the rest of the day's discussions. Finally, at the conclusion of our time together, I asked the students, "So, what do Jesus' words mean – 'For what does it profit a man to gain the whole world, yet to lose his soul in the process?'" Their response was short and sweet: "There is no right way to do a wrong thing."

January 29
A Safe Harbor

One day, when I was pastor at Saint John Church in West Chester, Ohio, I was walking slowly around our church as I said my morning prayers. While looking at a series of *bas reliefs* that were part of the walls, I stopped in front of an image of Sister Thea Bowman. As I paused there I felt myself pulled deeper and deeper into prayer. I don't know why I was pulled into such deep prayer at that spot, but I certainly was. In fact it felt like I was standing on some extra ordinary holy ground. It was quite intense.

Late at night on that same day, I was sitting in my chair at home reading when I came across a little booklet about, you guessed it, Sr. Thea Bowman. Because of my morning prayer experience I knew I had to read that little booklet. In it I came across a quote from Sister Thea, taken from an interview she had given just a few weeks before her death. In the interview she was asked about her image of God, and gave this enthusiastic answer:

"My people in life have blessed me with multiple images of the Living God. God is bread when you are hungry, water when you are thirsty, and a harbor from a storm. God is a father to the fatherless, a mother to the motherless. God is my sister, my brother, my leader, my guide, my teacher, my comforter, my friend. God is the way-maker and the burden-bearer, a heart fixer and a mind regulator. God is my doctor who never lost a patient, my lawyer who never lost a case, my chaplain who never lost a battle. God is my all in all, my everything!"

Aren't those wonderful images of God? I have spent many hours of deep prayer using each one of those images, and I want to offer them to you for your own deep prayer time. I want to encourage you to take some time to consider just how God has been each of those things to you in your daily life. For example, when was God a safe harbor for you in some terrifying storm? Or when have you experienced God being your way-maker or burden-bearer? Do you need God to be your heart fixer now?

As you make your way through this day, why not take some time to consider how close God really is to you and try to spend some time in his safe harbor?

JANUARY 30
Take a Look in the Mirror

I attended a seminar a few years ago at which a Protestant minister gave witness to how God had used the people in his congregation to help him find what is really important in life. I don't remember much of what he had said during his talk, but I do remember one story he told.

A woman had come to see him on the advice of her doctor. Thinking of the many times local doctors had sent people to him in the past, the minister asked his visitor, "Have you been diagnosed with a terminal illness?"

The woman replied, "Oh no, I'm in very good health. I'm not here because of any illness. I am here because of the note my doctor gave me when he dismissed me. I have just recovered from some cosmetic surgery, a facelift to be specific, and he said the note was his prescription for my continued recovery. Here's the note; please read it and see if you can be of any help."

As the minister slowly opened the note, he advised all of us to pay attention. Here's what the doctor had written to his patient:

"My dear, I know that I have done an extraordinary job on your face, as you can see for yourself when you look in the mirror. I have charged you a great deal of money, and I know that you are more than happy to pay it. But I want to give you a bit of free advice, a kind of post-op care, if you will. Please, find a group of people who love God and who will love you enough to help you deal with all of those negative emotions that you are carrying inside you. Just from the conversations we have had together I know that you are filled with a bitterness that has taken a toll on you. If you fail to take my advice and don't find a group of people who will love you for you, then I know you will be back in my office in a relatively short period of time with your face in far worse shape than before."

When the minister had finished reading the note aloud, he looked up at us and said," I can see by some of your faces that this woman is not the only one who has carried a boatload of bitterness inside themselves. Why not decide today to let go of that bitterness and do your faces a favor?" We all laughed, but that was followed by a period of thought-filled silence. He had struck a note with many in the audience.

If you looked in the mirror, would your face tell the story of someone who has spent too much time carrying bitterness?

January 31
As You Fall Asleep Tonight

Recently I read a passage from a World War I soldier's diary. In that diary a wounded British soldier tells of a conversation he had with an army chaplain who came to visit him in a field hospital. The soldier had just turned eighteen years old and had been severely wounded. The soldier also wrote that since he had been shot, he could not stop shaking because he was so frightened.

When the chaplain asked the young soldier why he could not stop shaking, the soldier replied, "This is the first time in my life that I came to know the truth that something bad can, in fact, actually happen to me. Before all this happened, bad things only happened to other folks, not to me. I guess I thought I was in some way immune from bad things happening to me. Not only that, this is the first time I realized that I am going to die some day, and it might even be today!"

The soldier went on to tell of how the chaplain had spoken kindly to him and managed to calm him down. The chaplain told him that once you realize how fragile life is, how each day is not always guaranteed, it's then that you begin to treat your life differently. You begin to see that each day is quite literally a gift. Finally the soldier asked the chaplain a question: "What am I supposed to do from now on?"

I like what the chaplain told him: "Son, from this day on, at the end of every single day as you are trying to fall asleep at night, ask yourself this simple question: 'God gave me this day, what the heck have I done with it?'"

That's not a bad way to end any day, is it? Perhaps tonight, as you are trying to fall asleep you too might ask yourself that very same question. Every day is a gift. What are you doing with the gift you have received today?

February

FEBRUARY 1
A Row of Medicine Bottles

I stopped by the public library the other day to return some books and look for some new ones. As I was browsing through the stacks I came upon a copy of *Treasure Island*. It had been a long time since I read that book, so I picked it up and read a few chapters.

I remembered that in college I had written a paper on the book's author, Robert Louis Stevenson. What I recall most about him is that all who knew Stevenson saw him as an eternal optimist. This was significant because Stevenson spent much of his time confined to his bed with chronic illness. Those who knew him best found it remarkable that he never let his constant bouts with poor health stifle his optimism.

One contemporary of Stevenson wrote about an incident he witnessed when visiting with the great author. During their visit, Stevenson began to cough violently for several seemingly long minutes; the man thought Stevenson might even pass out or expire. As Stevenson's wife helped him sit up and catch his breath, she said with a bit of sarcasm, "I suppose even now you still believe it's a wonderful day." Stevenson is said to have looked around his room, saw sunlight coming through the window, bouncing off the walls, and calmly remarked, "I do think it's a wonderful day! I'll never permit a row of medicine bottles to block out my horizon."

I love that simple image of a row of medicine bottles having the potential, if we let them, to obscure our horizons. Robert Louis Stevenson knew the secret of coping with chronic illness and seemingly everlasting pain or suffering. He knew from his own life that pain, sickness, or loss can easily block out the horizon and steal our hope – or we can see a row of medicine bottles as a means to consider life in a new and different way.

Suffering has the potential to make us completely absorbed in ourselves, our wants and our desires, or it can open up a new awareness of how much other people are suffering too. Our pain can help us feel empathy for other suffering folks, and it can help build a bridge to them so that neither they nor we have to feel isolated, frightened, or embittered by what has befallen us.

If you find yourself feeling isolated by pain, suffering, loss, or even by simple depression, why not take a few moments this week to look at the row of medicine bottles in your life and ask yourself: "Am I letting these few bottles block out my horizons, and all of my hope and joy?"

FEBRUARY 2
High-Speed Good Intentions

I read an article the other day by a woman who is worried for her children. She thinks the world is moving so fast that children can no longer be properly cared for. She put it this way: "Our children lie wounded on the ground, run over by our high-speed intentions. We all want to do good for them, as long as it doesn't take too long."

To illustrate this point, she described the experience she had at a recent school open house, noting, "The place was abuzz with people darting from classroom to classroom and from gym to auditorium." At one point, the principal made an announcement: "All parents are asked to assemble in the auditorium to hear the school band play some Mozart. Don't worry, it won't take too long."

When all of the parents had been seated, the band director welcomed everyone, and was very careful to point out that the Mozart piece would only take two minutes. With that said, the band played. Parents applauded, then moved on to the next event scheduled for the night.

One parent stopped by to thank the music director for the evening's performance. The director thanked the parent but went on to say, "I would have prepared a longer program, but when you look out and see all of those tight-lipped parents looking at their watches, positioning themselves to be nearest to the exits, I just lose heart and offer a two-minute selection. I just wonder to myself, 'If we don't have time for our children to play Mozart, what *do* we have time for?'"

This is a very important question for each of us to consider as we try to live our faith in this fast paced world of ours. If you looked at your calendar and calculated the time you give to various activities, what gets most of your time? Is that activity truly the most important thing in your life? Are the significant people in your life getting enough of your time? Does God have a place on your schedule? And finally, are there things on your schedule that you could let go of so that you could live at a more reasonable pace that doesn't leave significant people in your life lying wounded on the ground, run over by your high-speed good intentions?

FEBRUARY 3
Set Free

I was flipping through some old books the other day when I came across a passage in one of them that made me stop and think. The author's name is Mary Barnes and in her book, *"Two Accounts of a Journey through Madness,"* she wrote this very striking description:

"I was very frightened of this big bomb in me, all my anger. It was sapping my life away. Everything seemed to go into this terrible thing inside me. I couldn't spew it out.... There was the urge to throw it out, to explode it outside myself. As if trying to tear it out would get rid of it.... It's a terrible experience, the shattering of the bomb, and the more you try to throw it out by violence, the more it seems to cling, to stick inside you."

That description caught my attention because in recent weeks I have been speaking with quite a few people who feel like there is a ticking time bomb of anger inside them. It amazes me that these people do not know each other, yet each of them described their anger in almost the exact same way. Each of them was frightened that their anger might explode on someone they love deeply and cause terminal damage. All of these people were living in fear and felt trapped.

As I listened to these people, a story from the Gospels kept coming back to me, the story of Jesus calming the storm at sea (Mk 4:35-41). Do you remember that story? It's the one in which the apostles are in a boat being tossed around by a mighty storm. These apostles are fisherman by trade, yet they are terrified and certain they will die unless Jesus does something quick. The problem is, Jesus is asleep in the back of the boat! There is nothing they can do but wake him and get his help.

The truth of the matter is that when a bomb is ticking inside you, you are not the best person to diffuse it. It requires a far more steady hand and greater confidence than yours. For sure, there are many things -- be they fears, emotions, illnesses, or terrors of any kind -- that are bigger than us. But nothing is bigger than God's love for us. Only Jesus can step out into the middle of a fierce storm and with two calmly spoken words – "Be still!" – bring immediate tranquility to the situation.

Are you feeling overwhelmed and trapped? Perhaps today is the day you might go to the back of the boat to wake Jesus. Even if he seems to be asleep and unaware of your fears and worries, he is truly ready to help. He is willing to step out into the midst of your personal storm, and with his calming words restore you to peace of mind and heart. Take a moment right now to approach Jesus. Let him diffuse that ticking bomb so the wind and waves will subside and you will be set free.

FEBRUARY 4
Salt

There is an old story about a king who once asked his three daughters how much they loved him. According to the story, one of his daughters said that she loved him more than all the gold in the world. In response to her sentiment the king gave her a large sum of gold coins. The king's second daughter said she loved him more than all the silver in the world. Again, the king was so happy his second daughter placed such a high value on her love for him that he gave her a huge sum of silver coins. Finally the king's youngest daughter said she loved him more than salt. The king was not pleased with this answer. In fact, he was so insulted by her remark he sent her away from court.

The king's cook had overheard the conversation, so the next day he prepared a wonderful meal for the king and left out the salt. The food was so insipid the king couldn't eat it, and he was enraged that the cook would serve him such a terrible meal.

The cook was summoned and told to explain himself. He said, "Sire, I overheard your youngest daughter say that she loved you more than salt. I know the value of salt, as does your youngest daughter. Unseasoned food is not worth eating. Salt makes food so much more exciting. Your daughter was not insulting you; she was saying that you make life worth living!" The king was overwhelmed with emotion. He now understood the value of salt. Even more importantly, he knew the true depth of his youngest daughter's love for him.

Is there someone in your life whom you love more than salt? Who "seasons" your life in such a way as to make it truly worth living?

FEBRUARY 5
Planting Good Old Seed

I was thumbing through an old *National Geographic* magazine the other day, and came upon this story. A group of archeologists discovered a large jar of seeds in one of the tombs they were excavating. The tomb was about five thousand years old, and so these seeds were probably from that time as well.

One of the archeologists wondered whether the seeds still had any life in them, so he found some rich soil, filled several small pots with it, then planted several of those ancient seeds. He watered them and placed the pots in the sun. After a few days he noticed little shafts of green coming up out of the soil. Those ancient seeds still had life in them! As the days passed it became apparent that the seeds were wheat seeds. The archeologist said that if he had planted enough of those seeds, he could have made some flour and used it to make bread from the fields of some ancient pharaoh.

As I read that article, I wondered if there were any ancient seeds in me that needed to be planted. Might you too have some ancient seeds within you that could come to life and produce good fruit if you put them in rich soil, and nourish them with water and sun? Are there good intentions within you that you've always wanted to bring forth but haven't found the time to do so? Perhaps today is the day.

If five thousand year old seeds could sprout with new life, I'm sure our inner seed that aren't quite that old can certainly bring new life. Go ahead and plant some good seed today!

FEBRUARY 6
The Treasure of Good People

How aware are you of the people in your life? Who are the people who make a difference to you? You might be quick to think of your spouse, your children or grandchildren, or your parents. You might think of relatives, good neighbors, friends you've had for years, college roommates, or even co-workers. But maybe we need to think again. Let me explain.

It might have been former Mayor Michael Bloomberg of New York who told this story, though I'm not certain of this. According to the story, an older, married couple was walking in New York City one evening. As they walked, they came across an electricity generating station, quietly humming along. The wife turned to her husband and said, "We've lived here for years now; have you ever noticed this station?" He replied, "I never knew it was here; I can't believe I never stumbled over it before, but it does look like it's been here a long time."

Bloomberg's comment was this: "Some people among us are just like that hidden generator station – people who quietly go about doing their jobs, running farms, pumping gas, fixing shoes, cutting hair, teaching children, cleaning buildings, driving a truck that delivers goods. Like that station, there are people who keep the city running, inconspicuous people who make the world a better place to live."

Who are some of the quiet, inconspicuous people in your life who make your world a better place? Is there anyone who has made a big impact on your life that you may have taken for granted because they are unassuming? Are you aware of all of the people who really are a gift to you?

As Lent approaches, it's a good time to become more aware of the gift and treasure of the good people in our lives.

February 7
Looking at the Stars

I was going through some old files the other day, and came across a notebook from a college philosophy course I had taken back in the 70s. In it I had jotted down some thoughts about the famous philosopher Soren Kierkegaard. He often taught his students by using parables, and in one of his most famous parables he told the following story:

A wealthy man is driving along at night in his well-lighted carriage, looking comfortable and secure. But because of the light that fills his carriage, and because of all the material things that he has gathered around him on the seats, the wealthy man is unable to see outside his own carriage. Therefore he never even notices the beautiful stars shining above him. He never sees beyond his well-lighted, warm, and secure little world. In contrast, a poor peasant who also is driving along that same night is not in a warm, secure carriage. Rather, he is driving a rather primitive wagon in which he sits out in the open. From his vantage point he is able to see the vast array of stars that fills the Heavens, and his thoughts immediately turn to the maker of those Heavens.

Kierkegaard concludes his parable by commenting about how tragic it is for our life when we allow the false sense of security we get from material things to obscure our view of the stars, cutting us off from a wonderful view of God's goodness.

I used that parable in my prayer this past week because every day recently there are more and more people telling me they have lost their jobs. What a terribly frightening thing it is to lose a job. Yet perhaps Kierkegaard has some light to shed on difficult times such as that. He taught his students that big changes in life, like losing a job, a divorce, or even a death, can become opportunities to see life in a whole new way.

If you are going through a rough time right now, perhaps it is time to pay attention to how you are looking at things. Maybe God will use your present difficulties to give you a new view of the stars -- maybe even a new way to live your life.

FEBRUARY 8
Trying to Read the Book

There is a story told of Saint Anthony the Great, the desert hermit. It happened that one day he was sitting by the side of the road, reading a book under an old tree. A stranger happened by and said, "Oh, you are that holy man everyone talks about. What are you reading?" Anthony replied, "I am reading an old sacred book."

"So, what is that book about?" asked the stranger.

"It's about God himself," answered Anthony.

"Who is God?" the stranger asked.

"God," said the saint, "is the Lord of the Universe."

To this the stranger replied, "I only believe in those things I can see with my own eyes. Where is this God you are reading about? Where does this Lord of the Universe live? Like many things in my life, this makes no sense to me."

With that, Saint Anthony stood up, walked ten paces away from the man, turned around, and held the book open for the stranger to see. "Read this book to me," Anthony commanded.

"How can I read that book to you when you hold it at such a far distance from me?" asked the stranger.

Then the saint held the open book so close to the stranger's face that it literally was touching his nose. "Read the book to me now." Anthony said.

"But how could I ever be able to read this book when it is so close to my face? I cannot see anything clearly," the stranger replied.

"Indeed you cannot see," the saint said. "You cannot see and you cannot focus your eyes on the print because you are blinded by faulty perspective."

If you are going through a period of time in which you find yourself questioning things or not fully understanding what is happening in your life, perhaps you, like the stranger above, are finding it difficult to read the book. Maybe this is a good time to check your perspective. Maybe it's time to read some Scripture and pray with it. Maybe this would be a good time to consult with someone whose perspective you trust. Talking things over with a good friend may give you a new way of seeing things, a new lease on life. Give it a try and see what happens.

FEBRUARY 9
Make This Day Really Count

There is an old story about a teacher who, each morning after he had greeted his students, would ask them to be as quiet as they could be. After they had all calmed down and were sitting quietly in their places, he would turn to them and say, "In the quiet that we all experience, I want you to picture the pile of words that are in your hearts and your minds, but not yet in your mouth."

"Think for a moment of all of the words you might say today. You have many words to choose from; more importantly, you have decisions to make about how you will use those words. Will you use them to make others feel good about themselves, or will you use them in such a way that others will be hurt – like throwing a stone at those around you? There are words in your heart and in your mind that can make a very sad person a lot happier. There are also words there that could make a discouraged person see things differently simply because you kindly spoke some well-chosen words to them. Be sure to make this day count by choosing words that make the people around you better off for having been with you today."

Why not take a few moments to be quiet, to consider the pile of words in your heart and mind. What words could you choose to use this day with your loved ones, co-workers, classmates, friends, or those you meet for the first time today that would make them better off for having been with you? Choose to make this day really count for yourself and those you come in contact with.

FEBRUARY 10
Take Good Care of Your Teeth

A group of fourth graders were asked to write a paragraph about how to take care of their teeth. One student wrote a long paragraph on the importance of brushing your teeth after every meal. Another student wrote a paragraph in which he said there are three things you must do if you want to have good teeth. "First, "he said. "You must make sure you have a very good dentist who can take a good look in your mouth to see just what you have in there." He went on, "Second, you have to make sure you brush your teeth a whole lot. Then the most important thing you can do to keep your good teeth is to watch out for shovers at the drinking fountain!"

Isn't that great advice? I loved reading that little essay because I could immediately see a homily in it. Looking out for "shovers" is probably one of the most important things we need to do in life. Just take a few moments to consider your own experience. In the past, when you have gotten into trouble or when you have been hurt, wasn't there some kind of shover involved who pushed you into bad decisions or who caused you some kind of painful loss because they forced you into something before you were ready for it?

That little fourth grader was wise beyond his years. Taking good care of your teeth involves not only brushing and flossing, but also being vigilant to what others may carelessly do to your teeth as well. And while vigilant care is important for our teeth, it is even more important for our hearts and souls.

Maintaining a healthy spiritual life is not only about being faithful to our good practices, but also about being vigilant to what effect other people might have on our hearts and souls. Looking out for shovers is good advice indeed.

February 11
Like Someone Was Watching Me

I had an interesting conversation this week with a guy who had just come back from a wonderful vacation with his wife and children. As we talked about all the things they had done on their vacation, my friend stopped and looked at me with a rather strange look. "I need to tell you what happened to me while I was on vacation. It's shaken me up a bit," he said.

"Tell me what happened," I said.

"We were up in Michigan, and I decided to get up early, before my family got out of bed. I wanted to take a walk in the woods and experience nature. So, I got up at about 5 a.m., got in the car, and drove a few miles away from where we had rented a cabin. I got out of the car and walked into the woods. It was absolutely beautiful, peaceful and so still. You could hear just a faint breeze through the trees, and maybe a bird or two chirping. Then all of a sudden, I felt as if someone was watching me."

"Were you afraid?" I asked.

"Absolutely, more frightened then I have ever been," he said.

"Did you think it was a wild animal out to get you, or did you think there were people out there who might harm you?" I asked.

After a long pause, my friend said, "It didn't feel like something hostile watching me. It was a kind of presence. When things got really quiet, I could feel this very strong presence. I knew it saw me and was looking at me, but I got scared and ran back to my car. I quickly turned on the radio so I could get out of the quiet."

"Was it an evil presence that you felt out there in the woods?" I asked.

"No," he said. "I really think it was God. I got scared because I've never felt God so close to me before. I thought he might be mad at me, or that somehow I didn't measure up. I know this sounds weird, but it happened and I can't get it out of my mind. I keep thinking that I wish I were a better person. I wish I had been able to stay out there in the woods, but I just got scared. What should I do?"

My response was simple: "Go back. Go find some woods, take a walk, and when it gets quiet again, don't run. Stay put. When God looks at us, it's with love. You don't need to be afraid. Go back. You'll see that the one who was looking at you loves you just the way you are. Go back. Don't run this time."

I've been thinking a lot about this conversation recently. This week, I went out early in the morning for a slow walk on our nature trail here behind the church. It was very quiet. There was a gentle breeze (although it was a humid, hot morning), and then it happened – I felt like someone was watching me. I stopped and began to tell God all my troubles.

When was the last time you felt like someone was watching you?

FEBRUARY 12
A Life Sentence

There is a story that tells of a man who, while walking on the beach, found a used, magic lamp washed up on the beach. After dutifully rubbing the lamp, he saw before him a genie who told him that the lamp contained just one more wish. "Choose wisely!" the genie warned. The man pondered this for a moment, and finally requested a copy of the stock page from the local newspaper dated for exactly one year from the present date. "I'll make a financial killing with that kind of knowledge," the man thought.

There was a puff of smoke, and he genie was gone. In his place was the financial news for the date requested. Gleefully the man sat down to study the paper and plot his new financial course of action. He made copious notes, growing more and more excited as he garnered all kinds of useful information. Finally, he turned the page and was shocked to see what was on the very next page – the obituaries! And the name at the top of the obituaries was, as you might have guessed, his.

The man was angry yet frightened. He began to scream, and yelled for the genie to reappear – and in a sudden flash, he did.

"How dare you pull such a miserable trick on me, to grant me such valuable information and then to show me how little good it will do me as a dead man!"

"I gave you one of God's greatest gifts!" the genie replied.

"What kind of gift did you give me? You gave me a death sentence!" the man screamed back.

The genie tried to calm the man down, but the more he tried the unhappier the man became. Finally, the genie said, "Let me explain what a valuable gift you have just received."

"The valuable knowledge in that newspaper is not the financial information, even though that is precisely the information you had been seeking. The truly valuable information is the knowledge that you have just one year left of life. Now, knowing that you have just one year left is a blessing because it is a reminder of just how precious are your life and your time here. You now have a choice to make. You can either take this knowledge as a 'death sentence,' or as a 'life sentence.' If you take it as a death sentence, then you will waste this valuable time being angry and bitter, complaining about how life has cheated you. This will be a year of misery, and you will end up isolating yourself from every family member and every friend you have. You will die alone, full of rage."

"On the other hand, you could accept this knowledge as a life sentence, in which you have been given the gift of a year to make a difference, to make your remaining time here on earth truly remarkable, rich, and rewarding.

You've been given the gift of knowing that every day is precious. You've been given the knowledge that you cannot afford to waste a single one of those days in anger, bitterness, pettiness, or meaningless spats. No matter how much time you have left, remember: life is truly a gift. You have been given a life sentence. Use it well."

The time we have to live is truly precious. Choose today to use your time well.

FEBRUARY 13
Endangered

A few weeks ago I stopped over at the Cincinnati Zoo to take a bit of a break and look at some of my favorite animals. Near several enclosures in which some of the more exotic animals were being displayed, I saw little signs reminding zoo patrons that the animals we were viewing were endangered species. As I was looking at a black rhino, I overheard a man talking to his little girl about how some of these animals are very rare, and that we may be the last people to ever see them. The little girl's eyes got very large as she looked at the rhinos. "Are they leaving right now?" she asked. "Will you take their picture with your phone, daddy? I want to remember them."

The other patrons around the rhino exhibit smiled as they listened to the little girl's worried questions. One woman in the crowd looked at the little one and said, "Don't worry, honey, the zookeepers will take very good care of the rhinos so that they will be here for a very long time. Don't you worry about Mr. and Mrs. Rhino!" Then she glared at the little girl's father and walked away.

As I continued to look at other exhibits, I kept thinking of all the "Mr. and Mrs. Rhinos" in our world that are endangered. It occurred to me that there are lots of things that are endangered, and not all of them are plants and animals.

One thing that is endangered for many of us is peace and quiet. We all live at such a hectic pace, our minds filled with so many worries and anxieties, that we can never really find a moment of solitude or quiet. I read an article that said most of us live in a TGIF world and therefore, we will never be able to have any peace and quiet because our peaceable existence

Fr. Mark Burger

is invaded by TGIF. So what is TGIF? It's an anagram for Twitter, Google, iPhone, and Facebook. All those wonderful electronic connections that make it possible for us to stay in touch, stay on top, stay informed, stay current 24/7, also make it almost impossible to have peace and quiet.

Take a step to preserve an "endangered species" in your life. Perhaps today is a good day to take a half hour or so to turn off all of those devices and take a break so you can have that rare, exotic gift: peace and quiet.

FEBRUARY 14
What Happens When We Ignore Our Faults?

I was at the public library the other day looking through some of the periodicals when I came upon an article written in 1998 about a little village near Istanbul. According to that article the government had advised the leaders of the village that official government surveyors had determined that their village was situated precisely on the middle of an earthquake fault.

Realizing this was a rather serious situation, the leadership of the village called all of the people together to advise them of the situation, and determine what action the villagers should take. Everyone was allowed to speak and offer his or her advice as to what should be done. Almost every person present had some comment to make. Finally, four hours later, the village leadership composed a letter to the government surveyors to advise them on what the villagers wanted the government to do on their behalf. The villagers said, "Our advice is to tell the government to please move the earthquake fault." The letter was signed by the village leadership as well as by the head of each village household, and was dated April 1998. In the summer of 1999 one of the largest earthquakes ever to hit Istanbul struck and wiped out that entire village.

If it were not so tragic in its results, the attitude of the villagers would be almost comical. Those villagers had not heeded the warning. They refused to see the facts straight on and instead wanted the facts altered to fit their desires. Rather than move themselves they demanded that the fault be moved. In a sense, they thought they were at the center of the universe and that everything should conform to what they wanted. The result of such shortsighted thinking was catastrophic. Many died and everyone lost everything they owned.

I'm sure most of us would say those villagers were simply foolish. Yet I wonder if we too might make similarly silly decisions when we are faced with unpleasant circumstances? How often do we try to alter the facts to fit what we want, rather than what's best for everyone?

As John the Baptist said, all of us are called to make a highway for our God (Mark 1:3). That means we need to remember we are not at the center of the universe, and not everything is conformed to what we want. We cannot afford to ignore our "faults." We may try to do things our own way, but wisdom has shown that God almost always has a better plan. John reminds us to trust what God is doing. It usually turns out much better for us when we do.

FEBRUARY 15
Considering Life's Dragons

Do you spend a lot of time being afraid? I'm sure we all spend some time being afraid, but I know that some people spend a great deal of time being afraid. Late last week, after I had spent an hour with someone who was very much afraid of what people thought of him, I happened on a parable about fear.

The parable comes from an ancient source out of China. According to the story, there once was a huge dragon in China who went from village to village, from countryside to countryside, killing cattle, dogs, chickens, and even farmers and their children. Obviously, all the inhabitants of the area were terrified. And so the people went in search of a great wizard in the hope that he could slay the dragon.

Finally, they found a wizard and told him what they wanted. But the wizard asked, "Why don't all of you band together and kill the beast?"

"We are far too frightened even to approach that horrible dragon. Please help us kill it!" the people begged.

The wizard said, "I cannot slay the dragon myself, magician though I am, for I too am afraid and trembling. But I will find you the man who will have the power to do so."

With that the wizard transformed himself into a dragon. He took up a position on a bridge so that everyone who did not know it was really the magician was too afraid to even go near the bridge. One day, however, a wise traveler came up to the bridge and spied the dragon sitting there. The traveler came closer, looked, then calmly climbed over the dragon and walked on.

At once the wizard transformed himself back into human form and called out to the traveler, "Come back, my friend. I have been waiting here for weeks for one who is not afraid."

The traveler replied, "Why, certainly I am not afraid. I learned long ago from a wise mentor that fear is really in the way you look at things, not in the things themselves. Just take time to consider the way you are looking at things and that dragon of fear will dissipate."

Jesus came and climbed over many "dragons." He will lead you and guide you so you too can calmly approach, climb over, and walk on from any fear that threatens to kill your spirit.

FEBRUARY 16
Every Day a Gift

Are you happy? So many people spend all their energy on the pursuit of happiness, and yet they seem unable to find it. The strange thing about happiness is that many people only recognize it years later. Many people find happiness only by looking back over their lives to times when they *were* happy, as if happiness only belongs to the past.

Most studies that have been done on happiness reveal that real happiness is almost always associated with times of struggle and difficulty, rather than times of success. Most folks look back fondly on the first years of their marriage as the happiest days of their lives, when money was scarce and burdens overwhelming.

It reminds me of a conversation I had with a young couple the other day. They were talking about how they had both lost their jobs and their house, and were now in a new place. The young woman then said, "You know, we just got a new place to live and it's a place I would never have accepted in the past as suitable. Yet now it's the most wonderful place, because in all our difficulties we still have a home. I realize that as long as we have each other we will always have a home. One day, when we have better jobs and money gets better, we might have a better house. Right now, though, we are happy just to be together, wherever we find ourselves."

So, are you happy? Are these present days, though they may be difficult in some ways, really the "good old days" you may one day look back on with fondness? Jesus taught us that every day is a gift from God, and within the confines of each day you can find true happiness. Are you aware of just how blessed you are? Are you aware that you may have one of the most valuable treasures anyone could ever imagine? That treasure, that blessing is simply summed up in one word: happiness. Take some time today to give thanks for the happiness this day offers you.

FEBRUARY 17
Solomon's Bees

The bible says that King Solomon was the wisest person who ever lived, and there are many stories the rabbis have told throughout the centuries that illustrate his wisdom. One of these stories is about the queen of Sheba, who came to visit Solomon on more than one occasion. She was quite taken with the wise king, and longed to see him display his wisdom.

One day she decided to put him to the test. She brought him artificial flowers that were so perfectly formed no human eye could tell them apart from real flowers. She put them in a vase on Solomon's table in his throne room, next to the flowers from his garden. As he came in, the queen of Sheba said, "Solomon, you are the wisest man in the world. Tell me, without touching these flowers, which are real and which are not?"

Solomon studied the flowers for a long time and spoke not one word, until finally he said, "Open the windows and let the bees come in; they will lead me to the truth!"

The rabbis would tell this story to their young students, and advise them that every young person needs to choose their friends according to Solomon's wisdom. When the students would ask what they meant by that, the rabbis would respond by saying, "Choose friends who really care for you and can lead you, like Solomon's bees, to that which is real and true.

Who are the "Solomon's bees" in your life?

Fr. Mark Burger

FEBRUARY 18
Pearls

    I was talking with a friend of mine the other day as we waited in line at a supermarket. She was telling me how she and her husband had been trying to come up with a name for their baby girl, who was due to be born in May. She told me that she wanted one particular name but her husband absolutely refused. "He just hates the name," she said. When I asked her what name she wanted, she paused and asked, "If I tell you, you won't laugh, will you?" When I finally convinced her that I would not laugh, she agreed to tell me the name. "I want to call her Pearl," she said quietly.
    I must admit that I was tempted to laugh at the name, not because there is anything funny about it, but simply because I had never heard any young mother say they wanted that particular name for their child. So I asked her why she liked the name. She said it was because her grandmother had given her a pearl ring for her First Communion, and along with it a small booklet about the Legend of the Pearl.
    According to the legend, a special oyster lived way down deep in the ocean, swimming around the muddy sand of seabed. One night there was a very bright full moon, and the most brilliant light penetrated all the way down to the ocean floor. The oyster was profoundly affected by the wonderful light, and felt itself being pulled to the surface by that light as if drawn by a giant magnet. As the young oyster broke the surface of the water, the beauty of the light overwhelmed her. She felt the beauty with a directness that was not possible in the depths of the ocean waters. There was a glory and a power in the light that was like a living presence. The oyster's shell opened ever so slightly, just enough to trap just a fragment of that wonderful light within. Eventually the ocean waves drew her back down to the seabed, but a pearl was formed within her, a pearl that reflected the brilliant light of a loving and living God.
    When my friend had finished telling me the Legend of the Pearl she said, "I love kids and I think they are a reflection of God. So I want to name my little girl 'Pearl'. I think it's a beautiful name."
    After she told me this story, I thought it was a beautiful name too. I began to think of the people in my life who are pearls, or reflections of God,

and I came away very grateful for the many pearls who have blessed my life. Who are the pearls in your life?

FEBRUARY 19
Precious

A high school teacher walked into the school cafeteria and saw some of his students making fun of an elderly woman who worked as a cashier in the food line. The woman was a volunteer, and sometimes she was a bit slow in making change; other times she was confused when the students asked her questions. On this day they were imitating her in a mocking way, then laughing. The poor old woman began shaking and her eyes filled with tears.

When the teacher saw what was happening, he immediately ordered his students back to their classroom. Once the students were in their places the teacher entered the classroom and closed the door. The students expected him to start yelling at them, but he didn't do that. Instead, the teacher looked around the room and held up a $100 bill. He said, "Who would like to have this $100 bill?" All of the students raised their hands.

Then he announced, "I am going to give this bill to you, but first, let me do this." Then he proceeded to crumple up the $100 bill, throw it on the floor, and stomp on it. Then he tore off one of its corners. "Who still wants this $100 bill?" he asked. Every hand was up in the air; everyone wanted the $100. "Well, what if I do this" And he dropped the money in a glass of water he had on his desk. Holding up the crumpled, torn, soggy $100 bill he said, "Do you still want this old bill?" Every hand still went up. "Why would you want this old soggy $100 dollar bill?" he asked.

One student shouted out, "Because it doesn't matter what it looks like, how old it is, or how crumpled up it is, it's still worth one hundred dollars." "Exactly!" the teacher replied. He continued, "It doesn't matter what it looks like, it's still valuable. That old woman you were all making fun of, she is more than valuable; she is precious. Whether you can see it or not, she is someone's wife, someone's daughter, sister, or friend; she is someone's mama or grandma. She is precious. She does not deserve to be the object of your cruel jokes. She is precious. Never, ever forget that."

That teacher taught his students a valuable lesson. It is a lesson that the prophet Isaiah taught his people thousands of years ago when he told them what God himself had said about them. Isaiah wrote this, "Thus says the Lord, 'You are precious in my eyes.'" We are all precious in God's eyes. The question we must all ask ourselves is, do we treat each other as precious gifts from God?

FEBRUARY 20
A Costly Bowl of Stew

In recent days, as part of my prayer time, I've been reading the story of Jacob in the Book of Genesis. You might remember him; he's the grandson of Abraham and Sarah, and the son of Isaac and Rebecca.

Jacob was a twin. The Bible says that Rebecca had a difficult pregnancy because the two babies within her were struggling with each other even before they were born. Esau was the older child by a few minutes. The Bible also details the fact that as Esau was being born, Jacob was holding on to his brother's heel. In fact, the name Jacob means "the one who trips up others" or "the trickster."

The two brothers were exact opposites of each other and, as siblings often do, they spent most of their lives fighting with each other. Esau was a man of few words, while Jacob was more of a speech-giver and much more articulate. Esau, a rough, very strong, and hairy man, was his father's favorite. Jacob was slight in stature and more refined, his mother's favorite.

One story in Genesis about their difference tells how Esau loses his birthright to his scheming younger brother. This is what happened:

One day Esau comes home from a rather unsuccessful hunt, and he is very tired and very hungry. As he arrives back at camp, he finds his brother Jacob cooking up a pot of stew. Esau is so tired and hungry that he begs his brother for a bowl of the stew.

Now Jacob knows his brother is not particularly bright, and that when he is tired he is easily tricked. So Jacob promises to give Esau some of the stew in exchange for Esau's birthright. This birthright gave the first-born son the bulk of his father's estate upon the father's death. Esau responds to Jacob's proposition by saying, "What good is a birthright if I die today of hunger?" With those words, Esau trades away his future because he cannot think beyond his immediate needs.

As I read that part of the story, I kept thinking about how ridiculously foolish Esau was. How could he give away his entire future for a meal? How shortsighted. How stupid. How could he do such a thing? The more I thought about this, however, the more I realized just how brilliant the Bible is in presenting this story, because Esau is a symbol for all of us. He represents the persons we are when we let immediate concerns keep us from thinking about anything else.

How many of us are shortsighted when we are in the middle of some disagreement with loved ones, friends, or even co-workers? It's so easy to be so concerned about our own immediate needs or interests that we fail to see the bigger picture, isn't it? In other words, to use an old expression, we may win the battle but lose the war if we don't pay closer attention to what life sets before us.

Esau fell victim to his brother's dishonest schemes because he could not see beyond the meal Jacob had put before him. Had Esau paid closer attention to what his brother Jacob was saying to him, he may well have thought things over, come to a different decision, and had a much better life.

FEBRUARY 21
Writing a Masterpiece

Last Summer I read a biography of Pablo Picasso. In it the author describes an incident in Picasso's life that has stuck with me. The incident occurred when Picasso was relaxing on a beach in the south of France. Picasso was already a world famous artist, and those visiting the beach that day easily recognized him.

A small boy clutching a blank sheet of paper and a marker rushed over to Picasso and handed them to the artist. The boy's parents had sent him to ask the artist for an autographed drawing, hoping to make some money from it. Picasso hesitated for a moment and looked at the little boy, who was dressed in swimming trunks. The artist took the paper, tore it into tiny pieces, and threw them into the wind. Smiling, Picasso then took the marker from the

Fr. Mark Burger

child, turned the boy around, drew a picture on the bare skin of the boy's back, signed his name, and sent the boy back to his parents.

Picasso turned to those watching all of this unfolding and said, "I wonder if that child's parents will ever wash him again, now that he is so valuable!"

Now we all know that the young child did not suddenly become more valuable because he had been autographed by a great painter. That child was one of God's masterpieces long before that painter of masterpieces ever wrote on the boy's back. The incident can, however, serve to remind us, whether we are great artists or not, that we "write" on each other's lives and hearts.

The way we treat people, the things we say to one another, the gifts we give each other -- all of these things write a message on that person's life. What are you writing on the lives and hearts of those whom God has entrusted to your care?

FEBRUARY 22
Think

I was talking with a college student the other day. As she described her first few years' experience of life at a university she began to tell me that, for the first time, her mind was being opened to lots of new ideas and new thinking. She said she had never met so many people who were so different from her. "It's like I've entered a whole new world that I never knew existed," she said. Then she added, "For the first time in my life I have to really think, and I don't like it very much. It's too hard."

I asked what was so difficult about thinking. She replied, "Well, it's like this stupid essay I have to write. It has to be on this one line the teacher gave us, and I can't figure out what it means. It's so frustrating. I just don't know what to say about it."

"What's the line you have to write about?" I asked.

"That just it, it's a stupid line. He just gave us a little index card with this one sentence on it: 'Pay attention to what you think.'"

"Why is that a difficult sentence?" I asked.

"It's because of that underlined word. I don't know what I think!" she said.

As our conversation continued, I told her the professor must be pretty smart because he is trying to protect his students from one of the biggest traps every new student can fall into.

"And what trap is that?" she asked.

"It's the trap where you just blindly think about things the way everyone else does without ever looking into things for ourselves."

"Can you explain that to me?" she said.

"I can do better than that. I can give you an old parable about it." Then I told her this story:

A philosopher who had only one pair of shoes asked the cobbler to repair them for him while he waited. "It's closing time," said the cobbler, "so it won't be possible for me to repair them right now. Why don't you come back for them sometime tomorrow afternoon?"

The philosopher replied, "I have only this pair of shoes and it will not be possible for me to walk anywhere without them."

"Very well," the cobbler said, "I shall lend you a used pair for the day."

"What! Wear someone else's shoes? What kind of fool do you take me for?" exclaimed the philosopher. The cobbler shook his head and said, "Why should you object to having someone else's shoes on your feet when you don't mind carrying other people's ideas and thinking in your head?"

When I had finished telling that parable, that university student said, "Hey, thanks for writing my essay for me!" The truth of the matter is that whether we are university students or out in the world, finished with our formal education, we all have to "Pay attention to what *you* think."

February 23

Watch Your Language!

I was reading the other day about a man in England who had fallen on some rather difficult times. Because things kept getting worse for him he began to drink, and it wasn't too long before he ended up living on the streets of London. One day, as he was looking for a handout, he came upon a pub with a rather classic English name, The Inn of Saint George and the Dragon. He knocked on the back door of the pub, assuming that was where the kitchen was. A woman answered the door, took one look at him and snarled, "What the hell do you want?"

"Please, ma'am, could you see your way to giving me a bite to eat? I am really hungry."

"A bite to eat?" she growled. "Do you expect me to give you, a sorry-assed, no-good, foul-smelling bum like you a meal? I won't give you a thing!" With that she slammed the door on his hand.

Stunned by the sudden stab of pain in his hand and arm, the poor man just stood there shaking, trying to make sense of what had just happened to him. As he looked up he noticed the sign hanging in front of the place: The Inn of Saint George and the Dragon. He thought for a moment, then turned back to the door and knocked on it again. The same woman answered the door, glared at him and said, "Now what do you want?"

"Ma'am, since I've already met the dragon, I was wondering if Saint George might be willing to come to the door this time. Perhaps I'll have better luck with him."

When I read that little scenario I immediately thought of an elderly priest who was a mentor to me. He would often say to me, "You can learn any number of languages in your course of studies, but there is no better language to learn than the language of kindness. It's the most important language for any disciple of Jesus to know and use."

I think the "dragon lady" in the story above could have benefited from my mentor's advice. If you were to judge from the incident described above, I'd say that she didn't know there is a language of kindness. In fact, I think she spoke an entirely different language altogether: the language of bitterness. And the language of bitterness produces a sour crop of misery where ever it is spoken. On the other hand, whenever and wherever the language of kindness is spoken an entirely different crop is produced. The fruit of kindness is love.

Every one of us has the potential to be either Saint George or the dragon when it comes to how we treat one another. It really is quite simple. We can choose, by the language we speak, to make the world a better place -- or a bitter place.

FEBRUARY 24
Holding Hands

Earlier this week I read about a man who had a massive stroke at the age of forty. He described how scared he was as the life squad arrived to care for him and get him to the hospital. He could speak, but not very well. He turned to his wife and asked her, "What do I do now? I'm so scared! What's happening to me?" The man's wife replied, "Joe, you will be okay. Just pray." "I can't think of any prayers, I'm so confused. Help me!" the man replied.

The man described how his wife sat down on the floor next to him as the paramedics were tending to him. He said that she took his hand in hers and said, "Joe, just say, 'Lord hold my hand.'" "I could hardly talk," the man said "but I could say those few words: Lord, hold my hand."

During the next few days and weeks after his stroke, the man found something rather interesting happening as family and friends began to visit him. Here's how he described it,

"I could hardly talk to anyone those first few days. I couldn't get the words to come at all. Then, I would just tear up and quietly sob. Internally I kept telling God, "Lord, hold my hand." The strange thing was that as I sobbed, every visitor had the very same reaction to my struggles – each one of them took my hand and held it in theirs. Each person would offer a prayer as they held my hand, and they would all say something like, "God has you in his hands and you will be okay."

"Day after day and visit after visit, everyone who came to see me held my hand and told me that God had me in the palm of his hand. I drew great courage from those visits, and I am sure that they were the source of the strength that led to my recovery. Today I thank God for the way he held my hand through the hands of every relative and friend who came to see me."

If you are going through a particularly difficult time right now, why not take a few moments to say a simple little prayer: "Lord, hold my hand." If you put your burdens and worries in his hands, you will in fact find a deeper peace and healing as well. Go ahead, ask the Lord to take your hand!

February 25
Odd Birds

There is a Sufi tale told about a man named Nasruddin who became an ancient king's prime minister. Nasruddin's duties were many and varied and he took all of them rather seriously. He wanted everything in the king's palace to be in perfect shape, and everything had to be in its proper place.

One day Prime Minister Nasruddin wandered through the palace taking in all that was before him. His eyes fell upon the Royal Falcon. He said to himself, "I have never seen this kind of pigeon before. This will not do here in our king's great palace. So he got out a pair of scissors and a pair of clippers and began to trim the bird's claws. Next, he noticed the bird's wings were not shaped like other pigeons he had seen, so he used the scissors to trim up those wings. Finally he noticed that the poor bird's beak was hooked in a way that he had never seen another pigeon's beak look. He took his clippers and trimmed that bird's beak until it was in the shape he thought it ought to have.

When Nasruddin had finished his work he said, "Now you finally look like a decent bird. Your keeper must have been neglecting you!"

A famous Sufi master would conclude this story by saying, "This is how we all act when we see someone who is different from us and conclude that since they are different then they must also be wrong."

Are there any Royal Falcons in your life? If you have come across a Royal Falcon or two among your friends or family members, do you accept them or do you try to do as Nasruddin did with that poor bird? The Lord's final command to us was to love one another. Look around at the people in your life. Those are the ones Jesus calls us to love. I sure he meant even those "odd birds" we come across now and then as well.

February 26
Mending

One of the Desert Fathers tells the story of a rabbi who was feeling a deep depression. According to the story, the rabbi was perplexed as to why he was feeling so lost, confused, bewildered, and overwhelmed. The rabbi consulted older, wiser rabbis to find an answer, but they offered little help.

Still feeling very low, the rabbi spent a long period of time in prayer asking God for an answer, or for at least a sign as to what the problem was. Shortly after his time of prayer ended, the rabbi was standing in the doorway of his little house when a shoe cobbler came down the road pushing his cart with tools and materials on it. When the cobbler came up to the rabbi's house and saw the rabbi himself standing in the doorway, he shouted in a loud voice, "Do you have anything that needs mending?" The rabbi felt as if the voice of God was falling from the Heavens. He suddenly saw clearly just what the problem was: his life needed mending because God was not at the center of his life.

The Desert Father who related that story would tell it to people who came to him seeking answers to life's difficulties. Over the years, as he told it more and more and grew tired of repeating it, the story got shorter and shorter until the holy man stopped telling it and just asked a simple question: "What needs mending?" "Answer that question," he would say, "and there you have the source of most difficulties in life."

As you look at your life right now, "What needs mending?"

FEBRUARY 27
Buddha Responds

I spent some time this past week reading about the life of Buddha. According to the little book I read, Buddha taught that one should never return evil for evil. One day, after Buddha had taught a rather large crowd some of his principles, a man came up to speak to him. The man had decided to see if Buddha practiced what he preached. So as soon as he came into Buddha's presence, the man began to spew out all kinds of insults, using foul language and calling Buddha many disrespectful names.

The whole time the verbal attack was taking place; Buddha sat quietly and listened attentively to the man. When the man was finally exhausted and had nothing more to say, Buddha then spoke. "My son, I would like to ask you a simple question. If a man declines to accept a gift from another, to whom does the gift go?" The man was quiet for a moment and then said, "Well, any fool knows that the gift would then remain with the giver. If it is not accepted it returns to him."

"My son," said Buddha, "you have just given me much verbal abuse. I refuse to accept your gift." The man made no reply. Then Buddha went on, "A man who slanders a virtuous person is like a man who spits at the sky. The spit doesn't soil the sky; it returns to soil the face of the one who spat. Do no evil to another, speak no evil to another."

The wisdom that Buddha passed on to that man was a spiritual principle that is common to almost every major religion. The Desert Fathers knew that spiritual principle as the Law of the Echo. Simply stated, the Law of the Echo says that whatever you send out will come back to you. It is rather important then for each of us to pay close attention to what we send out.

One Desert Father taught his disciples to start each day with the realization that God has laid out the world in front of us. "As you enter into your daily walk in that world," he would say, "be careful of the response you make to it. After all, the response you make will come back to you sooner or later."

What response will you make to the world you walk through this day? How will you speak to those you love? What kind of response will you make to them? Remember Law of the Echo and take care.

FEBRUARY 28
Remembering the Ring of Gyges

As I was sorting through a bunch of old files the other day, I came across a paper I had written for a college philosophy class. The paper itself wasn't all that good or interesting, but the title caught my eye: "The Significance of the Ring of Gyges". When I read the title I couldn't for the life of me remember just what the Ring of Gyges was, so I read my paper. Then it came back to me.

In one of the sections of Plato's *Republic,* the great teacher Socrates tells the story of the Ring of Gyges. According to that myth, the ring was a magic ring that made the person wearing it invisible. Socrates asks his students this question: "How would an honest man behave if he were to wear that ring?" When his students gave no answer, Socrates said that both the honest man and the dishonest man might act in the same way. He concluded by saying, "If a person truly understood his own self-interest, he would never take advantage of his invisibility to do anything wrong. Why? Because there would be nothing he could gain that would be worth the loss of his integrity, his right to think of himself as a good person."

If you were to make a long list of all of your blessings, I bet there is one blessing you would not have thought to include in your list of graces – the right to think of yourself as a good person. As a person who spends a great deal of time with troubled people, I can assure you this is indeed a real gift that should be at the top of everyone's list of blessings. There are so many people who cannot find any goodness in themselves and are therefore filled with despair and hopelessness. There are many people who cannot bring themselves to the point where they can begin to forgive themselves for past sins or mistakes, and they find it ever more difficult to cope with life.

Jesus came to call us to the truth that we are all made in God's image and are God's own beloved children. So, if you are feeling bad about yourself, remember that God has created you as a good person -- though still a work in progress. You are not perfect but you are God's own. You are good. God has created you that way and invites you to choose to live your life out of that goodness. If you fail, make mistakes, or in some way betray that goodness, remember: we all have in Jesus a good and loving savior who can restore us to sanity and integrity.

FEBRUARY 29
God Just May Be Getting Started

I read an article the other day about a Mr. Charles Darrow. In 1935, this unemployed heating engineer who in 1935 took an idea he had for a family game to the Parker Brothers Company. The experts at Parker Brothers informed Mr. Darrow that his game, which he called Monopoly, contained what they saw as "52 fundamental errors." They told him further that they saw no future in the game but thanked him just the same for his interest in their company.

Charles Darrow spent the next year selling his board game himself. Sales were good. In fact, sales were so good that in 1936 that same Parker Brothers Company, a tad embarrassed now, made their way to Germantown, Pennsylvania to ask Mr. Darrow if he would allow them to manufacture his invention. They eventually came to an agreement, and since that time, over

150 million copies of Monopoly have been sold in over thirty-one countries. The company prints more than 40 billion dollars worth of monopoly money each year. The article concluded by saying that since the first copy of the game was produced, 3.2 billion of those little green houses have been made, enough to circle the globe.

Evidently those millions of people who purchased all those games weren't too concerned about the "52 errors" that the so-called experts saw. Generations of folks have enjoyed the game for years, and have probably never noticed what the experts saw.

As I read the story of Mr. Darrow and his Monopoly game, I began to think of all of the people I have counseled over the years who were so disappointed because they didn't make a particular team, they didn't get the part in the play, or they didn't win the scholarship. I began to think of all the people I have known over the years who were so heartbroken because things just didn't seem to work out the way that they wanted. In almost every case, I seem to recall that something different or even better happened for each of those "rejected" people.

It seems to me that God often uses rejections to redirect us or bring about some good in another way, usually a completely unexpected way. If you are experiencing some sense of disappointment because someone or something is finding "52 errors" in you, perhaps this is a time that God is giving you new directions, and maybe even a better plan for your life than the one you had in mind. Take courage because the story, your story, isn't over yet. God just may be getting started.

March

MARCH 1
Look to the Night Sky

One of the Desert Fathers tells of a conversation he had one day with a Bedouin (a desert nomad) about God's love and care. The Bedouin had invited the monk to eat a simple meal with him. As they were sharing the meal, the monk asked the Bedouin, "As you wander through the desert with your animals and family, how often do you think of God?"

The Bedouin replied, "My life here in the desert revolves around my family and caring for them. It revolves around my herding of the animals, the camels, the sheep, and the goats. The sky above is the ceiling of my world; the sands make up the floor of my world. Throughout the day, the footprints of my animals, and even those of my family members, are my lifeline to them. I can keep watch over them and I know where they are by following their footprints. I am connected to each one of them by their footprints."

As the monk listened to the Bedouin, he noticed that the man was someone who was at peace with himself. That peace seemed to emanate from him as he spoke. The Bedouin went on, "As you know, holy monk, at night here in the desert, the skies are filled with many, many stars. I spend hours each night looking at them. Some of them move through the sky, some of them twinkle; some of them seem to fall out of the sky. As I am in awe of them, because of their beauty and the vastness of their number, I begin to see that these stars in the sky are very much like those footprints in the sand that keep me in touch with my family and animals throughout the day. The stars are God's footprints, and when I see them I know God is near. I look for him, and when I see his footprints I know he is looking out for me and watching over me. I think of him every night as the stars fill the sky."

The Desert Father concluded by saying that whenever he felt the need to feel God's presence, he would think of that holy Bedouin. Then he would wait for the stars to appear in the night sky, and peace would be his.

MARCH 2
Arriving

One fact about life today is that, for most people, it moves at a rapid pace. Although speed can be a good thing in some instances, when speed ends up becoming haste, it becomes caustic. It begins to eat away at one of the great gifts Jesus left us, the gift of peace.

Why is it that we all dart about so rapidly? For many of us, a great deal of energy and attention gets paid to saving time, yet what are we doing with all of that saved time? Not only that, at what cost have we saved all that time? We end up living life at much too fast a pace, and we pay the price of having less and less calm in our lives. To be calm in the whirlwind that many of us live in is a priceless treasure. How do we find this "calmness"?

The Desert Fathers and Mothers have much to teach about this, but the short answer is quite simple. The road to being calm is sure and straight. If you want to be calm, you must slow down.

The Japanese have a folk saying that can give direction to us: "The day you stop traveling, you will arrive." I would put it a different way: "The day you stop running, you will arrive." It is in arriving that we can come to pause long enough to catch our breath, let things settle down a bit, then patiently wait for the calmness that quietly brings peace with it. Spending time being calm opens up ways for us to experience God's presence or begin to discern his still and quiet voice.

Why not do yourself a great favor today? Why not take a few minutes away from your rushing around to sit quietly, put on some soothing music, and then let the calm settle around you? I can assure you, if you create that kind of space in your hectic life, the calm will descend and God will fill you with peace. When that happens, he will begin to speak to your heart and you will have arrived.

March 3
Doing What He Could

I read recently about an eleven-year-old boy, Trevor Ferrell, from Philadelphia, who went into the city one day with his parents. In the course of the day, Trevor came upon a homeless man sleeping in the street. Trevor was absolutely shocked that this man had no home, no bed or place to sleep.

That night, as Trevor was trying to sleep, he knew he had to do something. The next day he gathered up his own sheets and blanket and pillow and put them in a bag. He asked his parents to drive him into the city, where he gave his bedding to the first homeless person he saw.

Now that in itself was a remarkable act of kindness, but the story doesn't end there. Others came to find out about Trevor's act of kindness. Struck by his simple gesture, some folks from area churches and a few local businesses began to make some contributions. Soon medical supplies were donated, and some social services and legal aid folks volunteered to help out. Within a year of Trevor's simple act of kindness, a shelter for the homeless, named "Trevor's Place," was opened. All of this came about because one eleven-year-old boy was moved to respond to someone in need.

Isn't that a great story? It certainly can remind us that every act of kindness is important in God's kingdom; every gesture made out of love for others bears great fruit. So often we think the world's problems are so big that our meager efforts can't do much to make a difference. Trevor Ferrell would disagree. He did what he thought he could, and good things began to happen. What do you think might happen if you stepped out and did what you could to care for someone in need?

March 4
Heart Fires

Most teens to not like to hear the word "curfew." To them it implies an end to their fun and a time to be home. Many parents have struggled to enforce curfews as their children do their best to resist them.

The word "curfew" comes from the French words *couvre fe,* which literally means to "cover the fire." It refers to the days in times past when, at the end of the day, it was time to extinguish lamps, candles, and fires. To put it another way, it was the original form of "lights out!"

Although a curfew may seem an imposition to some, they serve an important purpose. They can remind us that we do not have unlimited resources of strength or energy or even time, and that if we are not careful, we will burn out much like an untended fire or candle.

Especially among the young but also in people of every age, there is a resistance to the idea that we have limitations. We cannot simply do all that we want to do as long and as often we want to do it without some long-term cost or damage. The next time a parent, a situation, or a responsibility imposes a curfew on you, take heart. In a real sense, a curfew is a gentle reminder that we must tend the fire within our hearts us to keep it warm, bright, and alive.

March 5
Levi's Jeans

I was in the doctor's office the other day reading some magazines when I stumbled on a piece about Levi Strauss. According to the article, Levi came to this country from Germany as a young man. He first worked in New York with his brothers, running a dry goods store. Then, after having become a U.S. citizen, he headed out West to make his own way in life. Because the Gold Rush was still in full swing, he decided to take some bolts of heavy canvas with him that he could sell in pieces to make tents and wagon covers for the miners.

Well, it wasn't long after his arrival that he met several miners, to whom he tried to sell a few yards of canvas. They all examined his fine heavy cloth, but they weren't interested. Levi Strauss saw his future crumbling in front of him. He asked one of the miners what he and the others might be interested in buying. The miner spoke right up and said, "Well sir, what you should have brought us is pants. We got no pants that will last out here doing the heavy work we do mining. What we need is some good pants."

And so Levi decided to turn his heavy canvas into pants. At the same time, there was a tailor who had an idea to add metal rivets to the seams of some heavy-duty pants to reinforce them, but he needed just the right kind of cloth. The tailor's business partner happened to hear about what Levi Strauss was doing, and brought Levi and the tailor together. They applied for a patent on the canvas pants that used copper rivets to reinforce the seams, and in no time at all they hit it big selling Levi Strauss jeans.

As I read about Levi Strauss, I was struck by the fact that he could have fallen apart when his dream did not happen. If he had been a defeatist, he probably would have packed up all the bolts of heavy cloth and headed back to New York, a failure in his own mind. Yet rather than let his first idea be his only idea, Levi Strauss was humble enough to ask the miners what they needed. Then he listened to what they told him. He focused on what they needed, not on what he wanted to sell.

There is some important wisdom here for each of us. First, it's important for all of us to remember not to let our first creative idea be our only idea. Second, humility can take us to places we never thought we could go. And finally, being willing to share what you have with others will always make the way forward much better.

March 6
Gathered Up

A few weekends ago at Mass, I was praying quietly after communion. The whole church was quite still, and a kind of peace had settled in. It was very pleasant. Then, all at once, a child began to cry. It was that kind of childhood scream that is followed by a long period of quiet that makes you stop and notice because the child has not yet taken a breath. Finally, after that seemingly eternal pause, a breath was taken and the true screaming began. The church, which one minute before was a real haven of peace, was now cast into such a din.

As everyone in the church turned to look in the direction of the screaming, the child's mother gathered her little one onto her lap and she began to make quieting, shushing sounds. In a moment or two, that young mother began to whisper into her child's ear. It wasn't long before peace was restored. You could almost hear the congregation utter a sigh of relief.

As I returned to my prayer, it became apparent to me that the attentiveness of that young mother was almost sacramental. The way she so calmly gathered up her screaming child into her lap and proceeded to speak words of comfort was, for me, a great image of what God wants to do for each one of us when we are screaming out in pain or fear. When we are truly hurting or in some sort of difficulty, God comes, like any good parent, to gather us up, offer words of comfort, and restore us to peace.

If you are going through some difficult times right now and you long for some peace, God already knows and has heard your cries. Even now he may be bending low to gather you into his lap to restore you to peace.

March 7
Take It When It Comes

A friend's daughter called from Summer Camp to tell him that she wanted to come home. He said, "I told her she was just a little homesick, and she would feel much better in a day or two." I asked him what his daughter said to that. "Oh," he laughed, she said, "Daddy, I am not homesick, I'm 'here-sick' and I want to come home right now!"

As we laughed about that little girl's reply, I began to think about the number of people I talk to who are experiencing a kind of here-sickness. The sickness they feel is an unsettling feeling that sucks happiness out of their lives. They feel that God must exist, but they feel very far away from him.

When people describe this to me, I often think of a book I read back in college called *The Great Divorce*, by C.S. Lewis. The book is not about the kind of divorce that happens between spouses but about the kind of estrangement or divorce that happens between people and God. In the book, Lewis pictures hell as a big city where the weather is always dreary and overcast. The light in that city always appears to be dim and murky. Each day the people in that hell-like city discover just how big a separation there is between them and God. Each day they feel like they are sinking into a deeper and deeper hole of despair.

As the novel continues, some of the people discover that there is a way out of this hell, this horrible gloom: God has provided a shuttle bus that travels from hell to Heaven. The bus comes regularly each day, and all you have to do is to get on it and let the power of God's love carry you out of the gloom and into the light. This is the way out.

The amazing thing, however, is that very few people bother to get on the bus, even though it comes and goes many times each day. They just keep putting it off until another day. Everyone keeps thinking that today is not a good time to get on the bus. They hem and haw about it, but they just don't make the effort to get on the bus. They miss the opportunity to allow the love of God to carry them away from the hell they are experiencing.

Are you experiencing a bit of "here-sickness" and feeling a bit blue or depressed by your life's direction right now? Perhaps it's time for you to look around to see if God might be sending you a shuttle bus out of the gloom and into the light. Whatever your situation or difficulties might be, know that God cares for you. Don't miss the bus!

MARCH 8
Stirring Up Your Spiritual Life

I just finished reading a little article written by Cardinal Roger Mahoney. In it he describes a rather striking image of Pope John Paul II from the time when the Pope visited the Archdiocese of Los Angeles back in 1987. The cardinal recalled one special night at around 10:30 p.m., when he went down to the kitchen. Mahoney said, "I came into the kitchen to find the Pope's secretary sitting at the table drinking coffee, and the Pope standing at the stove stirring a pot of leftover soup. The Pope just looked up and smiled at me. The Holy Father then remarked, 'I think I do some of my best thinking standing at the stove stirring soup!'"

Isn't that a great image? I love picturing that scene in my mind. I love it because I too do some of my best thinking and reflecting while stirring something on the stove. (I wonder if that means I'm going to be Pope some day?!)

How about you? Where do you do your best thinking? Many people tell me they want to spend more time in prayer and reflection, but they just don't have the time. My answer is usually the same: instead of looking for extra time, just begin to use those times and places where you already do your best thinking. If that is standing at the stove stirring a pot of soup, then begin right there. Deeper prayer and reflection can grow and develop where you already are doing rather ordinary things. Remember, Jesus taught us that God is the God of the ordinary.

So, whether you are standing at the stove or driving into work, whether you are shoveling snow or working out at the gym, wherever or whenever you find yourself doing your best thinking, why not invite God into that part of your day? I can assure you, the simple act of inviting God to be a part of that time will bear much good fruit. Your spiritual life can grow so much deeper, and it doesn't have to take a great deal of time. Simply pay attention to when and where you do your best thinking, then invite the Lord to be a part of it.

MARCH 9
They Feared a Great Fear

Recently, I took a morning off to make a kind of mini-retreat. The focus of that little retreat was a passage from the Gospel of Mark, which was told by a professional storyteller from West Virginia. The story is that familiar one of Jesus sleeping in a boat being tossed about by a great storm. The disciples are terrified. They awaken Jesus and ask him if he cares about what is happening to them. Then the storyteller said that Jesus "got up and hollered at the winds and then told the sea to be still." (I love the image of Jesus hollering at the winds)

I can remember to this day how that storyteller from West Virginia concluded his performance. He went on to say that Jesus eventually said, "Peace, be still." The storyteller continued: "And all at once the wind shut up, and then the waters relaxed, and then there was great calm. And then he turned and said to those followers of his, 'Why are you so fearful? How is it that you have no faith in you?' And they feared a great fear, and they whispered to one another, 'Who is this that even the wind and the sea obeys him?'"

Isn't that a great rendition of that gospel story? I have read that part of Mark's Gospel many times in the past, but this particular translation of it made it come so alive for me that my morning of reflection was a real blessing. I want to share it with you in the hope that you too will find in it a source of strength and peace.

The events of that story can serve as a parable for each of us when we find ourselves in troubled times. Think about it for a moment. When times get difficult for you, doesn't it feel like you are being beaten down by fierce winds, and that the boat of your ability to cope is filling up with so much turmoil it feels as if you are about to go under? Perhaps too you have felt that as you are going through some crisis or very difficult ordeal, God seems to be asleep. What are we to do in the face of such overwhelming feelings?

What we have to do is to do what the apostles did; they went immediately and woke Jesus up. They shook him awake, and because they were so afraid, they probably yelled at him. When Jesus was asleep all the way in the back of the boat, he probably seemed very far away even though he was just a few yards away. This is exactly how it is with us when life scares us to death. God can seem far away and asleep, yet he is very near.

The whole description of waking Jesus is really a description of prayer. It is the apostles (and us) turning to Jesus, begging him to help us with our fears. Jesus responds by yelling at the wind and speaking to the sea. Instantly there is calm. The calming that followed was found not only in the dying down of the winds and the sea, but also in hushing the panic-filled hearts of those apostles who had "feared a great fear."

Today, take some time to read and pray the translation of Mark's Gospel story above. It brought me a sense of the Lord's closeness, and a rather profound experience of the peace that only he can give. It can do the same for you, too, and there is nothing quite like experiencing the grace of his calming peace.

March 10
Leave Your Expectations Behind

I once went to a rather dull lecture on prayer. I didn't like it at all, and thought of five or six other people who would have done a much better job. I was getting a bit frustrated. Finally, about a third of the way through the talk, I stopped listening and began to think of things I'd rather be doing. I looked over at another priest, a friend of mine, and he looked as if he were in awe of what was being said. It amazed me that he was so absorbed by what I thought was a rather dull monologue.

The speaker eventually invited all of us to take a short break. I approached my priest friend and said, "What do you think of it so far?" "I think it's wonderful!" he said. "How in the world can you call a dull speech like that 'wonderful?'" I asked. "Well it is obvious to me that you haven't been listening. Your mind has been everywhere but here, and you've been spending your time just looking around. No wonder you think it's dull. The problem is not in the speaker, it is in you," he said quietly.

I suppose he saw something in my expression that made him back away from what he had just said. Then my friend reminded me that, although the delivery was, in fact, rather dull, what was being said was not at all dull. "You're letting externals determine what you hear, see, and even understand. You need a better attitude. I am going to send you a little parable to help you see what I'm trying to tell you," he said.

As the meeting was called back into session and we walked back to our places, I whispered to my friend, "Next time I go to a lecture, I'm going to go with a friend who will just agree with me!"

A few days later I received this little parable in the mail:

A man went daily to buy his newspaper at a local newsstand, whose owner was so surly that, while selling him the newspaper, he insulted and abused him. A friend of the victim noticed this and told him, "Why do you insist on buying your newspaper from that news dealer who abuses you so badly each time? You know that at the same distance from your house there is another newsstand whose owner is very kind and obliging and will be very happy to supply you with the newspaper every day without your having to endure the insults of that other madman." At that, the victim of the insults answered, "And why should that man, who according to you insults me, be the one who decides for me where I buy my newspaper?"

My priest friend wrote across the bottom of the page, "Expectations can make you deaf! If you would stop letting your expectations determine the value of what you see and hear, you may discover a whole new world of ideas that you never knew existed. All you have to do is leave those expectations behind, open your eyes and ears, and be ready to receive!"

I thanked my friend for the parable. He was right. I had missed a lot of what that lecture was teaching because my expectations plugged up my ears. I missed out on some important learning because I wouldn't keep my mind focused. Has that ever happened to you? Maybe the parable above could be of help to you too.

MARCH 11
A Nudge Toward Our Blessings

Here's a story to take to your prayer. A man runs to his rabbi, a very wise and holy man, and says to him, "Rabbi, you must help me. I am in misery! My house has become hell to me! We live in one room, my wife, my children, my in-laws, and me. This is pure hell. There is just not enough room for all of us in that room! What can I do?"

The rabbi studied the man's face rather intently and then finally spoke. "So you would like some suggestions as to what to do about this hellish situation you find yourself in today?" asked the rabbi.

"Yes, Rabbi, please, please help me!" the man cried.

"I will certainly help you, but you must promise me that you will do exactly what I tell you to do. Can you do that?" the rabbi asked.

"I am so miserable," the man replied, "I promise I will do whatever you tell me to do, no matter what."

"Okay then," the rabbi said. "How many animals do you have?"

The man answered, "We own a cow, a goat, and about ten chickens."

"Put those animals in the room with you, and then come back to see me in a week." the rabbi instructed.

Even though the man thought this was ludicrous, because of his promise he went home, gathered his animals together, and brought them into his one-room house. He was miserable, depressed, and overwhelmed. As soon as the week was up, he went right away to see the rabbi.

"I'm going crazy! This is going to kill me if something doesn't change!" the man whined as he poured out his soul to his rabbi.

The rabbi said, "There, there, my son, don't fret so. Go back home and put all of the animals out of the house. Come back to see me at the end of next week."

The man went running back home to get the animals out of his house. After the week was up, the man ran back to see the rabbi and exclaimed,

"Wonderful news, Rabbi, wonderful news! My house is a wonder. It's so clean and so spacious! My home is paradise!"

What's the moral of that story? The ancient religious leaders who told that story would give very cryptic answers when they were asked what it meant. One answer I have seen given for this story is this: "I didn't have any shoes, and I was always complaining and whining about it to everyone I could find to listen to me, until the day I met someone who had no feet. Then I knew I had little to complain about."

Are there things in your life that you find yourself muttering about or complaining about? Do you ever whine about things that aren't really all that bad? Perhaps the story above can be a nudge in the direction of looking for your blessings.

MARCH 12
What Would Old Diogenes Think?

I was searching through some boxes of books from my college days when I found an old assignment sheet from an undergraduate philosophy course. The professor had asked us to write an essay on personal integrity based on the following story about the philosopher Diogenes:

The philosopher Diogenes was eating his supper, a simple meal of bread and lentils. As he was eating, another philosopher, Aristippus, came to visit him. Now Aristippus lived quite comfortably and had grown rather wealthy by flattering the king. Aristippus said to Diogenes, "I have noticed that you eat a terribly meager supper. Let me advise you: if you would learn to be subservient to the king and meet his every wish, you would not have to live on lentils."

Diogenes then spoke to his friend Aristippus, "Let me advise you, sir: Learn to love lentils and to be content to live on them and you will not have to find ways to be subservient to the king, and seek to meet his every demand."

As a final question on our paper, the professor asked us to consider what part of our own personal integrity we may have learned to live without in order to cultivate someone else's favor. I looked through that box of books and papers for my essay but it wasn't there. Either the professor never returned our essays or I just threw it away. I can't remember what I wrote about, but I'm sure it would be interesting to compare to what I might write today, some forty years later.

Now I have a question for you. Having read the story above and my old philosophy professor's final question, what would you write about? Have you ever sacrificed a part of your own integrity to get ahead or win someone's good opinion? I think old Diogenes has something to teach us all.

MARCH 13
How About Taking a Break?

I want to tell you a story I read some years ago that has always stuck with me, especially when I get a bit weary or tired. A man challenged another man to an all-day wood chopping contest. The guy who had made the challenge worked very hard all day chopping like crazy, stopping only for a lunch break. He noticed that the other guy took a leisurely lunch break, but also several more breaks throughout the day. The challenger thought to himself that he would surely win the contest since his opponent never seemed to rush, and took many breaks throughout the day.

At the end of the contest, however, the challenger was very surprised and truly annoyed to find out that the other fellow had outdone him. The other man had chopped a whole lot more wood than he had, and not only that, he didn't look a bit worn out!

"Hey, I don't get it," complained the challenger. "Every time I checked, you were taking a rest, yet you chopped a hell of a lot more wood than I did. How'd you do that?"

The winning man grinned a bit and then said, "When you saw me resting, did you notice what I was doing while I was sitting there catching my breath?"

"All I remember is that when I was working hardest, you were sitting!" the challenger replied.

"Well, I'll tell you the truth of what you didn't notice. Every time you saw me sitting down resting, I was sharpening my ax so that every time I got up again, chopping wood became easier."

Fr. Mark Burger

What's the wisdom of that story? It is simple: We will find our work and our life much easier and more enjoyable if we take enough time for purposeful rest that sharpens the best in us.

When he sat down to rest after he had worn himself out with worry, fear, and anxiety, Saint Augustine said this: "Our hearts were created for You, O Lord, and they will always be restless until they rest in You." He learned from his own struggles that he was always restless and unable to find peace when he didn't take some time to catch his breath and literally breathe in God's peace. He said that when he allowed himself to be filled with that peace, the best in him came to the surface. In other words, time in prayer, time in God's presence, was his way of sharpening his ax.

If you are feeling tired, worn out, discouraged, or overwhelmed by the difficulties of daily life, maybe its because you aren't taking enough breaks during the days in which you could be sharpening your ax. Why not take some time today to do just that?

March 14
Thanking God for Sophia

According to an article I was reading the other day, many people only come to discover their true genius for something after they have experienced a very difficult failure or defeat. As I thought about that I remembered something I had learned way back in college days about Nathaniel Hawthorne.

Before he ever put pen to paper as an author, Hawthorne worked in a customhouse. His work there enabled he and his wife to have a comfortable life, and they were quite happy together. Then one day Nathaniel was fired from his job. He was devastated and felt like an utter failure. As he walked home, feeling lost and, as he put it, worthless, he worried over how his wife Sophia would take the news. He felt that she too would be quite devastated.

When he had finally told Sophia his bad news, she surprised him by exclaiming, "Now you can write your book!" "That's wonderful and easy for you to say," he replied. "But how are we to live while I write this book?"

Sophia replied by walking over to a desk, opening the center drawer, and pulling out an envelope containing a rather substantial amount of money.

"I have always known that you were a man of genius," she told him. "I just knew that someday you would write a great masterpiece. So every week, out of the money you gave me for housekeeping, I have saved a bit. There is enough here to support us while you write.

Because of Sophia's confidence and encouragement, Nathaniel Hawthorne was able to turn his job loss into a great opportunity to do what he loved most, to write. In a year's time he wrote his famous book, *The Scarlet Letter*.

Is there a "Sophia" in your life? Is there someone who has been a great source of encouragement and inspiration for you? Have you taken the time to thank them for all that they have done for you? Have you thanked God for all of the Sophias he has sent your way throughout the years?

One more thing: Is it possible that perhaps, God may very well be calling you to be a Sophia for someone in your life right now?

March 15
Just Like That!

I was in the library the other day when I came upon a description of something that happened during a rehearsal of one of Claude Debussy's works. The rehearsal was being lead by the famous conductor, Arturo Toscanini. According to the story, the rehearsal wasn't going very well, and Toscanini was growing more and more agitated with the orchestra's performance. They were all, as he put it, "playing the notes on the page, but not working together to make the music."

The more the maestro tried to explain what he wanted from the musicians, the worse they played. Exasperated, Toscanini thought for a moment, then had an idea. He reached into his pocket and pulled out a silk handkerchief. Then, with all his strength, he threw it up into the air.

The orchestra members were at first a bit shocked by his display, but that quickly changed as the silk cloth slowly and rather gracefully floated down from the ceiling. Each of the musicians was mesmerized by the beautiful way the handkerchief softly fell to the floor. As Toscanini caught their eyes, he whispered, "There, play like that!" And they did.

When I read about that rehearsal, I thought about how much Jesus' life and ministry was like Toscanini's illustration. Jesus' whole life of love and service was God's way of telling us to "Love like that!" If we are faithful to what the Lord asks of us, our lives will say, "Live and love like this!"

As you are thinking about that rehearsal, why not take some time to examine how you are living your life? Are you living in such a way that those around you would say to themselves, "I want to live and love just like that"?

March 16
Grounded!

When I was studying philosophy back in my seminary days, I always enjoyed reading Soren Kierkegaard, the Danish theologian and philosopher. He often used folk stories to illustrate some of his ideas. One such story was about a duck.

According to that story, a flight of ducks was sailing over a farmyard when one of the ducks looked down and saw a flock of chickens peacefully moving about the ground eating their meal. Since having a nice, peaceful meal appealed to the duck, it dropped out of formation and joined the chickens on the ground. The duck enjoyed the meal so much that he spent the entire winter with the rather well fed chickens. All seemed good; the duck was happy and well fed, too.

But eventually spring came. One day the duck looked up into the sky and saw the familiar V-shaped flight of ducks soaring overhead. The duck was immediately homesick and wanted more than anything to join the flight of his fellow ducks. Unfortunately, with very flabby muscles and a rather large belly, the duck could not flap his wings hard enough or long enough to get off the ground. He was grounded. Kierkegaard concluded the story by warning people to pay attention to what they allow themselves to fill-up on.

Any one of us can get "grounded" by the weight of what we carry around in us. I know lots of people who are miserable because every day they eat three full meals of bitter resentments that they continue to harbor. An unforgiving spirit or harsh judgments of people grounds other folks. Still others are grounded by an inability to forgive themselves.

There are many other "bad meals" we can fill up on that will lead us to just barely making it through life, scratching at the ground with the chickens. Kierkegaard was right; we need to pay attention to what we eat.

MARCH 17
Learning How to See

I've been thinking about a character in a novel I read a few years back, who was a prisoner in a Soviet work camp. Conditions in that concentration camp were absolutely horrendous and many inmates died due to the appalling conditions.

The man was awakened one morning at four o'clock, given a piece of bread, and sent out to work in a warehouse. The man thought to himself, "I had better hold on to this piece of bread because I may need it through the night. At night I am so hungry that I cannot sleep, and if I don't sleep, I'll never have the strength to endure tomorrow."

After working all day, the man fell exhausted into his bed and pulled the thin blanket he had been given up over his head to try to stay warm. He was famished. He thought of the piece of bread. Slowly he consumed each tiny morsel. As he savored the bread, he thought to himself, "What a good day this has been. I did not have to work out in the freezing wind and rain, but was permitted to work indoors. And now, when I am most hungry, I have these scraps of bread. Thank you, God, for blessing me so."

I don't know about you, but I'm not so sure I would be able to see myself as being blessed locked up in a concentration camp and slowly starving to death. Yet the character in that novel has much to teach us. His attitude and his thoughtfulness illustrate a basic spiritual principle that happiness is not found on the outside. It is not found in external things or in particular people. Changing where you live or changing jobs, even changing your appearance cannot necessarily make you happy. Many people assume that money, power, prestige and respectability will bring happiness. But none of these things do.

Happiness, in a sense, is an inside job. It is our inner "lights" or way of seeing that can determine whether or not we find happiness. Many well meaning people have set out on very long journeys in search of happiness only to discover that the path to happiness is a pilgrimage within. If you are looking for happiness, go within and learn how to see.

MARCH 18
Feathers

A woman once came to Saint John Vianney to speak about a problem she was having in overcoming a bad habit. She told Father Vianney that she was trying to stop gossiping about some of the people she knew, but she was unable to overcome it. No matter how hard she tried, she failed time and time again. After Father Vianney had listened for quite some time, he was silent. In fact, there was a very uncomfortable silence in the room, which made the woman a bit nervous.

Finally the priest spoke up. "This is what you must do to overcome your difficulties. I want you to go to the market and buy an unplucked hen and bring it back here to me. Now on your way back here, you are to pluck the bird a feather at a time and let the feathers be carried away by the wind." The woman did as the priest had asked her.

When she arrived back at the priest's office and presented the plucked chicken, Father Vianney said, "Now, there is one more thing you must do. I want you to go back along the way you came, and pick up all of the feathers belonging to that hen."

The woman was dumbfounded. "How in the world will I ever be able to find all of those feathers?" she exclaimed. "The wind will have carried them far and wide, it will be impossible to get every one of them back!"

"That is exactly true." John Vianney said. "Perhaps this will help you to see exactly what has happened as a result of your gossiping. It is virtually impossible to call back your words once you have sent them on their way. Be very, very careful what you say, and especially what you gossip about. It can be near impossible to repair all of the damage done by careless words."

Saint John Vianney was a wise man. He knew the power of words, and taught his people to use them with great care. We can all learn a great deal from him.

March 19
Being Awake Enough

How about a nice parable to think about today? A farmer awoke one Monday morning and looked out his window only to discover that overnight a giant field of daffodils had sprung up all around his house. "How beautiful!" he said to himself. "I really should stay home and walk through these wonderful flowers, but I have to plow the north fields today." When the farmer returned that evening, he discovered that all the daffodils had withered and died. He was disappointed.

The very next day, the farmer awoke and saw two small sparrows perched on the branch outside his window. Their feathers were smooth and dark, and their song soared joyfully above him. "Oh what beautiful music they make!" he sighed to himself. "I will come back to listen once I have milked all of the cows." When he had returned from work, the birds had flown away.

The following morning, the farmer awoke to the sound of clatter hooves on the front drive. He rushed to look out the window, and there it was. A great white stallion was dancing and cavorting in the sunlight, and it seemed as if the horse was inviting him to take a ride through the countryside. "You have to be the most beautiful and magnificent horse I have ever seen!" exclaimed the farmer "But I can't go off riding right now. I have to go mend the south fences. I'll be back, wait for me." When the farmer returned, the stallion had run off.

Each morning, for many years, the farmer awoke to witness some new wonder outside his window. Each was there for him, yet he would never really enjoy them because, well, he had to tend to the farm. Because he was so busy and had so many important things to do, he never took the time to enjoy the small miracles that were happening just outside his window every morning. He never took time to enjoy them because he never really saw them as miracles. Not only did he miss the miracles right outside his windows, I'll bet he also missed the miracles happening out in the north fields, or among the cows he went to milk, or the fences he went out to mend.

This parable serves as a reminder to us all to pay attention and be awake enough so as not to miss what is happening around us. There are miracles happening all around us each day, if we would just open our eyes wide enough to see them. We can't let our hectic schedules keep us from all God wants to give us.

March 20
Better or Worse?

I recently came across a modern parable about service to others. According to the parable, a commuter got on a train in New York and told the conductor that he needed to go to Fordham. The conductor looked at him and shook his head saying, "I'm sorry sir, but this train doesn't stop at Fordham on Saturdays." "But I must be at Fordham today!" the man pleaded.

"Well, I'll tell you what we can do." the conductor instructed. "As the train slows down at Fordham, I will open the door and you jump off. Make sure that you're running along with the train when you hit the ground or you will fall flat on your face."

When the train reached Fordham, the conductor opened the door and the commuter jumped out as instructed and hit the ground running alongside the train. As the train began to pass him, however, another conductor a few cars back noticed the man running alongside the train opened the door and reached out and grabbed the commuter and pulled him back on the train. That conductor looked at the man and said, "You are mighty lucky I saw you mister, you know this train doesn't stop here at Fordham on Saturdays. If I hadn't pulled you onboard you would have had to wait until Monday for the next train!"

What is the moral of that story? It is this: People who try to improve things frequently achieve remarkable success in making things worse rather than better. Before one tries to improve things, one must first understand what is truly going on before they take action.

Have you ever been that second conductor, thinking you are working on improving things only to find out that you've made them worse? Probably every one of us has made that kind of mistake. The parable above can serve to remind each of us that the first task of reaching out to help others is to do no harm. In this season of Lent, where we focus on doing good for others, it is important to pay close attention to how we are helping others so that in the end, we truly are being of help.

MARCH 21
Fun with Math

I was having breakfast the other morning with some friends, two of whom are schoolteachers, and we began talking about the beginning of a new school year. One of the teachers was telling us that she always likes to begin the year in her math class with what she calls a fun formula. "What's a fun formula?" we asked. She gave us the following example: Think of a number between one and ten. Then multiply the number by two, add ten, and divide the result by two. Finally, subtract the number you initially thought of. The result will always be the same: it will be five. It works every time.

After we all tried out that fun formula and were amazed by it, we asked that teacher why she began her class that way. She said, "I do it because I want my students to be in awe of the wonder of learning. I want them to get excited about discovering amazing things. I want them to love learning. I want them to be full of expectation."

Wouldn't you love to have her as your teacher? I know I would. One of the greatest gifts we can give each other is the gift of enthusiasm and joy. Why not make a point of passing on some enthusiasm and joy to the children in your life? In fact, pass it on to the adults too!

MARCH 22
Which Is It?

In my meditation this week I have been using a story that date's from the teaching of Confucius.

According to the story, a fire broke out in the house of a rather huge man who was fast asleep inside. Rescuers arrived and tried to get him out. They tried to carry him out through the window, but he was just too big to fit so they gave up on that idea. Next they tried to carry him, bed and all, through the front door, but again they could not do so because of his size and weight. They were pretty desperate until someone asked the fire captain what to do. His reply was simple: "Stick him with a pin and that will wake him, then when he sees a fire coming after him, he'll find his own way out!"

When folks would ask Confucius what that story meant, his response was this: The solution to most folk's problems is that they have to either wake up or grow up.

If you are wrestling with issues in your spiritual or personal life, or if you are trying to help someone else through some confusing times, perhaps the above story can be of help to you. As Confucius would often teach, in most situations, the difficulty has arisen because someone involved either has to wake up or grow up.

March 23
A Sheltering Tree

The other day I had lunch with some of my closest friends. Every time I'm with them I think of a line from a poem by Samuel Coleridge, *Youth and Age*. I don't remember much of the poem but I do remember one simple sentence: "Friendship is a sheltering tree."

Isn't that a great image? The professor who made us read that poem in college asked us to consider how our friends are like the branches of a tree that provide not only shade, but also refuge and comfort when life is full of dangerous, irritating, or wearyingly hot times. He had us write an essay about how our friends, like trees, not only have provided us with cool shade in the heat of the day but have also provided us with nourishing and strengthening fruit when life begins to drain us. The professor told us that when we matured one day, we would know just how truly important good friends are in life. He made us promise not only to make it a goal in life to find good friends, but also to always try to be a true good friend to others.

As I drove away from lunch that day, the image of a sheltering tree and the promise we made to our English professor came rushing back to me, and I spent some time thanking God for each friend. What a gift each one is to me.

Have you thought about how blessed you are with your friends? If you think about it, I'm sure you would find that each of your friends has been and continues to be a sheltering tree for you. Take some time this week to give thanks to God for your friends; maybe take some extra time to be with them and to be a good friend to them, as well. I know one thing for certain:

When you take time to be with your friends, you'll find yourself under a real sheltering tree.

March 24
Discovering Your Coaches

I read an article recently about words, which pointed out that there are words we use every day and think nothing of what those words might mean or how we have come to use them. The article urged readers to pick out a word, research it to discover its various meanings, and then see what it has to teach you about yourself. Well, I decided to do just that, and the word I chose to research was "coach." Here's what I discovered.

The word "coach" first appeared in the English language in the 1500s, and it was used to describe a carriage drawn by a horse that was used to convey a person from one place to another. Apparently this was the only way the word was used until the 1880s, when the word took on new meaning. In the last years of the nineteenth century the word coach started to be used in the athletic sense, but it still had a similar meaning of moving a person from one place to another. In this case, the new use of the word meant to move a person from one level of ability to a new level of ability. Thus a coach moves an athlete from one skill level to another, from one level of play to another.

As I continued to research that word, it dawned on me that the word "coach" could be applied to so many different areas of life beyond athletics. In terms of our health, how many doctors and other health practitioners have coached us from illness to health? How many teachers have transported us from ignorance to knowledge and wisdom? Think of the many ways your parents or spouse, children and grandchildren have coached you to new experiences and new places. Our friends have a great ability to coach us as well. In the same way, Jesus is our coach who can lead us out of darkness into light, from despair to hope, from death to life.

When I had finished researching that simple word, I came away with some rather profound and unexpected insights. I discovered how incredibly blessed I have been throughout my life to have so many wonderful coaches who have helped to make me the person I am today.

Why not take some time today to do a little research of your own? Who have been your coaches throughout the years? How have you been carried to new places and new insights by the coaches God has put into your life?

MARCH 25
Morning Stillness

In my reading this past week I came upon an interview with George Washington Carver, from many years ago. During the interview Carver was asked if he had any routine that fed him and kept him excited about the work he did. Before he could even answer the question the reporter said, "I've been told you have come up with over 300 uses for peanuts; just what is your secret to discovering such information?"

George Washington Carver paused before he answered, then said, "I get up before the sun comes up, usually around 4:00 am."

"And do you go directly to your laboratory to begin your work in the quiet of the early dawn?" asked the reporter.

"Oh no, no. I don't go out to my workshop at that hour. No, I go deep into the woods. I find a place to sit and then I just pause in the morning stillness. I take a few moments to calm myself, then I listen to God and little by little he tells me of his plan for me. From there I go to the lab and what happens, happens."

During these beautiful spring mornings, are you spending any time in the morning stillness, listening to God and his plan for you? What do you think would happen to your day if you took a few moments to calm yourself in the stillness that allows one to hear God's voice?

MARCH 26
Rabid People

I recently heard a little story about a man who had been examined in an emergency room because of a mysterious illness that seemed to be getting worse. After a battery of tests a physician came to him and announced, "Our tests confirm it: you have rabies."

The patient asked the nurse standing nearby if she would get him a pad of paper and a pen. When the nurse brought the requested materials, the patient began writing down names. Thinking that the man was writing out his Last Will and Testament, the doctor said, "Listen, this doesn't mean you're going to die. There is a cure for rabies."

"Oh, I know that," said the man. "I'm just making a list of all the people I want to go and bite!"

I had an experience a couple of weeks ago in which I was having lunch with friends, two families and me. The conversation was lively and a lot of fun, and we spent a good deal of time laughing.

At one point in the evening, a son from one of those families came to join us after he had gotten off work. We welcomed the newcomer to the group and he said hello to everyone. Then he launched into a diatribe about how he hated his boss, he hated his job, and he hated life, too. All attempts to console him were rebuffed. He sat there looking rather sullen and you could almost feel the heat coming off him.

The whole atmosphere of our evening radically changed after that. There was a long, awkward silence. Soon the other children present began to be unsettled and started whining. The fun part of the evening was obviously over, and it wasn't long before we all headed home.

As we were walking toward our cars the mother of the sullen young man leaned over and whispered in my ear, "It's like a rabid dog or a vampire just came in and bit us all, and now we've caught what he's got!" We laughed and headed our separate ways.

On my way home that night I thought of the story of the man with rabies. Isn't that a great metaphor for the damage we can do to one another with our unchecked anger? We often forget how powerful an influence we are on one another. If we don't pay attention to what we are doing we may inadvertently bite and infect those we love the most. A good question to consider today might be, "Have I bitten anyone lately?"

March 27
What Treasure?

A few years ago I was asked to take over an eighth grade religion class for a teacher who had been called home for a family emergency. I began the class by asking the students to listen to a story; here it is.

A young couple was given a new, leather-bound Bible as a wedding present by the groom's grandfather. The Bible was an extraordinary book. Not only was it bound in tooled leather, but its pages were edged in fine gold leaf. In addition, it was encased in a finely crafted wooden box that had been richly decorated with painted scenes from the Bible. It was a very expensive edition of the sacred Scriptures. The couple thanked grandfather for the nice gift and put it with the other gifts that would be moved into their new home.

A couple of weeks after the wedding the grandfather asked the young couple how they liked the Bible he had given them. The couple told him they liked it very much. The truth was, however, that they had not even taken the book out of its box. In fact, neither of them could recall exactly where they had even put it. "You know that it's a very valuable book, don't you?" the grandfather said. "Oh yes, we really appreciate your kindness," they replied.

About six months later, at a family gathering, grandfather again asked how they liked their new Bible. "I like it just fine," said the grandson. "I read a little of it every day," said the young wife. "I so glad you like it!" the grandfather replied.

Two years later the grandfather died. On the way home from the funeral, the couple began to talk about how much they loved grandfather. When they got home, they decided to look for their "treasured" Bible. For the first time they took the Bible out of the cardboard box it was in. Then they opened the wooden case and removed the leather-bound book with its gilded pages. When they opened the book and began to flip through its pages, to their astonishment they discovered that grandfather had place one hundred dollar bills between many of its pages. For the two years they had owned the Bible they had never once opened it. Now, as they counted the hundred dollar bills, they realized that grandfather had not only given them an expensive Bible, but also ten thousand dollars!

The author of that story concluded his tale by saying, "That young couple had no idea what a great treasure that had in their possession."

When I finished reading the story, I asked the eighth grade students what the treasure was that the young couple had received. Most of the students answered, "It was the $10,000!" Others said that it was the expensive Bible. No one gave the correct answer.

Do you know what treasure the couple had in their possession of which they were unaware?

MARCH 28
God Behind the Scenes

Last week I spent some time in Washington D.C. As I was working my way through the Smithsonian Air and Space Museum, I noticed a display dedicated to Neil Armstrong's landing on the moon. Looking at a moon rock, special landing gear, and other memorabilia from his successful mission led me to a display of the words Neil Armstrong spoke as he put his foot on the moon's surface: "That's one small step for man, one giant leap for mankind."

What I found very interesting however, was not so much what Armstrong said at that moment, but rather what it took to get him to the point where he could say those words. The display indicated that, although it was one small step that one man took on that fateful day, July 20, 1969, there were many other people involved in making that day happen. In fact, it took over 218,000 people working behind the scenes to make it possible for Armstrong to be on the lunar surface. That's a lot of people putting their skills and talents together to create something remarkable.

Have you ever taken the time to consider how many people and events God has put together to make it possible for you to be where you are today? Is it possible that God may have been doing a lot more behind the scenes work than you know, getting the right people in the right places at the right time under just the right circumstances, to bring you to where you are today?

The Lord has each of us in the palm of his hand and he is always at work in our lives, creating and re-creating us. Take some time right now to give thanks to the Lord for all the many and varied behind-the-scenes ways God has been taking care of you.

MARCH 29
Opening a Restaurant

Recently a friend called in the middle of the night in a daze. He said that he needed a cup of coffee and a friend because his son had overdosed. I asked if his son had passed. There was a long pause. Finally, in a very tired whisper, he said, "Thank God, no." Another long pause, tears, and then three words, "I'm so tired." "Love can do that," I said.

We met in a little restaurant and talked for quite a long time. As my friend drank his coffee, ate a little and talked, he began to look a bit better. I noticed something as he was talking. On the wall directly behind him was a chalkboard that listed the daily specials. At the top of the board were these words: "If you're tired, our soups can restore you!"

Those words reminded me of something I read while on vacation with friends. We were in a little cafe and the menu had an explanation of the word "restaurant," which was first used back in the 1700s. In those days everyone ate at home. If they traveled and stayed at an inn they ate whatever the innkeeper chose to serve. It was in Paris that a chef first opened a little room where he served customers a variety of soups. To attract passersby he painted a little sign with the word "restaurant" on it in big letters, a word that means, "to restore." In a short time many such dining rooms opened in Paris. Each one would put that same word in their windows to let people know that the food they served would restore their energy.

As my friend was regaining his strength after his son's brush with death, I told him what I had learned about the word restaurant. He looked at me for a few minutes and said, "You run a good restaurant."

Is there someone in your life right now who needs you to open a restaurant for him or her? When you have been worn out by life's burdens, was there someone who opened their heart to you and restored your energy?

MARCH 30
God and Your Cat

I was at my mom's one day feeding her cat, and I began to wonder what kind of life a cat has. Do you know that cats spend eighty-five percent of their time doing absolutely nothing? The experts say that cats spend five percent of their day eating, drinking, grooming, killing things, visiting the litter box, and on the availability of another cat, mating. The remaining ten percent of their day is spent just moving around or "visiting." Experts also have discovered that when your cat "disappears" for a day or two, it is not off on some grand expedition hunting game; more than likely it is three or four doors down the street with another family who thinks your cat is their cat that has finally come home from some great hunt out in the fields.

The Egyptians are said to have domesticated the cat. The truth, however, may well be that it was cats who domesticated us. One recent study has shown there are many more people who claim to own a cat than there are actual cats. How do the experts explain this? They discovered that if your cat is an outside cat, or even a cat that gets out once in a while, it is probably one of those cats that have "adopted" or "domesticated" other families. In other words, if you own an outside or occasionally outside cat, your cat has been cheating on you and leading a double or triple life!

If you need proof of this, how often does your cat eat? The cat folks will tell you that a healthy feline needs to eat the equivalent of five mice a day – but they will only eat the amount of food the size of one mouse at a meal. If your cat eats only twice a day, guess what? Someone else is feeding it three other times during the day or night. The truth of the matter is that your cat has adopted or domesticated other families who have gladly agreed to feed, nourish, and pamper it.

Now why do I even bring all of this up? Because we often think of God the way we think of our cats. Many people assume that God, like their cat, belongs only to them, that in some way we have invited God into our lives and because God has accepted the invitation, he has therefore declined all others and will be there only for us. Little do we realize that God has a much bigger worldview than we do. The truth of the matter is, there is much more to God than we could ever imagine. Although we have invited God into our world, can you even begin to imagine the bigger world God invites you to share?

The gospels of the Easter season are a reminder to us that even though we think we have "domesticated" God by bringing him into our world, it is really God who is domesticating us and bringing us into his world.

MARCH 31
How Far Away Are You?

I've been thinking about one of the exhibits that came to the Museum Center in Cincinnati some years ago, a national tour of artifacts from the *Titanic*. In that exhibit were artifacts from some of the lifeboats and stories that went with those items. A survivor by the name of Eva Hart told about her experiences after the huge ship had gone beneath the surface. At least twenty lifeboats had been launched prior to the sinking of the ship, but many people chose not to board them. The result was that very few of the lifeboats were full.

After the Titanic had slipped from view, it was lifeboat number 14 that rowed back to the scene to search for other survivors. It made its way through the darkness, chasing the cries of those in the water. Many were rescued from those frigid waters. All of the other lifeboats, however, remained at a distance because they feared the people in the water would swamp them, which might cause their boat to sink. Fear kept nineteen of the twenty lifeboats that had been launched at too far a distance to do what they had been created to do: save lives.

Isn't it amazing what fear can do if we let it take charge of our lives? What happened back in 1912 on the night the *Titanic* was lost can serve as a great metaphor for what can happen among us if we let fear keep us at too far a distance, to do the good that we have been created to do.

The question we have to ask ourselves is, "Am I allowing fear to keep me at a far distance from the people God is asking me to serve?" Is there anyone in your life or some situation in your life that needs the "lifeboat" of your love? The great gift we have all received is that God chose to be with us when he sent Jesus.

April

APRIL 1
Loose Cannons

I was reminded the other day of a novel I read as part of a history class in college. The class was on the French Revolution and the novel was Victor Hugo's *Ninety-Three*. I honestly don't remember much about that book, but I do remember one particular scene in it because I used it in a presentation I gave as part of that class.

In that scene a war ship is caught in a terrible storm, tossed about in the roaring waves so violently that the crew begins to fear for their lives. In addition to the roar of the sea and very loud cracks of thunder, the captain becomes aware of a terrifically loud banging sound below deck. In an instant he realizes that the sound coming from below is an unchained cannon rolling freely from one side of the ship to the other.

Two sailors are ordered to go below to secure the cannon; the mission given those two sailors is the most important of all at that moment. The captain knows better than anyone else on that ship the greatest danger to them is not the storm on the outside of the ship, but the loose cannon within the ship that could sink them.

I remembered that scene this week as I was listening to a young man describe his craving for a drink. He said, "When I'm with my friends, all I want is to be a part of the group. If I can't have a drink, I don't think I can be myself and be accepted by them. I just know I need something to get me relaxed. This voice in me says, 'Have a drink and you will loosen up; then everything will be just fine.'"

As I listened to him, the scene from that novel just came to mind. That young man had a real "loose cannon" banging around within him. Had that young man not been able to speak with his sponsor in his AA group, he probably would have lost his sobriety. An honest talk with his sponsor helped him to secure that loose cannon within him.

Is there a loose cannon within you that threatens to sink your future? Why not take some steps to secure that cannon by talking honestly with someone who cares for you? Why not approach God in prayer and ask his help with securing the loose cannons within you?

April 2
He Has Work

Recently I've been working with several people who feel that God might be calling them to some kind of ministry. One person, in fact, is beginning to believe that God is calling him to be a missionary preacher to the poor. A curious thing happened during our conversations, however, that took me by surprise. All three of these people are truly feeling called, but each of them also doubts the call because they are ashamed of something in their past. As one young woman said, "I'd really like to do God's work, but I am hardly a good example of what someone who works for God ought to be."

In response to this I dug out some of my old class notes from my biblical study days in the seminary. These notes helped me when I was trying to discern my calling, and I think they helped my three friends. Maybe this will be of some help to you, too.

The next time you begin to feel unworthy, unfit to be one of God's friends and disciples, remember these folks from the Bible: Noah was a drunk. Abraham thought he was too old. Isaac was a daydreamer, and Jacob a liar. Leah was ugly. Joseph was hated by his brothers and sold into slavery. Moses was a murderer. Gideon was terrified. Sampson was a womanizer, and Rahab was a prostitute. Both Jeremiah and Timothy thought they were too young. David had an affair and murdered to cover it up. Elijah was suicidal. Isaiah ran around preaching naked. Jonah ran from God. Job went bankrupt. John the Baptist ate bugs. Peter denied he even knew Jesus. The disciples fell asleep when Jesus needed them most. Martha worried about everything.

Zacchaeus was too short. Paul murdered Christians. Timothy had an ulcer and Lazarus, well, Lazarus was dead!

It's important for all of us to remember that God has a plan for each of us, and he knows everything about us. There is nothing in us or about us that will keep God away. So if you ever get to thinking you aren't good enough to serve God, think again. He has work for you to do.

April 3
Old Pictures

The other day I found an old photo album, and I spent quite a bit of time looking at it. It was fun to go through those images, some of which were very old, and recall past events. There were some pictures of relatives who have died, and recalling memories of those folks made me realize how much I miss some of them.

The experience reminded me of a book I had read a few years ago, *The Cloister Walk*, by Kathleen Norris. In it there is a passage in which Norris talks about visiting a monastery. The guest master of that monastery had given her a tour of the grounds, then introduced her to the monks who lived there. After she had had some tea with a few of the monks, the guest master then said to her, "Kathleen, would you like to meet the rest of the community?"

When she heard that question she wondered what the monk meant, because she thought she had met all of the residents. Her guide then proceeded to take her outside and led her to the monastic cemetery, where he pointed out the graves of departed monks. He told a little story or anecdote about each one, and explained to her that their community consisted not only of the monks who lived in the monastery but also those who now live in Heaven.

Kathleen Norris learned that day about our belief in the Communion of Saints. Our family does not just consist of those living here on earth but also those who have gone on ahead of us and live with the Lord in Heaven.

If you haven't looked through some of your family photo albums lately, I recommend that you do. It's a great way to rediscover how blest you are with the people God has placed in your life. It may also give you an opportunity to revisit some of your friends and relatives who may no longer live here on earth. Sometimes we need gentle reminders of the gifts that have been bestowed on us throughout the years.

Remember to give thanks to God for the gifts you have received through those family members here now on earth, and don't forget to give thanks for the gifts you have received through those who now live in Heaven.

April 4
Introducing a Failure

I had a conversation with a friend of mine a couple of weeks ago, and I'm still thinking about that little talk. He had been telling me about how he felt like a failure, and that he thought he was a person of no significance making little difference in the world. As he continued on and on about the many times he had failed in his life, my mind went back to something I read years ago that had been written by Erma Bombeck. For anyone who feels they have made way too many mistakes, failed way too many times, or just feel small and insignificant, listen to what Erma has to say:

"I have several reactions when I hear people introduce me as a speaker. Sometimes the accolades are so glowing that I don't even recognize myself. I just figure that Mother Teresa must have flown in to give the invocation before the speaker and it's she they're talking about. Other times I feel like bolting while I'm still ahead. But most of the time I feel as if the only decent thing I can do to justify such a tribute is to die!

"I would like to propose a new wrinkle to introductions. Instead of listing a speaker's successes, why not list the failures? Something like this, 'Born average, our speaker tonight never rose above it. Her first and last comedy album raced away from the charts to oblivion. She has written numerous plays no one has ever heard of because none of them ever made it to the stage. She has never won a Pulitzer Prize, has never been invited to the White House for dinner, and has never been interviewed by Barbara Walters.' Failure is what most of us do. We do a lot more failing than succeeding.

"So, if the speaker really is a loser, what IS the point of the crowd listening to what she has to say? Well, the very point is that, despite all of the disappointments and failures, she still has the gumption to put them all aside and manage to go on breathing and working and loving and caring in some imperfect but heartfelt ways to reach out to all of those around her that she loves so dearly."

If you are at a point where you feel overwhelmed, overburdened or maybe even a bit undone by some of your past mistakes or lack of success, take heart: you are not alone. You, like most of the people around you, can and have taken the next step. You go on breathing, and in many loving and caring ways, imperfectly forge ahead, reaching out to those around you whom you love so dearly. If Jesus taught us nothing else, he taught us that failure is often a road to new life.

April 5
Can You Remember Why?

I received the following little vignette in the mail the other day, and it gave me a good laugh. According to the story, three sisters, ages ninety-two, ninety-four, and ninety-six, lived in a house together in upstate New York. One night the ninety-six year old drew a bath. She put her foot in and then paused to think. She yelled down stairs to her sisters, "Was I getting in or out of the bath tub?"

The ninety-four year old yelled back, "I don't know, I'll come up and see." She started up the stairs and paused a bit to think. "Was I going up the stairs or down?" she yelled to her sister. Now the ninety-two year old was sitting at the kitchen table having some tea, listening to her sisters yelling. She shook her head and said, "I sure hope I never get that forgetful!" With that she knocked on wood for good measure. She then yelled to her sisters, "I'm on my way up there, but first I have to stop and see who's knocking on the door!"

As I was thinking about this little story, I began to consider how many people I know who find themselves in the middle of some very complicated situations. One man came to talk about all of the stress he was under. He talked for an hour without pausing, then, after taking a deep breath said, "I am in so deeply that I can't remember how I ever got into this mess! Can you remember why I decided to do all of this in the first place?"

This reminds me of a conversation I had with a parent who was complaining about how many activities she had to drive her daughter to each day. "I can't recall why I ever agreed to all of this," she said. "I can't remember when I said yes. I guess I did, but I don't really recall it. My daughter insists that I agreed to all of this. I just can't remember."

This is a great time of year for us to do a kind of memory check and ask ourselves why we are doing what we are presently doing. It's a great opportunity to see if how we are living matches up with what we had originally intended for ourselves, our families, and others.

Perhaps if we recall the decisions we made that brought us to the way we are presently living and why we originally made those decisions, we may find that a new decision is in order. Could you use a good memory check?

APRIL 6
The Law of the Echo

I read about a farmer who always won first place at the local county fair competition for the best corn. He was very proud of the fact that year after year he was able to produce the best corn in the county, and he would tell people he would do everything he could to make sure his corn was always the best. He also made sure he gave some of his best corn seed to all of the farmers in his neighborhood. He was praised by one and all for his truly generous spirit.

Each year, as his neighbors thanked him for sharing his wonderful corn seed with them he would simply reply, "My corn is your corn too!" When he was asked by his young son why he shared his best corn seed with the neighbors, the farmer replied, "Listen, son, although it looks like I'm being very generous in sharing our corn seed with all of the neighbors, I'm really just practicing the "Law of the Echo."

"What is the Law of the Echo," his son asked.

"Well, the law simply says that whatever you send out will always come back to you. So when it comes to corn, what I give out will eventually come back to us," the farmer replied.

Because his son looked more confused than before, the farmer went on to explain what he meant. "You see, son, when our neighbors plant the seed I give them, the corn grows. Then the wind comes and picks up the corn plant's pollen and carries it from field to field, including our own. Because we know our corn seed is really good, we can be sure it will be good corn pollen that is spread around, and we will maintain our good crop."

"If our neighbors were to plant inferior corn, those plants would be spreading inferior pollen and the quality of our corn, because it had been pollinated by inferior corn, would be brought way down. So by sending out good seed, we grow better corn. What we send out comes back to us, just like the Law of the Echo says."

That story can be a good reminder to all of us to consider what kind of "seed" we are giving to those around us. The seed we send out will surely come back to us in some way or other, just as the Law of the Echo dictates.

APRIL 7
Without Wax

I recently went to the Cincinnati Art Museum. In one of the rooms, which had statues carved in ancient Rome, I noticed a group of art students sitting in a circle around a particular statue. A teacher was with them giving a lecture on Roman sculpture, and as she was talking, the students were sketching the statue in their sketchbooks. I continued my own tour of the sculptures in that room, but listened in on what the art teacher was saying. One thing she said was very interesting.

According to the teacher, sculpting was a very popular and lucrative profession in ancient Rome. It was quite fashionable for every Roman citizen to decorate their homes with statues of various gods or with images of personalities from popular myths and legends. Because of this, many people chose to become sculptors. Not all of these people were good at the profession, however, and there were many poorly done works created. One thing these less qualified artists did to cover the mistakes in their marble sculptures was to hide the cracks with wax. Unsuspecting customers usually could not see the wax cover-up, and ended up with very inferior works.

The best artists were appalled by this practice, so to make sure people knew that their works of art were truly works of great skill, they would mark each of their pieces with the words *sine cera*, meaning "without wax."

I listened closely as the teacher finished up by saying, "And so even today, when you or I send a letter to someone and we want to make it very official, we sign the letter 'sincerely.' By that we mean we have written from our hearts what we truly believe and feel. There is nothing fake about what we have said. Like those artists from the past, we are saying that there is 'no wax' in what we have written."

As I finished my own tour of the art museum, I continued to think of those old Latin words –*sine cera* – and I began to see how our English word "sincere" came to be. I used that little part of the art teacher's lecture in my meditations for a week or two. It's a helpful way to take stock of our own life and practices from time to time, to make sure that what we do and what we give each other is "without wax" and is truly sincere.

If you were to stop and consider your own life and work, your attitudes and the quality of the things you do, could you say they are "without wax"?

April 8
Do You See Now?

This week, as I observed parents getting their children settled in at church before Mass, I recalled something I had read years ago when I was studying some Zen Buddhist stories.

A famous Zen teacher once shocked his students by saying, "A child will rarely find a greater enemy than a parent." Now this saying confused all of his students. "How in the world can a parent be such a great enemy?" they asked. The Zen master thought for a moment, then his eyes lit up with a twinkle and he went on. "I met a woman on the street pushing a stroller with two little ones in it. 'What cute children you have,' I said. 'How old are they?' The mother replied, 'The doctor is three and the lawyer is two.'"

Turning to his students, the Zen teacher said, "So do you see it now?"

April 9
Go Off Schedule

I came across a news item the other day about some difficulties one of the bus companies in London was having. According to the article, complaints were coming in from bus riders all over London who had been standing in large crowds at various bus stops only to see completely empty buses drive right by them. As many as twenty-five to thirty people would be waiting at a stop yet not one of these empty buses even slowed down, much less stop, to take on waiting passengers.

After a thorough investigation the bus company officials discovered the root of the problem: bus drivers were purposely passing up the crowded bus stops so they could stay on schedule. Picking up all of those people would have put them behind schedule, and that was forbidden.

As I read that article it dawned on me that, although it may have been some ridiculous logic on the part of the bus drivers, it's the kind of logic we all fall into from time to time. Think of it for a moment: Has the hectic pace of your schedule ever caused you to ignore the needs of your family? Have you ever allowed your schedule to become more important than the relationships you have with your friends? Have you ever found yourself feeling isolated from family and friends because you have too rigidly kept to a schedule and made little or no provision for the people who mean the most to you? Sometimes we forget that our schedules are meant to serve us, and not the other way around.

In the weeks ahead, why not look for an opportunity to go "off schedule" and spend some quality time with those you love? I don't think you will ever regret the effort you make to do so.

APRIL 10
Knock, Knock, Knocking

I happened to catch a news report this past week in which the news anchor was interviewing an expert on the economy to get his views on current economic conditions. As I listened to the interview I recalled a famous parable from the Sufis, titled "The Experts."

According to that parable a dead man, who had already been placed in a coffin, suddenly awoke, came to life, and began pounding on the lid of the coffin. The lid was raised. The dead man sat up and looked around, and saw that he was the main attraction at his own funeral. "What are you people doing?" he said to the assembled crowd. "I am not dead. I am quite alive!"

The people gathered there were startled by all of this. In fact, they were all quite stunned and sat in silent disbelief. Finally, one of the mourners screwed up enough courage to approach the dead man. "Sir," he said, "I would like to have a word with you if I may. My friend, both the doctors and all of the priests here have certified that you are, of course, dead. That is why we have gathered here today for your funeral. You're sitting here, speaking with us, and this is, to say the least, a bit disconcerting. Nevertheless, all of the experts have agreed that you are dead. So dead you are; that's it. Please lie down and let us continue."

The "dead man" listened attentively and spoke, "Well, if the experts have agreed to the fact that I am dead, I must be dead." At the end of the service he was duly buried.

When I first heard that parable I thought it was the dumbest thing I had ever heard. I thought it was complete nonsense, and in fact, I asked the professor who told the parable to explain it. Here's what he said:

"You may think this is a nonsensical story and just blow it off, but I assure you there is great wisdom here. How many of you in your 'expert' opinions have ever made a judgment about a family member or colleague of yours, assuming that your appraisal was accurate and true? For example, have you ever written someone off as dishonest or not very intelligent, and then from that moment on refused to see him or her in any other light? If you have, you are much like the people in that Sufi story. You are an "expert" who puts up his or her own ideas against the truth and chooses to ignore the truth."

The professor went on to tell us that if we insist on making judgments about people we can expect from time to time that those people will be knocking on the lid of the coffins you put them in. I guess there is something to be said about that parable after all.

APRIL 11
He Is Risen! Now What?

While doing some research at the public library the other day, I came upon a book entitled *Aging Well*. The book was the result of a decades-long study done by a psychiatrist named George Vaillant. In his long term study, Dr. Vaillant sought to identify traits of men in their teens and twenties that would predict successful careers and home lives when they reached their forties and fifties, into old age. The study showed that for many people the last years of life did not have to be seen as a time of loss, regret, and waiting for death. In fact, many of the men in the study saw the later years of life to be their best years.

Dr. Vaillant wrote that he had identified two traits that seemed to be the key to contentment later in life. The first trait was that the men who, throughout their life, seemed to have a growing circle of friendships were much happier in later life. The men who would continue to make new friends, as old friends died or moved away, were men of hope and vitality. Because of this finding, Dr. Vaillant suggested that everyone make a point of doing a friendship inventory on a regular basis and ask themselves, "Have I made a new friend recently?"

A second important trait that points to a future filled with hope, joy, and contentment is the choice to forgive slights and hurts. The study suggested that if you spend a lot of time looking back over your life, look back with gratitude more than with regret. We can look back with thankfulness for blessings received or we can choose to look back with bitterness and regret over disappointments.

It seems to me that these two traits – a growing circle of friends as well as nurturing the ability to forgive and be thankful -- are a good description of what we are called to do as disciples of Jesus. As we enter into this Easter Season and celebrate Jesus' triumph over death, we may be asking ourselves a simple question: "Now what?" What are we to do with what Jesus has done for us and in us? The short answer is also simple: We are to live the resurrection.

What does it mean to live the resurrection? In a very real sense, it means that we live out the two traits identified by Dr. Valliant as key to a happy life. We are called to build an ever-widening circle of friendships in which we can share blessings, burdens, and our faith in Jesus. We are also called to actively cultivate and nurture a spirit of forgiveness, to foster an attitude of letting go of the slights and wounds that come our way and be people who look for the good in others.

The season of Easter is the season of joy and hope. If we live our daily lives according to the two traits identified by Dr. Vaillant, we will certainly become agents of that joy and hope.

April 12
Time to Glow

All human beings have a need for silence. Because we live in a world full of noise, however, we can find ourselves trying to make some noise if we find ourselves in a quiet place. Think about it: How often do you get in your car and turn the radio on rather than ride in quietness? If you find yourself alone at home, do you turn on the TV or radio or play music because the silence makes you feel uncomfortable? For many people, silence is unnerving and downright eerie.

I was thinking about this the other day when I read about a famous site, some sixty miles from Auckland, in New Zealand, called the Waitomo Glowworm Caves. When you travel to this cave you are asked to be completely quiet during the tour of the caves. You get to the caves by a boat that is pulled by a wire so there is no engine noise.

As you move along on the stream running through the cave you enter into a completely dark world. Little by little you begin to see a soft gleaming light in the distance; then you enter a mystical world. From the roof of the cave, thousands of long threads of light hang down about three or four feet. The threads are made up of glowing insects. The light glows and then brightens to the point where you could easily read a book. The light is warm and almost holy in the way it reflects off the waters below it. One feels like they are in another world.

If there is the slightest noise in the cave, the bright light instantly goes out as if someone had flipped a switch, and it becomes pitch black. This causes most people to scream in fear, and the light does not come back on as long as there is too much noise. Once people calm down and begin to be quiet, a small soft light starts to appear. Then, in a short period of time, the insects begin to glow again and light is restored.

Isn't that a great image of what can happen to each of us if we spend too much time in a world full of noise? If we can't find some quiet, our "light" will go out. If we don't try to find some quiet time, our lights may be a long time in coming on again. Why not take some time for yourself this week to find a little bit of quiet? Just imagine the mystical world you may enter if you let the quiet provide the right atmosphere for the light inside you to begin to glow.

APRIL 13
Show Me the Way

Have you ever thought to yourself, "I wish I knew what to do or which way to go"? Have you ever wished you had someone who could just nudge you in the right direction?

I was thinking about this very thing the other day as I read a book about plants. It wasn't a particularly exciting book, but I did find an intriguing description of a plant that grows out on the plains of North America. The plant produces a strange flower with petals that always point toward the north. I'm not sure what the botanical name for the plant is, but its common name is the compass plant. Obviously, it's called that because, like the magnetic needle on a compass, the flower petals always point north. The author of the book said that no matter how much rain falls, no matter how severe a storm may be, nothing seems to affect that plant's ability to point north. Hikers who find themselves lost out on the plains can use the plant to get their bearings and find their way home.

As I read about that plant, I began to think for a moment of the people in my life who serve as compass plants for me. These are the people I can turn to at any given moment to give me direction. Are there people like that in your life? Are there people who, whenever you need direction, just seem to know the right thing to do, the right words to speak, and the right way to go? Isn't it amazing how God seems to provide such people at exactly the right moments in our life! If there are people like that in your life, pause right now and give thanks to God for granting you such blessings.

Of course, the other side of that coin may be the fact that you, yourself, may actually be serving as a kind of compass plant for your friends or family members. You may well be a great blessing to the people right around you who are relying on your wisdom and insight to guide them along the right way. This is, I think, one of the wonderful ways Jesus shows us the way home to the Father. Jesus' life and ministry was all about seeking out the lost. During this Easter season, may you always be aware of his great love for you, and may you always know that if you or a loved one is ever lost, it will be his love expressed in the actions of his disciples that will lead you safely home.

April 14
What Will It Take?

During his annual physical, a man was shocked to learn that he had a rare disease and had less than a year to live. He was devastated, and wondered just how he could go on knowing that he had such limited time left. His wife convinced him that even though he had limited time, he didn't have limited faith or hope. With this, the man realized that he had to see things in a new way.

Not even a month later, however, the doctor discovered he had made a mistake in his diagnosis, so he quickly summoned his patient and told the man that he would live a long life.

Although the doctor's error caused many negative feelings during the month after the initial diagnosis, it also had its positive side because the patient's wife had convinced her husband that he had unlimited faith and hope. He later reflected, "After I had that conversation with my wife, I began to see the beauty of God's creation in a way I hadn't seen it before. When I thought the length of my life was limited, I began to make the most out of every moment."

The man learned that before he was "sick" his busy life actually blinded him to the beauty of a budding tree, the ever-changing formations of interesting clouds, or a spring rain making small circles in a mud puddle. He began to realize that God is performing miracles every day, but we are so caught up in ourselves and our problems that we no longer see the beautiful robin sitting in a nest with her young. He began to see that, when we wake up each morning we need to really open our eyes to God's miraculous world. If we do, we will discover the miracle that awaits us every day. Looking a little harder, we will certainly see a whole lot more.

What will it take for your eyes to be opened?

April 15
Fretting About the Future

Do you ever get nervous about the future? The ways things are today I think most people are a bit worried about it. Some folks seem to be almost paralyzed by their anxiety about the future.

In the past week or two I've spoken with several high school seniors who are trying to determine which college they want to attend. I also have spent time with several college seniors who are worried about the job market and what the future holds for them. All of these students remarked that they wish they could see years into the future, but since they cannot they just don't think they can make a good decision about what to do with their lives.

One student concluded by saying "Since I can't know the future and so can't know what to do about it, I guess I'll do nothing until someone tells me what to do!" That student's buddy, who was sitting at the table with us, said, "My dad told me if I needed someone to tell me what to do I should join the Marines because they have no difficulty in telling you what to do!"

The very next day after I had that last conversation, I came upon something from the life of one of the founders of Johns Hopkins University. That man was one of Canada's most famous doctors, Sir William Osler. He wrote that in the final days of his schooling, as he was about to graduate, he became overwhelmed by fear, worry, and anxiety. He said that fear controlled him because he was so uncertain as to what would happen after graduation, and because he could not see the future he felt totally lost and full of despair.

As Osler was preparing for one of his final exams he came upon a quotation from a nineteenth century English poet, Thomas Carlyle that calmed his restless spirit. Carlyle said, "Our main business is not to see what lies dimly at a distance, but to do what lies clearly at hand.

Later on in his life Sr. William Osler was given many awards for his work, and was even knighted by the King. In his acceptance speech on the day he was knighted he said that he owed every success in his life to the fact that, just before he graduated college, he learned the importance of settling down and doing the work at hand, leaving the future to take care of itself.

That's good advice, especially if you believe that both we and our future are in God's hands. We must simply be alert to the people and tasks at hand and tend to them, rather than fretting about the future.

April 16
A Sheltering Shade

What do you think makes a person holy? I've been thinking about this lately because several people have been telling me that they just don't think they are good enough to please God. They speak as if they have to earn God's love by being good, yet the reality is that God loves us just as we are, sinner or saint. We are his children whom God loves very deeply.

So what does it mean to be a good or holy person? All the religions of the world answer that question in a different way, and in my reading this past week I came across three separate passages that speak about this.

A mystic from India said this: "A holy person, a good person, is like a rose." The mystic went on to say that no rose ever says to itself it will only give its wonderful fragrance to the good people of the earth. No, because the rose is good by nature it gives away its great gift of a beautiful aroma to all who pass by, good as well as bad. "This," the Indian mystic explained, "is just like God himself who sends rain on both the good and just as well as the bad or evil folks of the world."

A Christian saint once said, "The truly good disciple of Jesus is like a lamp lit in the center of a really dark room." That holy woman would go on to say that the lamp gives light to all in the room, and in no way could shed its light only on those who it deemed as worthy or good enough. According to that saint, the good person is like God, who shines his sun down on both the good folks and the evil folks of the earth.

A Sufi holy man put it this way, "A truly good person, one who is very close to the almighty, is just like a big shade tree. It provides its shade to all who come under it, both good folks and bad folks. In fact, it will even provide shade for the very person who is in the act of cutting it down!"

God's love is deeper than any one of us could ever even imagine, and the shade provided to us all by that love is truly a rich blessing. In the very same way, a holy and good person is the one who, in the tiniest details of their daily life, reflects some of the immensity of God's love to those around. Look in your own life for the folks who provide you a real refuge under the shelter and shade of their love. Take some time right now to thank God for those precious "shade trees" of your life.

April 17
Hey, Listen Up!

I read a rather interesting article this week. The author began by saying that most human beings are born with the ability to hear very well. Even infants can distinguish fairly soon between the voices they hear. Yet although it is true that most of us are born with the ability to hear well, it will take a long time for us to learn to listen well. Hearing and listening are not the same things.

The author of the article, who was described as an expert on listening, went on to explain that the reason most of us are not good at listening is that we think four or five times faster than we can speak. This means, of course, that if someone speaks at about 120 words a minute, the audience listening to him is thinking at about 500 words a minute. The result is that many listeners will be tempted to take a side trip in their brain as the speaker drones on. The speaker might be pouring out his or her heart to the crowd, but after having listened for a minute or two, many in the crowd have already moved on to thinking about what they will have for supper or what they need to pick up at the grocery store, or to what they forgot to tell their mother when they last spoke on the phone!

The researchers found that when most people listen to a ten minute talk they only get about twenty-eight percent of what was spoken to them. In addition, the longer the talk we are "hearing" the less we are able to understand it, since our minds are off to the races! If we are going to understand what we hear, we have to cultivate an ability to concentrate so we can truly listen.

Perhaps taking stock of how well we listen to those who are closest to us would be a great spiritual practice to take up. How well do you pay attention when your spouse, children, parents, siblings, or friends speak to you? How much of what your co-workers say do you actually take in? These are important considerations. We may hear perfectly well without ever really listening!

April 18
Stupid Thoughts

I was sitting with a young couple at a wedding reception not long ago when our conversation turned from small talk to more profound matters. They had been married for just six months, and they were telling me about all of the adjustments they both were making in getting along. I asked them if things were going well. There was a pause, and then the young woman spoke up. "Things are pretty good but I notice that he keeps hurting my feelings." Before I could say anything, the young man spoke, "She's right. I don't know how it happens, but I keep saying stuff that hurts her. I don't mean to do it, it just happens.

I was about to respond when an older woman sitting at our table, who apparently had been eavesdropping, spoke up and said, "That same thing used to be a problem for me and my husband. For years he would say things that hurt me, then I'd find myself not thinking and end up saying something terrible to him, and then he'd have his feelings hurt."

I asked the woman, "So what did you two do about it?"

Without taking a breath she replied, "Well, we ended up talking with my mom. She told us that we had to learn the fine art of shutting the heck up! Then she gave us a little plaque with a saying from Benjamin Franklin on it."

"What saying was on that plaque?" I asked.

She began looking through her purse until she found her keys, which were attached to a fancy key ring. On that key ring was this quotation from Benjamin Franklin: "Remember not only to say the right thing in the right place, but far more difficult still, to leave unsaid the wrong thing at the tempting moment." "That saying," she said, "has served as a reminder to both me and my husband to think before we speak, and to pay attention enough to not speak when it is really important to not speak. It has saved both of us from a world of hurting."

Turning to that young couple she said, "You just have to learn when to keep your stupid thoughts to yourself!"

Sounded like good advice to me.

April 19
Right Side Up

Human beings have five senses – at least that's what I learned in grade school science. Recently, however, I've learned that we humans have some additional senses that were not included in my grade school science books. In addition to our sense of sight, hearing, taste, smell, and touch, we also have within us a sense of balance, which goes by the fantastic name of "equilibrioception."

Most of us know about the sense of balance simply by the times we may have lost that sense. If you've ever had an inner ear problem, been seasick or drunk, you know the feeling. Having a sense of balance, it seems to me, is just as important to a fuller experience of life as those other five senses we learned about in school.

Thinking about the sense of balance our bodies possess has led me to the realization that our souls possess a sense of balance as well. All of the great spiritual leaders in just about every religious tradition speak of this spiritual sense of balance when they speak of what we Christians refer to as the virtue of temperance.

By definition, a virtue is a good habit and a vice is a bad habit. To live the virtue of temperance then is to live a balanced life, and to practice the virtue of temperance is to live a life that does all things in proper moderation. For centuries spiritual masters have taught that true happiness comes from listening to your soul's directive to do all things in moderation. If you live an unbalanced life, then you may end up living a life of excess, falling into bad habits or vice.

I suppose the moral of all of this is simple: Just as our physical sense of balance keeps us standing upright, so too does our spiritual sense of balance. Put another way, temperance keeps us spirituality upright. As you think about your life right now, are you spiritually upright?

April 20
The Years of Your Life

How often do you think about your age? I'll bet that, other than in the days before an upcoming birthday, you probably don't spend too much time thinking about your age or the passing of the years.

I thought about my own age recently after I visited a local nursing home where a woman was celebrating her one-hundredth birthday. As she ate her birthday cake she said, "I have been through a whole lot of stages in my life. Some of those stages were pretty good, some not so good, but they all led me here to all you good people who surround me." She was a very sweet old lady.

I was reminded of her comments later in the week when I was browsing through the books at the library, and came across a copy of Grimm's fairy tales. As I was flipping through the pages I found something really interesting and funny. It made me laugh. I had flipped open to the page with a passage entitled, "The Duration of Life." Here is that passage, and see if it doesn't make you laugh, too.

God originally determined thirty years as the ideal span of life for all animals, including mankind. The donkey, the dog, and the monkey considered it much too long, however, and begged God to reduce their years by eighteen, twelve and ten. Being healthy, vigorous, and somewhat greedy, the man asked to be given those extra years. God agreed, so man's years totaled seventy.

The first thirty years of his life are man's own, and they pass quickly. The next eighteen are the "donkey years," during which he has to carry countless burdens on his back. Then come twelve "dog years," when he can do little but growl and drag himself along. This is followed by the "monkey years," his closing ten, when he grows rather strange and does things that make children laugh at him."

Did that story make you laugh? If you were to think about your life right now, what "stage" or "age" are you in? Are you in the "donkey years," "dog years," "monkey years," or still in your own years? Whatever age you may find yourself in, it's always good to take the time to thank God for every stage and age because, as that sweet, hundred-year-old lady said, they have led you here to all the good people who surround you.

Why not take a few moments to thank God for all the years of your life?

April 21
A Wonderful Place to Be

I read recently about a man who traveled with Christopher Columbus on his voyage to the New World. The man was a dedicated crewman, but he was always preoccupied by one thought, a thought he couldn't get rid of no matter how hard he tried. The tormented man spent his entire time on that voyage worried about when they were going to get back home. He worried about this because he thought that the village tailor was quite old and would probably be unable to continue working because of his age, or because he might even die. "If I'm not home when he quits or dies, someone else will take his job and I'll be left out in the cold!" the man thought to himself.

Because of thoughts like that, the crewman never really saw any of the New World. He might have been physically there when Columbus made his discoveries, but he certainly was not there mentally because his mind's eye was set on that little village he called home, and on the one job he longed to have. Imagine for just a minute: That man was along on one of the greatest adventures of all time, and he spent his time looking back in a fit of worry and anxiety. He really was never on that trip at all. He was there but he missed it.

Has that ever happened to you? Have you ever been on a trip but because of a preoccupation with home, or work, or other worries, could never be present to what you were doing? I can assure you that many people have had exactly this experience. They sign up for a great adventure but can't step out of their routine or worries long enough to experience all that is being offered them.

During this Easter season the Lord invites us into a great adventure. Jesus, who laid down his life for us, invites us to lay down our worries, fears, anxieties, and preoccupations so we can receive all that he wants to show us. I think the old saying, "Let go and let God," is an invitation to trust God with your future and to stop trying, by your worrying, to control it. The bottom line is that the Lord has all of us in his hands, and that's a wonderful place to be!

April 22
Rounding the Bases

Time and its effect on us is an interesting thing to consider. I was in a conversation the other day with some men who were lamenting the fact that they were getting older and not able to do all they used to do. As the conversation continued, one of the guys remembered something from the late 1980s that happened to him and his young son.

He said, "I remember taking my youngest son to a Major League baseball game. It was one of those games in which they honor some of the great ball players from the past, and there was time set aside for fans to get autographs. So I took my son down to the field, and there was Mickey Mantle! When we got up to have a baseball signed by Mr. Mantle, I said to my son, 'Joey, this is the greatest baseball player who ever lived!' My boy's eyes were wide as he said, 'Wow!' Mickey Mantle signed the ball and handed it back to my son. My boy was thrilled and so was I. As we made our way back to our seats, my son asked, 'Dad, how does that old guy run around the bases without falling over?'"

Isn't that a great story? I was thinking of it when I went to anoint someone at a local nursing home last week. As I looked at the person, I wondered what she must have been like when she was at the top of her game. I wondered what life experiences she carried around in her heart, and what fond memories of the past she may have been turning over in her mind. I thought also about how differently people might treat her if they knew her story, and all she had done and been through.

When I had finished the anointing, I mentioned my thoughts to a nurse's aide who was helping me and praying with us. The aide smiled and said she often thought the same thing, then added, "Whenever I come into a patient's room I always say to myself, 'Be sure to treat them as if they are at their prime!' That way I can remember to give them the respect and kindness they deserve. They were not always as we see them now. I try to honor both who they were and who they are."

That nurse's aide has some great wisdom that we can apply to anyone we meet. Time takes its toll on every one of us. We can also apply that wisdom to ourselves when we start feeling the effects of time. You may not be as great a baseball player as Mickey Mantle was, but then maybe you can still run around the bases without falling over!

April 23
Be Careful of How You Treat Your Camel!

I was at the library the other day looking through some magazines when I happened on a small article about animals and their memories. When I was growing up we were told that elephants never forget, and that they have the best memories of all of the animals. The article I read, however, said the ancient Greeks believed that, even though elephants appeared to have very good memories, they studied the matter and discovered that camels had the best memories of all.

Now I don't know just why the Greeks thought it was important to determine which of the animals had the best memories, but I did find something interesting in what the Greeks recorded about camels. According to their studies, camels not only have long memories, they hold grudges! If a trainer mistreats a camel, hurts it in any way, or treats it unfairly (how do you know when a camel feels it has been treated unfairly?) the camel will find a way to get even.

The Greeks observed that the camel would take just so much abuse before the resentment built up in them like a giant pressure cooker. Then the lid blows off and the camel goes berserk! The Greeks also noted that the camel might give a hint from time to time that it is unhappy with its trainer by spitting at him. Next comes a bit of biting or nipping at the trainer. But then, after the internal pressure gets to be too much, an attack of real meanness erupts.

The Greeks also learned that trainers could protect themselves from their foul-tempered camels by providing a kind of safety valve. They instructed the camel trainers to pay attention, so when they see their camels begin to show signs of resentment, they can calm the animal down with a simple gesture. They are to give the camel their shirt or coat. If the camel is resentful or angry the animal will immediately pounce on the article of clothing that smells of its trainer. It will jump up and down on it, tear it with its teeth, spit on it, throw it up in the air, and rip it to shreds. When the camel has vented in this way, it immediately calms down and all is well again. The trainer and camel can work together again; all appears to be forgiven.

Isn't that amazing? I had no idea that camels (or any animal other than humans) carried resentment around in them.

As I read that little article and began to think about it, I came back to a truth that I've known for years: resentment is the cause of much destruction in all of our relationships. Think about your own life right now. Are you like a camel slowly boiling away inside because of what someone said or did to you? Has the resentment been building up to the point where you are already spitting at them or biting and nipping at them? Perhaps now is the time to let go of those resentments before they boil over in a hurtful and destructive way. Camels are not the only ones with long memories.

April 24
A Special Blue Pennant

At a retreat a few years ago, a well-known spiritual master told us a story about a new army recruit who was assigned guard duty by his sergeant. The sergeant led the recruit to the entrance of the army base and gave him these instructions: "Private, your orders are to stand guard here at this gate, and you are to let no one pass if they do not have the special blue pennant attached to the car." "Yes, Sergeant!" the recruit answered.

Then, after thinking about it for a minute, the recruit asked, "Sergeant, what should I do if someone without a blue pennant tries to pass?" "Well, son," the sergeant replied, "if someone without a blue pennant tries to pass after you've warned them, you are to shoot them dead. Do you understand?" "Yes, sergeant, I understand. If they try to pass without a blue pennant, I will shoot them dead."

The recruit was on duty for about an hour when a car approached. He stopped the car and noticed that there was a driver in the front seat and a general in the back seat. The recruit told the driver that he could not enter the army base because he did not have a blue pennant attached to the car. The general was not happy about the delay so he shouted at the driver to continue on, then yelled at the recruit to get out of the way. The new recruit cleared his throat, raised his weapon, and said to the general, "You'll have to

Falling Awake

pardon me, general, sir, but I'm new to this. Could you please tell me whom do I shoot dead now; you, sir, or the driver?"

When the spiritual master finished telling us that story he looked at us and said, "As you begin this retreat, you must realize there is a general inside you that will want to bark at me to 'get out of the way' because I may be telling you things you don't want to hear. You may, while you are on this retreat, see me as a kind of 'new recruit' or a greenhorn who has to prove that I know what I'm talking about. You may be tempted to disregard what I'm saying because you think you have captured the whole truth about life, and you are merely looking for me to confirm what you already think."

"You also must beware of thinking that I will let you pass by if you do not have the special blue pennant of openness to God as he is, not as you want him to be. That new army recruit was entirely ready to do his duty; I am entirely ready to do mine. On this retreat, it's not about what you want; it's entirely about what God wants from you. It's not about what you want to tell God; it's entirely about what God wants to speak to your heart." With that, the retreat master left the room, and we were left to consider how open we would be to what God wanted to say to us. It turned out to be one of the best retreats I have ever been on, and it opened my mind to discover God in many new ways.

I was thinking about this the other day after one of the younger priests in the diocese told me he thought I could be in danger of losing my soul because he had heard that I had quoted Gandhi, whom he considered a pagan. He was also shocked that I quoted something attributed to the Buddha, and that I even spoke of having studied the Sufi mystics. I told him I would spare him the stuff I'm reading right now (he would have had me in hell if he knew!). We had a very lively conversation, and we were friends by the end of it.

I assured him that my soul was not endangered by my love of Gandhi or Buddha or the Sufis. I also was impressed that he really was concerned for me. Then I told him a story I had heard from a Jesuit friend of mine, who had been criticized at a retreat because his superior found the poetry he was reading "unspiritual." The superior asked my friend, "Is this poetry going to save your soul?" My friend's response was great: "Father, it may not save my soul, but it can make my soul worth saving!"

People often ask me how they can get closer to God. I usually tell them that one of the most common obstacles to getting closer to God is our own attitude. Each of us needs to have a "special blue pennant" of openness to what God wants to show and teach us. Everything in creation has something to teach us about God, and we can't be afraid to look, to see, and to try to understand. Even the people who do not share our way of life or thinking have something to teach us. Sometimes we have to stretch a bit to begin to see what God is already doing in our lives.

April 25
It Was that Kiss

Have you ever stopped to consider why you have become the person you are today? The other day, I was reading about a famous British artist, Benjamin West, who, when asked how he came to be an artist simply replied that it was because of a kiss.

When pressed for more information he told of a time when, in his adolescence, his mother went out, leaving him at home to take care of his little sister. In his mother's absence he discovered a few bottles of ink. There were several different colors of ink, and Benjamin became fascinated with them. He began to draw and to paint with those inks. As he looked around for something to draw, he noticed his little sister, asleep. He began to sketch her, and then began to color in the sketch. He became completely absorbed in what he was doing and was not aware that as he painted, he was spilling ink all over the table and floor. In short, the room in which he had been working was a real mess.

At one point he heard a noise and looked up. There stood his mother staring at the ink spills that covered the table, chairs, and floor where Benjamin was working. As he looked around and saw the mess he had made, he thought for sure he mother would be quite angry. He expected her to scream at him, but she did not. Instead she picked up the picture he had been creating and said with awe, "Why, it's Sally, your beautiful sister Sally!" Then she looked up from the painting, smiled at her son Benjamin, stooped, and kissed him. Benjamin West would often tell his friends and students it was his mother's kiss that had turned him into a painter.

If you were to look back over the years of your life, who or what has turned you into the person you are today? Is there someone who opened your eyes to show you the hidden talents you didn't know you had, or helped you have the confidence to follow your dreams?

On Pentecost Sunday we are made aware of the fact that God has poured out his gifts on us. There are many gifts, but one gift we may overlook is the gift of people whom the Lord sends our way to help us to discover the treasures within us. Are there such people in your life? Why not take a few moments right now to thank God for them?

APRIL 26
Hands or Feet?

A couple of years ago I went to a monastery for a few days of prayer. It was the week before Holy Week, and I was pleased to have some time to prepare for this important occasion. On the second morning of my time at the monastery, I went to Mass. The abbot gave the homily, and during it he looked at each of us and reminded us that the great season of Lent was coming to a close. And so as Holy Week was approaching, he wanted us to make an examination of our lives.

"I want to give each of you a question to take to your prayer," he said. "Here's the question: What kind of "basin theology" do you live by?"

We all must have looked incredibly puzzled because he went on to say, "Well, if you don't know what that means, I guess I'll have to tell you!" He continued: "Do you remember what Pilate did when he had the chance to acquit Jesus? He called for a basin and washed his hands of the whole thing -- that's what he did."

The abbot paused for a moment, then went on again. "Now take a minute to consider what Jesus did the night before he died. He called for a basin and proceeded to wash the feet of the disciples. This all comes down to what might be called "basin theology." Which one will each of you use in your life?"

What kind of basin theology are you going to practice today with your family, at work or school, or with friends? Will you choose to wash your hands, or the feet of others?

April 27
Which Bucket?

I read a story recently that, it's been said, was often used by Saint John Vianney when he preached to his catechism class. In the story there are two angels who were sent to earth by God the Father to gather up the prayers of the human race. One angel was ordered to gather up all the prayers of petitions that people throughout the world were offering. He had many huge buckets filled to the brim when he returned to the Father.

The second angel was sent by the Father to gather up the prayers of the human race as well, but this angel was instructed to gather up the prayers of thanksgiving that men and women all over the world were offering. That second angel returned to God the Father with just a single huge bucket of prayers.

John Vianney would conclude his little story by asking his students a single question: "Which would be visiting you the most, the angel of petitions or the angel of thanksgiving?" Then he would tell his class about the time Jesus cured ten lepers of their terrible disease. "And do you know what happened?" the saint would ask. The children were puzzled because they could not remember, then John Vianney would continue. "Jesus cured ten people, but only one came back to thank him. Make sure you are the one who comes back to thank God for every gift he gives you."

It might be good for each one of us to take a few moments to consider how greatly each one of us has been blessed by the Lord. Are you the one who has come back to thank Jesus for all he has done for you? Are you one of the nine who have forgotten to return and give thanks? If the two angels visited your house, which angel's bucket would be fuller after they had visited you?

April 28
Out of the Box

While reading a biography of Theodore Roosevelt this past week I came upon an interesting anecdote. According to that biography, President Roosevelt was interrupted during a campaign speech by a heckler who kept yelling out and calling the president bad names. The heckler continued on so loudly that Roosevelt stopped speaking and turned to address the man. The man screamed, "I'm a Democrat and I have had enough of you!" The President paused a moment, swallowed hard, then asked, "And why, sir, are you a Democrat?"

The heckler replied, "My grandfather was a Democrat and my father was a Democrat, in fact, my whole family are Democrats! That's why I'm a Democrat!" Roosevelt shook his head and replied, "And suppose your grandfather was a jackass and your father was a jackass, and, in fact your whole family were jackasses. What would you be?" The heckler replied, "Well, in that case Mr. President, I'd be a Republican!"

Teddy Roosevelt never tired of retelling that story, and when he did it always brought great roars of laughter. He would often conclude by saying that one thing he had learned over the years was to never try to put people into categories we won't let them out of. What he meant, I think, was that we have to let people, especially the ones we love dearly, be truly free to grow and become whatever they feel called to be. He said that it was not fair to box people in and then leave them there in that box for all eternity.

I suspect he had been a victim of this himself when he was growing up. As a child, because his health left him somewhat frail, people often thought of him has weak both in body and conviction. Yet time and his continuing struggles to overcome hardship proved all of his detractors wrong.

Every morning we are given a new day, and one way we can all make the world a better place is to make a resolution to not box people in. Sometimes we think we know someone, and we make conclusions about him or her that may not be fair or accurate. Perhaps this year we can all let one another out of the box, and make room for each other to be free to be ourselves.

April 29
Asking for a Gift from the Holy Spirit

I asked a group of college students who were on retreat to think of one talent they wished they could develop to improve their lives. After a few of the students had spoken, one of the senior girls raised her hand and said, "I wish I had the ability to truly appreciate what I see, what I hear, and what I experience. There is so much going on around me I'm sure I'm missing something significant, but I can't be sure. I just don't seem to be able to appreciate what's happening in me and around me."

I really liked that response because it is the one gift or talent we all need. That young woman's comments brought to mind two stories I had read some years ago. The first concerns a tourist who is visiting the tropics. As she visited a few villages she came upon a man wearing what she thought was a very beautiful necklace.

"Oh, sir, what a beautiful necklace you are wearing!" she said as she pointed to the string of objects around the native man's neck. "What is it made of?" she asked.

"Alligator teeth, ma'am," he said in reply.

The tourist was a bit surprised to hear that the necklace was made of alligator teeth, so she tried to make a little more conversation: "Oh, I suppose these teeth have the same value to you and your people as pearls have to me and my people."

The native thought for a moment and replied, "Not quite, not exactly – anyone can open an oyster to pick out a pearl. Alligator teeth require a bit more effort, I would think."

The second story concerns a young college graduate who had just landed a clerical job at the White House. According to that story, the young man had just finished attending his first reception for White House staffers given by the President of the United States himself. The young staffer was so thrilled to be working so close to the seat of power that he knew he had to call his mother to let her know just how far her son had come, exceeding his humble beginnings. As soon as the reception was over he placed a call to his mother. "Mom," he said, "this is a big day for me! I'm calling you from the White House!"

The mother sent her love to her son and gushed over him for a minute or two. Then she said, "Well, it's been a big day for me too!"

"Really? What's happened?" he asked.

"Well, today I finally managed to clean out the attic."

Both stories illustrate how we can miss the significance of the things that are happening around us if we do not have the gift of appreciation. Wouldn't it be a great idea to ask God to give each of us that gift which, like that young college senior said, would afford us the ability to truly appreciate what we see, and what we hear, and what we experience as well

April 30
The Next Best Time

Isn't it amazing that tomorrow we start another new month? Time really seems to rush by us at a faster and faster pace, yet we know that time really moves at its usual steady pace. It's our hectic pace of life that is speeding up, not time.

Whenever I pause to look at my calendar and all the things I have scheduled, I often think of a sign I saw a few years ago at a local plant nursery. The sign was displayed over the entrance to a section of the nursery containing hundreds of young trees of just about every variety, and it proclaimed this simple truth: "The best time to plant a tree was ten years ago. The next best time to plant a tree is today." That sign reminds me of a truth many of us often forget: Although time is limited, today offers us a fresh start.

How often have you looked over your shoulder at your life only to realize some of the things you should have been doing or could have been doing for someone else? You come to realize you should have been helping someone out for years now, yet somehow time got away from you and here it is, weeks, months, or even years later and you still haven't done anything about it. That kind of realization can lead us to feel lost and paralyzed, not knowing how to make things right again.

If that has ever happened to you, take courage. Like that sign in the nursery stated, perhaps the best time to have done something was years ago but that may not be the end of the story. The truth of the matter is that even though we may have missed it ten years ago, the next best time to do it is today. You still have today. Although time is fleeting, you still have today and you can still accomplish a lot of good.

As each day seems to fade away, each new day is a gift from God to each of us. Each new day is God's invitation to make a fresh start, a new beginning. If you have failed to act in the past, let it go. Tomorrow we start a fresh, new month. Use that precious gift of a new day and a new month as the next best time to begin again to make things right.

May

MAY 1
Ever Feel Like a Loser?

I had a conversation with a young couple recently about some difficulties they were having with one of their children. They were concerned because their young son just would not admit when he made a mistake. They had caught him several times hiding his mistakes or even lying about them.

As we discussed the situation I remembered a story I had heard on a local news broadcast. According to the news report, a professional carpet layer had just finished a job for one of his customers. He was rather pleased with himself because he had finished the job a bit early. But as he looked over the room, he noticed there was a little lump in the carpet near the far corner of the room. He didn't really want to rip up the rug, however, and so he was a bit frustrated.

That's when he reached for a cigarette from the pack in his pocket, but they weren't there. He thought to himself, "So that's what the lump is!" Quickly he decided what he would do. He picked up his rubber mallet and began pounding the lump flat. Within no time at all the carpet was nice and flat, as it should have been.

When the carpet layer got to his truck, he noticed his pack of cigarettes on the dashboard. Just then his customer called out the door to him, "Have you seen my parakeet?"

The couple laughed when I told them that story, and they decided to use it with their young son. Later on in the week they told me that their son laughed too when they told him the story. They said it was a perfect way to open a discussion with him about how human it is to make mistakes, and that there is no reason to run from them or hide them.

I asked them how their son responded to their discussion. His mom said, "Oh, he told me that for once in his life he doesn't feel like such a loser! I told him he wasn't a loser," she said. "I told him he was just like all the rest of us, a human being who can learn from their mistakes."

May 2
Clock Watching

While visiting my aunt in a local nursing home, I found myself a bit bored as she slept. I was sitting in a chair next to her, staring at a large clock on the wall opposite her bed. As I watched the second hand go around the clock, I began to wonder why we divide an hour into sixty minutes and a minute into sixty seconds. (I told you I was bored!) Since there was little else to do while my aunt slept, I took out my smart phone and looked it up.

It turns out that the division of time goes all the way back to about 2400 B.C. The ancient Sumerians used the number 6 as their mathematical base to calculate time. They divided a circle into 360 degrees, then divided each degree into sixty smaller parts. The Romans called these units *minuta prima*, meaning "first part," and the next unit they called *secunda minuta*, or "second part." This system was said to be a perfect way to divide the face of a clock, and that is how we ended up using minutes and seconds as units of time. How's that for some useless information!

After I did my research and my aunt had still not awakened, I began to think about time. While it is relatively easy to consider how time is divided into minutes and seconds, it is far more difficult to consider just how we, ourselves, divide up our time. The Desert Fathers often spoke about time and its importance. They said that what we give most of our time to usually shows what we think is most important in life.

If you were to divide your time into categories, what do you spend the most time doing? Is most of your time spent on what you think is most important? Is there a way to make one period of your time, no matter how long or short its duration, mean more than other times? What do you suppose gives time its meaning? Is sitting by the bedside of an old lady in a nursing home a good use of time? I think it is, don't you?

Take some time this week to consider how you, like those Sumerians centuries ago, have been dividing up the circle of your time. Would you change how you are using your time if you could? Why or why not?

May 3
Funny Things

I was visiting some parishioners recently. As I sat on the couch in their family room one of their little daughters joined me and asked if I would read her book to her. The book was *One Fish, Two Fish, Red Fish, Blue Fish*, by Dr. Seuss. Probably just about every parent, grandparent, or child in the country knows that book and may even be able to recite it from memory.

As I read the book to the little girl I asked her to read along with me. It was obvious that she didn't need to read the book at all; she knew it by heart. When we finished reading I asked her what were her favorite lines from the book. Without pausing she shouted out the lines with a kind of giggle: "From there to here, from here to there, funny things are everywhere!"

I asked her why she liked those lines and she answered very quickly, "Cause laughing is fun and funny things make me laugh."

That answer got me to thinking about laughter and happiness and joy. When was the last time you had a good belly laugh? When was the last time, in your going "from there to here, from here to there," that you discovered something really funny? I'm sure you've found something funny along the way; after all, Dr. Seuss did tell us, "Funny things are everywhere!"

Saint Francis of Assisi used to say that one of the marks of a true follower of Jesus is they are filled with joy, mirth, and much laughter. When was the last time you lived up to that description?

May 4
Hissing

I've been thinking lately of an old story about a snake that lived on a path along the way to a famous temple in India. A friend of mine had reminded me of the story as he talked about his divorce, and how an overwhelming bitterness was becoming unbearable. He said he felt "beat up," and was wondering what he ought to do about it. I asked him what his heart told him and he immediately reminded me of that old story, which we had talked about years ago when he had some personal problems.

"Do you remember the snake story?" he asked me. When I said that I did, he asked me to tell him the story again, because he thought he needed to hear it.

According to the story, many people would walk along the path to worship at a famous temple in India, and this angry snake would often bite people with his poisonous bite. One fateful day, a swami was on his way to the temple and the snake pounced on him. Before the snake could bite him, however, the swami put the snake into a trance and ordered him to stop biting people.

"It is not right for you to bite people with your poisonous teeth," the swami told him. "From now on, you shall not bite anyone." From that moment on, the snake did not bite anyone.

A few months later the swami was passing that way again, and he noticed the snake lying in the grass beside the path. The snake was all cut and bruised and in a terrible condition.

"Whatever has happened to you, my friend?" the swami asked.

"Well, since you have put your forbidding spell on me," the snake explained, "I have been unable to defend myself. Many people have beaten me. Please, give me back my bite."

"You foolish snake," the swami answered. "I told you not to bite anyone. But I never said that you couldn't hiss!"

When I finished telling the story, my friend said, "That's it! That's exactly what I needed to hear! My ex-wife and some of her friends and family members have been saying very hurtful things to me and about me. I feel really beaten-up. I guess God would not want me to bite them and fill them with my own poison, and neither does he want me to just submit to their bitter words. I had better develop my own 'hiss' that will let them know I still deserve to be respected and not abused."

"It's a great story, isn't it?" I asked.

"Yes it is!" he said.

Do you need to find your "hiss" in your own life now?

May 5
Hang On to Your Serenity

I was shopping in the grocery store the other day when I heard a great commotion going on in the produce section. A man was yelling at his wife. He had a very hateful look on his face, and everything in the store came to a standstill. Everyone who was watching looked quite uncomfortable as the man called his wife one name after another. For her part, the man's wife just went about putting some oranges in a bag as if nothing was happening. She didn't appear to be upset, ruffled, or disturbed by his outburst at all. Finally the manager came over and asked the man to either act civilly or leave the store.

As I went on with my shopping, I recalled something I had read from the life of the Buddha. It happened on one occasion that a group of people was making fun of him. When the Buddha didn't react, they began to hurl insults at him. Still there was no response from the Buddha, and he just went about his business. Later on, when he was alone with his disciples, they asked him how he could remain so serene when such terrible name-calling was all around him.

The Buddha responded by saying, "Imagine what would happen if someone placed an offering in front of you but you did not pick it up. Or what would happen if someone sent you a letter but you did not open it. If you did not open the letter you would not be affected by its content, would you? Every time you are insulted or abused by someone or they say hateful things to you, and you refuse to pick it up or open it, then you too will be able to hang on to your serenity."

I spent a lot of time thinking about that as I finished my grocery shopping. Think about your own response to hurtful situations: Are you able to hang on to your serenity?

May 6
It's Very Near

As I was flipping through the channels the other day I came across a program about the history of the space program. I don't know the name of the astronaut who was being interviewed, but I do remember what he said. The man was talking about what a privilege it was to actually walk on the moon, and to stand and look back at the earth. He said, "I was so overwhelmed by its beauty that I was speechless, and finally, after a few minutes, all I could mutter was, 'How awesome!'"

The interviewer then asked him, "So what did you do next?" "Oh, I quickly shook the mood off and said to myself, 'Stop wasting time and get over there and start collecting rocks!'"

I laughed when I heard that response because it sums up what I come across when I try to teach people about contemplative prayer. Many people tell me they are so busy with work and family and other aspects of life that they don't have time to notice God. The next time one of my students or someone at a retreat says something like that, I'll tell them about that astronaut standing on the moon, thinking it's a waste of time to notice God's handiwork.

Each new day gives us an opportunity to do something new. Why not take time this week to stop long enough and notice the beauty God has placed right around you? You don't have to go to the moon to find God's handiwork; it's very near to you. Just take some time, open your eyes, and see!

May 7
Restoration

Quite a few years ago, an angry man ran through the Rijksmuseum in Amsterdam until he reached Rembrandt's well-known painting, *The Night Watch*. After he caught his breath, the man took out a knife and slashed the painting repeatedly before he could be stopped. The canvas hung in shreds. The world was shocked at the devastating damage done to the work.

In a similar way, not too long after that, a distraught, angry, anti-religious man walked into St. Peter's Basilica in Rome with a hammer and began to smash Michelangelo's beautiful sculpture, the *Pieta*. The world was again shocked, and stunned that in a very short period of time, two priceless works of art were so viciously attacked.

Experts were called in to determine if those precious works of art could be saved. Many people feared that the works had been ruined and were beyond repair, yet restoration experts concluded that all was not lost. Working with the utmost care and precision, they made every effort to restore the treasures. In the end, they were quite successful; the priceless works of art had indeed been restored to the world.

As I read about how those two famous masterpieces were vandalized and then restored, I was reminded of the fact that every one of us is a masterpiece of sorts. We too can often be "vandalized" in the give and take of everyday life. If you were to stop and think about your own life, has the day-to-day stress of living taken a toll on you? Have you ever felt vandalized by life?

I know from the counseling work I do that many people are battered by life. The good news is, just as there are experts and ways to restore priceless works of art that have been damaged, so too there are folks and ways that can restore us when we have been battered by life. In these revitalizing days of spring, perhaps it would be a good time for you to recover and find restoration from the hardships and difficulties of life.

May 8
Burning the Ships

Recently I watched a History Channel program on ancient Rome, which described something amazing that happened when Julius Caesar landed on the shores of Britain with his Roman legions. Because Caesar knew what monumental task it would be to conquer Britain, he took a decisive step to ensure the success of his military venture. He began by ordering his men to march to the edge of the Cliffs of Dover. Next, he commanded them to look down at the water below. To their amazement, they saw that every ship in which they had crossed the channel was engulfed in flames.

Caesar had deliberately cut off any possibility of retreat. Although his troops were stunned by the move and even sickened by it, Julius Caesar knew exactly what he was doing. He well knew that because his soldiers were unable to return to the continent, there was nothing left for them to do but advance and conquer. And that's exactly what they did.

Caesar knew that when someone is faced with the real truth that there's no going back, no retreating from the road ahead, they will more than likely summon up the inner fortitude to put their entire mind, strength, and will into what must be done.

Is there a situation in your life right now that overwhelms you and makes you want to run away and hide? Are there difficulties in your life that make you want to retreat into your own little world and ignore the needs of those around you? Do you keep looking back to "the good old days" when life seems to have been better?

How different would your attitudes about the future be if you burned the ships that would allow you to retreat?

May 9
Finding Peace in his Footsteps

About a year ago I was at a Presbyterian Church for a wedding. The minister was very gracious and welcomed me by giving me a tour of the church. The facilities were beautiful, and there were many spacious meeting rooms, classrooms, and offices.

One room I remember well was the nursery. It was divided into two major rooms, one a playroom and the other a room in which there was a long row of cribs lining the wall. Above the cribs hung a large, beautifully painted sign that read: "Not all of us shall fall asleep, but all of us are to be changed."

The minister and I laughed as we read the sign aloud. It's a quote from Saint Paul's First Letter to the Corinthians. Paul wrote those words to reassure the people of his time about death and Second Coming of Jesus. He meant that when Jesus returns, not all of us will have died (fallen asleep) but all will be changed when we go off to glory in Heaven.

As the minister and I laughed about that sign, I reminded him that while that sign is funny in a nursery, it would also be funny if it were engraved on the pulpit from which we preach. He replied, "Certainly no one would dare fall asleep if either of us were preaching, would they?"

Although Saint Paul meant those words for the end of time, they apply to each one of us as we try to live out the Gospel each day. From time to time we may grow weary in our daily struggles, and may even for a time "fall asleep" and lose our way. But Jesus is a shepherd who seeks us out and calls us into a deeper relationship that brings about real change. As Paul says, though not all of us shall fall asleep, all of us, in fact, shall be changed.

Just being in the presence of Jesus, listening for his voice, changes us. When we spend time with the Prince of Peace, a change begins in us that bring peace. It's the gift he came to give. Why not take some time to consider what change Jesus might be asking you to make as you walk in his footsteps?

May 10
Saving the Scene

On these beautiful days in May I like to do my morning prayer out on the porch where I can watch the day slowly awakening. This morning, as the gentle breezes were blowing, I asked God for an image to use in my prayer. Immediately my mind was filled with the memory of a children's Christmas pageant that was part of the Christmas Eve Mass at a parish where I served as pastor. It was a wonderful parish in the poor section of town, where people would describe themselves as "just plain folks." I really loved those folks, and the memory that came flooding into my mind of a Christmas spent with them brought tears to my eyes.

In the scene I remembered, the children were acting out the Christmas Gospel, and it was at the point where Joseph and Mary are looking for a place to stay. The innkeeper, who was inside of a decorated refrigerator box, stuck his head out the window and said to Mary and Joseph, "No room for you two here!" Joseph put his arm around Mary and said, "Come on, Mary, there's nobody who wants us. They won't make room for us!" With that, the folks in the congregation collectively sighed and uttered a very loud, "Awww."

The little girl playing Mary became a bit overwhelmed by all this, and her bottom lip began to quiver. Then tears came, and there was a profound silence in the church. Finally, the little innkeeper looked out from the refrigerator box and said, "Oh, don't cry, there's a lot of room in this big box! You can come in here." There was another collective sigh in the church, then Joseph said, "Look Mary, there's a stable! Let's go there!" The little boy playing Joseph had recovered the scene. Everyone laughed and Jesus was born.

As I thought about that Christmas pageant from years ago, what came back to me was a sense that in the midst of our most difficult times, God puts the right people in the right place at the right time who do something to "recover the scene." They reach out, just like little Joseph did in that Christmas play, and in their own sweet way, say the right thing or offer just the right help. This is God's way of walking with us in hard times.

But there is still another blessing that may well be offered us. God might put us in circumstances where it will be quite obvious that a "little Joseph" is needed to save the day. It is then that we can step up and save the scene for someone else.

May 11
Is Your Parrot Coughing?

Here's an interesting story for you: A retired sailor decided one day it was time for him to quit smoking. He made this decision because he noticed that his favorite pet parrot had developed a persistent cough. The poor bird sounded pitiful as it went into long coughing fits, which were becoming more frequent, lasting longer and longer each time. Finally, he decided he had better get the bird to the vet before it was too late.

After a thorough examination of the parrot, the vet made his diagnosis. "Your parrot does not have cancer or even pneumonia," the vet explained to the bird's owner. "Well, that's a relief!" the owner said. Then he added; "Now that I know my parrot is healthy I don't have to give up smoking. What a great day this is!"

"Now hold on now," the vet answered. "I said the bird ain't sick, but what it is doing is imitating someone who is sick – you!"

This story reminded me of a conversation I had recently with a recovering cocaine addict. He asked if I ever did a moral inventory of my life the way that alcoholics or drug addicts do when they are working a program. When I replied that I found moral inventories to be a great tool for spiritual growth, he was surprised. "I didn't think they were for spiritual growth. I thought they were meant to show you that if you don't stop doing stupid stuff, you'll end up dead."

My response to him was this: "I can't think of a better definition for a great spiritual tool than that, something that shows you the stupid stuff you are doing that could end up killing you."

Take your own moral inventory by asking yourself this question: "Is your parrot coughing?" If it is, which one of you is really sick?

May 12
Polished By Experience

I met recently with a parishioner, a young college student who was very excited to be headed off to China as a part of an overseas study program. His enthusiasm and excitement was contagious, and by the end of our conversation I was almost as excited as he about his going to China.

There was one thing I noticed as he spoke. It was evident that although this was a great adventure and a valuable opportunity for him, he also knew this trip would stretch him in many ways. He knew his time in Asia would challenge him, test him, and even change him; for that reason, he seemed a bit frightened. He was wise to be a little afraid.

As I observed him I thought of an old Chinese proverb that a friend of mine embroidered and hung on a wall in her office. She works with troubled folks in the inner city, and she uses the proverb when she speaks to her clients who are in difficult situations. Here's the proverb: "A diamond cannot be polished without friction, and neither can a person know the best that is in them without trials."

I am sure that my young parishioner will learn a lot during his overseas adventure. The long journey and the encounter with a new world are bound to teach him not just about China, but give him a whole new way of seeing himself. He will not return from China the same person he was when he sets out to go there. He will be polished by the experience.

May 13
Ambassadors for World Peace

Someone recently sent me a story about a lion that was very insecure about his status. He wanted people to think that he was really something and acknowledge him as "king of the beasts."

So one day as he was making his way through the jungle, he grabbed a tiger passing by. The lion put a stranglehold on the tiger, snarled ferociously, and said, "Who's the king of the jungle? Who's the king of the beasts?" And the tiger, trembling and shaking, said, "You are, Mr. Lion. You are the king of the jungle!" Right after that there was a bear passing by. Again the lion grabbed him, put a stranglehold on him, growled ferociously, and said, "Who's the king of the beasts?" The bear, trembling like the tiger, said, "OK, you are, Mr. Lion. There's no question about it in my mind. You are the king of the jungle!"

Finally, the lion came upon a huge elephant, mighty and massive, towering many feet above the lion. And once more the lion asked with a ferocious growl, "Who's the king of the beasts? Who's the greatest beast in the wild?" The elephant didn't say anything. He just picked up the lion with his trunk, whirled him around several times, and smashed him into a tree. As the lion got up, broken and bleeding, he said to the elephant, "Look, just because you don't know the answer is no reason for you to get so rough!"

Do you know anyone like that lion? Is there someone in your family or among your friends, co-workers, or classmates who seems so desperate to be liked and admired that they go to great lengths to get you to say something complimentary? How would you respond to them? Hopefully you don't respond as the elephant did.

These folks are crying out to us for affirmation, respect, and perhaps even love. A priest and mentor of mine used to tell me all the time that one of the greatest gifts we can give people is the gift of appreciation. He would often say, "A well-placed word of affirmation and encouragement can do more to bring about peace to the world than any other human endeavor."

Why not take some time today to be an ambassador for world peace by letting the "lions" in your life know how much you appreciate them?

May 14
Real Love

A college student was home on spring break, walking his farm-girl sweetheart down a country lane on a beautiful spring afternoon. "Look at those beautiful flowers!" the girl said softly. At that the young man jumped over the fence to pick some of the flowers just for her.

At about that time he spotted a huge, mean looking, snorting bull a short distance away. "Is that bull safe?" the boy asked his girl.

"Yes," she replied, "I'd say he's a lot safer than you are right now."

Has your love for someone ever gotten you into what seemed like a whole lot of trouble? Just the other day I was meeting with a young couple who are making plans to get married. At one point in our discussion the young man said, "I had no idea when I first fell in love with her that it could lead to so much commotion! I know I love her more than anything, but once this wedding stuff got started everything's been turned upside down and full speed ahead!"

That got all three of us laughing. Then he stopped laughing and said, "Got any advice on how to slow all of this down? How can we be sane again?"

My advice was simply this: "Take a deep breath and think long term. Think about your life together as lifelong best friends. Think about who walks with you and will love you for you alone. Don't think about the wedding: think about your marriage. You are marrying your best friend.

Have you ever been afraid that you had stepped into something that threatened to cause you great harm? Most people have that feeling when they take the first steps into making a life-changing commitment. It can seem like everyone else is a lot safer than you are! The truth of the matter, though, is that whenever you give your heart away, nothing is ever the same again. It's not about being safe. It's about real love.

May 15
The Right Direction

When you were young, did you ever think about running away from home? I've been thinking about this because during our second grade First

Confessions, one of our young folks asked me if running away from home is a sin. I assured him that it probably was not a sin. Then I told him about a saint who is rather famous for running away, and did it a lot.

Saint Gregory, who might be called the patron saint of runners, died on November 17, 270 A.D. He was a student of another saint named Origen. They lived during the times when the Romans were persecuting Christians, and when Origen got in trouble with the emperor, he went into hiding. Gregory, on the other hand, simply ran as fast as he could to get out of town. He kept running for almost three years, but eventually came back home.

A few years later, Gregory was chosen as bishop, and guess what he did in response? He ran away again. Members of his church, however, were as fast as he was. They caught him and made him bishop anyway. Near the end of his life, Saint Gregory advised his church members to flee from the wrath of the emperor Decius, and was himself the first one out the door. Running away had become a way of life for him. He certainly lived a saintly life, but so much of it was lived on the run because he was, as his contemporaries put it, an easily frightened person.

Have you ever felt like running away from your life? Much as we might have when we were children, I think all of us have thought about running away. The truth of the matter, however, is that running away from problems or frightful situations seldom works. We eventually have to come home again, as Saint Gregory did, to face our problems. That's because most of the problems we try to avoid are within us, so that however far away we run, the problem is still right there inside us.

Jesus taught his disciples to stop running away and start running toward God and his love. He taught that when the storms of life start blowing around us, we are not to run away from the storm in terror, but rather to run to the one who can command the winds to be silent and turbulent seas to be still.

Ever feel like running? Be sure to run in the right direction.

May 16
Sunday School Lesson

A parishioner told me that her granddaughter attends Sunday school, and that she had been invited to observe the class as part of a "Grandparents Sunday Celebration." I asked her if she enjoyed it. She said that the whole experience had been truly a blessing.

The woman went on to tell me that the Sunday school teacher is known for his elaborate object lessons that are intended to help the little ones remember important spiritual truths. I asked her if the teacher had used an object lesson the day she was there. She replied, "Oh yes, and it was so powerful I haven't been able to get it out of my mind! I knew something different was going to happen as soon as I arrived in his classroom, because tacked up on the bulletin board in front of the classroom was a big target," she said. "And on the table next to the target was a huge pile of darts!"

"Darts and children don't sound like a good combination," I said.

"Well, I thought so too, but then who was I to tell this teacher how to run his lesson?" she said. The woman went on, "Just as I was thinking about how dangerous those darts might be for the little children, the teacher stepped forward and began his class. The teacher told the students to draw a picture of someone they disliked or someone who had made them angry. Then one by one, each child was allowed to put his or her drawing on the target and throw darts at the person's picture."

"One little girl had drawn a picture of a former friend, putting great detail into the drawing. The pictures were tacked over the target, the class lined up, and each person took turns throwing darts at the pictures. Some kids threw their darts with so much force that their targets were torn apart. Before long everyone was screaming and laughing and having a great old time."

"When each child had finished and been able to throw their darts, the teacher began removing the tattered pictures and target from the board. Suddenly, as the torn pictures were removed from the target and another layer of paper was removed, a new picture was revealed. It was a picture of Jesus. The room got very quiet. Because of all of the darts, the picture of Jesus was covered with holes. Under the picture was a Scripture verse: 'Truly I tell you, whatever you did to one of the least of these brothers and sisters of mine, you did to me.'"

The woman concluded her story by telling me that she had not been able to stop thinking about that Sunday school class.

May 17
Are You An Intellectual?

I enjoy reading biographies because they usually contain a lot of wisdom. One of the people I love reading about is Albert Schweitzer. His life and work are full of great insights and sage advice. In one of the biographies about him, there is an account of a time when Schweitzer was out working in the hot African sun, building his hospital at Lambarene with his own hands. A large timber had to be raised into place, and try as he might, Schweitzer could not manage to move it at all.

Taking a breather, he looked up and saw a well-dressed African man standing in the shade of a tree. He asked the man if he would lend a hand. "Oh, no," the man said, "I don't do that kind of work. I have studied and now I am an intellectual."

Albert Schweitzer, who had earned five doctorate degrees over the years, paused to think for a minute. He then said to the man, "I used to be an intellectual, but I found I couldn't live up to it. Today I am a follower of Jesus, and I just do what he sets before me to get done. It's all God's work and therefore, I gladly join in."

Is there any work that has been set before you that you find yourself reluctant to do for various reasons? Have you decided that you are now an intellectual, and are somehow above certain kinds of work? If so, perhaps a visit with Albert Schweitzer might change your perspective.

May 18
Good-bye

I was having lunch with a good friend the other day when my cell phone rang. I answered it, had a brief conversation with the caller, then said "good-bye" and turned off the phone. When I looked over at my friend on the other side of the table, he was smiling at me and said, "Do you know what you said to that caller when you said 'good-bye?'"

I thought a minute and replied that I said "good-bye" because the conversation was ending and the caller had first said good-bye to me. My friend then said, "I'll bet that both you and your caller have no idea what the expression 'good-bye' even means."

I said, "It means good-bye; our conversation is over. Like the military guys say, 'over and out,' or something like that."

"I'm surprised that you, a priest, don't know the origin of the expression you're using every day," my friend said.

"So, I guess you're going to tell me what it means then, aren't you?" I asked.

He said, "The phrase, 'good-bye' is a corruption of the sentence, 'May God be with you.' It comes from an age when the struggles of daily living were so intense that friends always offered a kind of blessing when they left one another to confront the world alone. Thus, they said, in essence, 'Don't go out there alone, it's too dangerous. May God be with you in your journeys when you are alone.'"

I had no idea I was saying all of that when I simply said good-bye to end a phone call. I must admit that I like the sentiment. Our world is no less dangerous or intense than it was in days past, and every one of us needs the blessing of friends and loved ones when we go out on our journeys alone. I'll try to be more aware of the real meaning of my "good-bye" when I come to the end of a phone conversation or leave the company of others. To say good-bye to someone is to say a lot. By the way, if I haven't said it to you lately – good-bye! May God be with you.

May 19
What Are You Saying?

There's a story about Saint Francis that a Franciscan priest at the high school I attended told us on the very first day of school. According to that priest, one day Saint Francis informed his brother Franciscans that he planned to go into the nearby village on a preaching mission, and he invited a novice to go along.

As they journeyed to the village, the novice noticed that Francis walked very slowly and stopped a lot along the way to talk with folks. At one point, they passed an injured man and Francis promptly stopped. He saw to the poor fellow's needs and arranged medical care for him. They went on a short distance further, and soon passed a homeless man who was near starvation. Again, Francis stopped his journey, reached out to the hungry, homeless man, and fed him. So it went throughout the day, encountering people in need and Francis caring for them as best he could until the sun was low in the sky.

As the sun was finally setting, Francis told the novice it was time for them to return to their base camp for evening prayers. The young man replied, "Father, you said we were coming to town to preach to the people. We haven't preached or said one word all day!"

Francis smiled, then said, "My friend, everything we've been doing today has spread the Gospel of Jesus. We have been doing the best kind of preaching."

In your walk through life today, tomorrow, and the day after, what kind of preaching will be heard in the way you treat those you encounter in the world?

May 20
Finding a Reason

In church last Sunday I was introduced to the grandchildren of one of our parishioners. Since they were on vacation, they had stopped to spend a few days with their grandparents and it was obvious to me that everyone was glad to be together. They were all full of smiles as they left church and headed off to have breakfast together.

On my way home from that scene, with the image of those very happy people in mind, I remembered something from my days at St. William. It was a conversation with Father Kennedy, the pastor of St. William. We had been talking about some of the happiest people we had known and as our conversation came to a close I remember asking him what he thought was the key to finding happiness in life. He paused for a moment and then said,

Fr. Mark Burger

"Mark, if you want to be happy, you've got to always find a way to be grateful for whatever happens. You have to find the blessing in everything."

Then he told a story from when he was a younger priest. He said that there was grandmother in his first parish who came to church one Sunday morning all excited that her grandchildren were coming for a visit. She told the pastor that she was going to write a check for fifteen dollars as a thanksgiving gift to God and put it in the collection. The following Sunday she came back to church, her grandchildren had spent the week and had just gone home. She spoke to her pastor, "Father, my grandchildren have just spent a week at my house and now I am going to put a check for $100 in the collection in thanksgiving!"

Father Kennedy concluded his story by saying that he and his pastor weren't quite sure exactly what that grandmother was thanking God for – was it that her grandchildren had visited or that her grandchildren had finally gone home! Father Kennedy then said, "So, the moral of the story is that in every situation you can always find some reason to give thanks!"

May 21
Who Will Know?

After years of watching the missionaries who had been living in his village, a Chinese man decided to ask for baptism. Because of their conduct, he knew the missionaries were people of honesty and integrity, and he wanted to be like them. After his baptism, the man was overjoyed to be, as he put it, a brother and friend of Jesus. Many of his fellow villagers were shocked that he had become a Christian, but they knew he was a good and honest man. If he said that this was what God wanted him to do, then it must be so.

About six months after his baptism, the new Christian was tempted to cheat by one of his countrymen. Upon his refusal, his tempter asked, "Why won't you do what everybody else does all the time? We all do a little bit of cheating just to stay successful in business. No one need know, and even if they did, they wouldn't hold it against you."

The new Christian stood up straight and said, "I won't cheat because three people will know that I cheated. You will know, and I will know, and Jesus will know. Jesus is my brother, and I would hate for him to find that he has befriended an untrustworthy friend. I cannot be dishonest without bringing dishonor to my brother and friend."

If those with whom you live and work were asked what they know about you, would they say they know you to be a person of honesty and integrity, someone who can be trusted?

May 22
When the Sun Shines

When I was in the public library the other day, I came across an anecdote from the time of the Roman Emperor Hadrian. According to the story, the Emperor invited Joshua, the chief rabbi in Rome, in for a meeting. When the rabbi arrived, Hadrian immediately asked him, "I know you Jews only believe in one God. I want to see this God of yours. You must show me your God!" Rabbi Joshua calmly replied, "That is impossible."

The Emperor, who was not accustomed to being told no, was irked by the Rabbi's response. "I demand that you show me your God!" the Emperor screamed.

Unshaken, the Rabbi calmly replied, "Come outside with me, and I will show you why this is quite impossible." It was summer. When they were outside the Rabbi said to the Emperor, "Sire, stand here and look directly into the sun." "I cannot do it! It would destroy my eyes," the Emperor replied.

Rabbi Joshua said, "If you, the most powerful man on earth, cannot even look at the sun, which is just a mere creature made by the great Holy One, Blessed be he, how could you ever look directly at the Holy One himself? We lowly folk often forget just how powerful the Holy One, Blessed be he, truly is. If you were to look directly at the Holy One, you could not endure it."

The Emperor Hadrian was said to have been very impressed by what the Rabbi had said. He was also a bit frightened by it as well because he realized he did not know this God of the Jews.

This week, if the sun should come out, why not take a few moments to go out and bask in its light and in its warmth? This "mere creature" of our God can serve to remind each of us just how powerful and mighty God truly is. There are no problems or situations too big or too overwhelming for him. As you feel the warmth of the sun, remember what Jesus has taught us about this all-powerful God, that he is also all loving, gentle, forgiving, and kind. Remember those words of Jesus, "The Father knows what you need.... consider the birds of the sky and how your Father feeds them."

May 23rd
Maybe You Can Show Me

The other day I was listening to a young student describe his difficulties in getting along with people at school and at home. I asked him, "Why do you think things seem to be so hard for you?" He thought for a moment, then said, "When I'm at school the teachers and my classmates tell me how wrong I am about stuff. When I go home, everyone tells me how messy I am. I just can't seem to make anybody happy with me."

We had a long conversation after that, and as I continued to listen and talk with him I remembered something I had read from the life of Andrew Carnegie. When asked how he went about developing good talent to work for him, Carnegie's response was simple: "You develop people the same way you mine for gold. In gold mining you literally move tons and tons of dirt to find a single ounce of gold. However, you don't look for the dirt, you look for the gold!"

The next time you begin to think about your family members, your friends, fellow students, or co-workers, why not consider Andrew Carnegie's words? Instead of looking for and pointing out the "dirt," why not take a few moments to look for the gold?

As I finished my conversation with that student, I told him about Carnegie's gold mining ideas. He asked me if I found any gold in him, and I told him I did. I asked if he thought he might be able to find gold in himself. "May you can show me," he said.

May 24
Do You Want to Be Rich?

The Desert Fathers warned their followers to "run as fast as you can away from the slightest whisper of greed." They taught that one of the easiest temptations to give into is the prospect of becoming rich. They warned their disciples that the slightest hint of the possibility of vast wealth has caused many good people to betray themselves and everyone they love. This came to mind the other day when someone gave me the following rather humorous story.

A mobster discovered that his deaf accountant had cheated him out of ten million dollars. So he decided to confront him, and took along a sign language interpreter. "Ask him where the money is," said the mobster. The interpreter did as he was told, and the accountant signed back, "I have no idea what you're talking about." The interpreter told the mobster, "He says he doesn't know what you're talking about." The mobster put a pistol to the accountant's head, and said, "Ask him again!" The interpreter signed, "Tell him where the money is. He'll kill you if you don't!" "Okay, okay!" the accountant signed. "The money is buried behind the oak tree in my backyard!" "What did he say?" the mobster asked the interpreter. "He says you don't have the guts to pull the trigger."

Have you ever been tempted by the prospect of becoming rich? Have you ever felt a slight whispering voice teasing you with the prospect of becoming wealthy? I think it was Saint Anthony who said that it's okay for people to own things, as long as the things don't end up owning the people. Ask yourself this question: Do I own things or do they own me?

May 25
Stubborn as a Donkey

I've been reading about donkeys lately because of an off-handed remark I heard when I was doing some counseling with a family. One of the people in the group had looked at her family members and said, "You're all as stubborn as donkeys!" The remark made me wonder if donkeys really are stubborn, and I decided to find out.

It turns out that there is a lot to know about donkeys. For one thing, they have a whole bunch of chromosomes that enable them to be crossed with horses and zebras, which produces some hybrid animals. I found out that the offspring of a male donkey and a female horse is called a mule. A male mule is called a john, and a female is called a molly. (Who knew?) Then I found out that the offspring of a male horse and a female mule is called a hinny.

Now what I thought was funny is that when you cross a zebra with donkeys, the offspring are called zebrasses and zonkeys! I am not making this up; that really is what they are called.

As I read further I found out that while donkeys may have a reputation for being stubborn, they really are not. One author said that donkeys are rather sure of themselves, and they can be of great help in warning you of danger. They are very sure-footed and are not easily spooked. Unlike horses that run away when they are frightened, donkeys stand their ground. In various countries in Africa they act as an alarm system and are often used to guard cattle because they bray so loudly when threatened. It is also true that they are the only animals their size who will stand their ground against a lion. They will not back down. Their greatest weapon is their kick, which is extremely accurate. In short, don't mess with a donkey!

So, do donkeys live up to their reputation for being stubborn? The research I did says that by no means are they stubborn; they actually are very smart. If they refuse to do something it may well be that they deem it too dangerous – or maybe just plain dumb! Those who keep donkeys say the animals are very sensitive to danger as well as to the world around them.

As I was listening to the family I was counseling fight, I began to see that maybe the stubborn donkeys one family member was attacking weren't all that bad. First of all, they may well teach us that, just because someone does not agree with us or will not necessarily do what we want them to do, it does not indicate they are stubborn. They may well be sure-footedly smart and aware of dangers you or I may not be aware of. They show us how to stand up for what we believe in when they refuse to back down from the lions that want to attack them. Donkeys have much to teach us.

May 26
Masterpiece

James Whistler, the well-known American artist, once wrote about an incident from his own life that had taught him a lesson. He had ordered a set of blank canvases that were to be shipped to him for his use in his studio. As it turned out, those canvases got lost in the mail and so Whistler contacted his local postmaster to report the matter.

The government official was very kind to him and began to write down all of the pertinent information about the situation. At one point the postmaster asked Whistler, "Are these canvases of any great value?" Whistler's reply was, "Well, no, not yet."

When Whistler reflected back on that conversation he had an insight. He said that, just as a blank canvas can have limitless value if it allows an artist to create a masterpiece on it, so too can each of us be like a blank canvas if we allow the masterpiece God has created in us to come forth. As he thought more about the value of those canvases he had yet another insight: "Each day is like a blank canvas that God puts into our hands to do with as we wish."

Why not take a moment and think about what kind of masterpiece you can create with the new day opening right in front of you?

May 27
A Way to Healing

Mary Lincoln, Abraham Lincoln's granddaughter, owned a small wooden box that was very dear to her. It contained the contents of her grandfather's pockets the night he was assassinated. No one knew that any of these artifacts even existed until Mary donated the box and its contents to the Library of Congress.

One of the things in President Lincoln's pocket the night he died was a letter to the editor that had been clipped out of a newspaper. The letter praised Lincoln as a man of pure heart and singleness of purpose. The letter writer had written it was because of Lincoln's perseverance that the nation had endured and survived the Civil War.

When asked why she thought the President had clipped and saved that letter to the editor, Mary is said to have replied, "Because everyone, even great men, need a word of encouragement from time to time. I bet it went a long way to healing a part of him."

We all need a word of encouragement from time to time. When was the last time someone gave you a word of encouragement? Did that bit of encouragement heal a part of you? When was the last time you provided a word of encouragement to someone? Do you think it may have brought them healing or comfort?

May 28
Flying Right

I was sitting out on my porch the other night just relaxing when I started to watch several moths that seemed to be attracted to the yellow porch light that was shining off in the distance. I have always wondered why moths are attracted by the light, and why they seem to fly in continual circles around them. After about twenty minutes of observation I decided to read up on those bugs.

It turns out that moths are not attracted to the lights as I have always thought. (That fact ruined a perfectly good homily I was forming in my head as I watched the insects flying around the light!) What researchers have discovered is that moths are not attracted to the light at all; they are disoriented by it. Imagine that! For countless generations moths and other insects have learned to navigate by the light of the sun and moon. As such, the artificial lights we humans have created mightily confuse moths and many other insects.

Scientists have learned that moths have evolved in such a way that they expect the light of the sun and moon to strike their eyes at a particular place depending on the time of day or night. This enables those insects to fly in a straight line. The problem arises when these new portable lights we have created make their appearance when we turn them on. A moth flying by all of a sudden thinks that somehow the sun or moon has changed position!

The bug thinks that it is no longer flying in a straight line and somehow has come to fly in a curved or circular direction. The moth then adjusts its course until it can see the light as stationary. The only way, scientists say, that this can happen for the poor bug is to just keep flying around in a circle. The moth thinks it is flying in a straight line, and we think the moth is doing that circling because it is attracted to the light. Both of us are wrong!

The point of all of this information is to remind us that it is rather easy not only for moths to be disoriented by the artificial "lights" of this world, but so too can we. How often have you thought you were doing a pretty good job of "flying in a straight line" in your relationship with your spouse or friends or with your children, only to learn that somehow you have veered off course because you had started to be disoriented by some artificial lights that the world has set before you? There are many things that can distract us from the important things in life. Perhaps the moths can teach us something. Perhaps we, like them, have to make sure that the "light" we are using as our guide in this life is the true light and not an artificial one.

May 29
Lunch with God

I had lunch this past week with an elderly man who wanted to talk about his relationship with God. This man is over ninety years old and still as sharp as ever. I felt blessed to be with him. In the course of our conversation, there were two sayings the man repeated several times. I asked him about them, and he said those two sayings are what kept his spirits up throughout his life.

The first of what he called "wise sayings" was this: "God called each of us to get in the game, not to keep score." He went on to explain that the one thing he found hurtful in so many relationships is when one or the other person begins to keep score of the wrongs and hurts that have happened over the years. He said, "Come to think of it, keeping score serves only to make yourself mad all the time, and who wants to be mad all the time? It's much better to just work to make life easier for each other. Giving each other some room to move about in is what makes friendships worth having. Keeping score is for idiots, and who needs an idiot for a friend?"

The old man's second wise saying was simply this: "We can complain because rose bushes have thorns or we can choose to be really happy that thorn bushes have roses." He explained that bit of advice by saying, "It's important to find the good things in life wherever and whenever you can. A sour outlook leads to unhappiness. I say, choose to be happy. I've learned that you pretty much find what you set out to look for, so why not look for the good things? If you do, you will find them, I'm sure!"

When we got to the end of our lunch, my older friend said, "I guess I didn't talk much about my relationship with God, did I?"

"I think that's exactly what you were talking about the whole time." I said.

Have you ever had lunch with someone like my old friend? I highly recommend it. I feel so blessed to have had the opportunity to be with him. His gentle conversation and kindness, along with his great wisdom, was really like having lunch with God.

May 30
The Gift You Have Received

I read an interesting thing about Leonardo da Vinci. According to the story, the great artist was at work in his studio, painting with great intensity and concentration, when he looked up and saw a young art student staring at him with his mouth open. It was obvious that the student was awed by da Vinci's work. Da Vinci asked the young man, "So what do you think of the work?" The young man continued to stare at the painting as Leonardo continued working. Finally, just before finishing the painting, da Vinci turned to the young student, gave him his paintbrush, and said, "Now, you finish it."

The young student began to back away, protesting that he could never be good enough to finish such a great work of art. Leonardo da Vinci then said, "I have given it everything my talent has to give, it will not be complete until you give it what only your talent can provide." With that he pushed the young artist toward the painting and said, "Now you finish this great work of art."

I love what da Vinci did for that young artist. He reminded the young man that, although he may not have had the same talent as da Vinci had, he did, in fact, have his own talent and that talent was no less valuable than da Vinci's.

Have you ever been intimidated by a friend or colleague's talents? Have you ever felt that somehow you don't measure up because you don't have the same abilities or level of talent as those around you? Perhaps da Vinci has something to teach you.

We all need to know what Leonardo da Vinci knew, and that is simply this: We are all gifted in some way. Our gifts were not given to us to put us into competition with each other, but rather, they are given so they may complement each other. We are not asked to live our life in comparison to others, rather, we are asked to work together, sharing the gifts we have so that a great masterpiece might be created. Each one of us has a talented hand to use in creating this work. Our differing talents were not given to us to divide us but rather to unite us. As Jesus told the apostles, "The gift you have received, give as a gift."

May 31
The First Day of the Week

Christianity began on Sunday, the first day of the week. It was the day when Jesus Christ, the Son of God, rose from the dead. It's a very significant day for all Christians.

Last Sunday, as I was praying before Mass, I was enjoying the peace and quiet of the early morning hours when I remembered something from my college studies in philosophy. It was a statement made by Voltaire, a famous philosopher from the Enlightenment period, who died in 1778. Voltaire had said he thought that within 100 years of his life, Catholicism and Christianity would be nothing more than history. This would happen, he said, because slowly and gradually Christians are being separated from their Sabbath. If Sunday is not acknowledged as sacred, holy, and belonging to God then those who call themselves Christians will simply end up hollow, without meaning. Without the Sabbath, the Christian faith will simply fade away into history and be no more.

As I recalled those words it dawned on me how true it is for each one of us as individuals. If we separate ourselves from a day set aside for God, soon our faith becomes hollow and slowly fades away into insignificance. Before long God becomes less and less real, and we end up having to cope with life alone, with little to no hope.

Sometimes people tell me they stopped coming to church on Sunday because it's their only day to "sleep in." Sometimes they tell me they find more meaning in life by walking in the woods, so they leave Sundays for the woods. Others tell me that Sunday is their day to golf. And still there are those who simply ask me if they "have" to go to Mass. They make it seem as if it is a terrible hardship or an annoying chore to attend Mass, and so they choose something else to do with the first day of the week.

When people say those kinds of things to me, I think of Voltaire. If we allow ourselves to be separated from the day God gave us for resting in him, we may soon find our faith and our relationship with God fading away into the past.

June

June 1
Are You Immunized?

Recently I've been reading a biography of John and Abigail Adams. At one point the book describes how John and Abigail tried to protect their children and themselves from the disease of smallpox by introducing each member of the family to a very small dose of what they called "cow pox." After receiving the dose, each of the family members got a fever but recovered. In a primitive way, they had immunized themselves from smallpox.

As I've been thinking about how someone can be immunized against a disease by getting a small dose of that disease, it began to occur to me this is exactly what can happen in our spiritual life. It is entirely possible that some of us have had so many small doses of God that we have become unable to catch the real thing. And so we end up with something quite different from what Jesus came to give us.

Perhaps many of us have had such a shallow experience of religion that we have never been truly introduced to the life-changing experience a real relationship with Jesus can bring. Many of us may never have been given the chance to, as Jesus said, "put out into deeper waters." We simply learn a few prayers, hear a story or two from the Bible, and put in some time at church, but nothing penetrates our minds or our hearts. Our everyday lives are not affected or changed by any of it.

As June begins and we look ahead to summer, as our schools are beginning to wind down the academic year and our families are getting ready for summer activities, I want to encourage you to take some extra time to go a little deeper in your walk with God. God has so much to say to each of us, and many of us are not hearing what is being said because we have never taken God or our faith seriously enough. We think that kind of faith is for "holy" people and not for us.

Deep faith and a closer walk with God are for everyone, not just an elite few. Please, treat yourself this summer to some quiet time with God. Don't let the small doses of religion that you might be experiencing now immunize you against God. Allow God to take you much deeper in your life with him.

June 2
Island Shell

Earlier this week a friend of mine was telling me of the wonderful vacation she and her family had just taken on a tiny island off the coast of one of the Carolinas. As she talked about their time away she began to describe how calm she had become during her time on that island. She wished she could capture that calmness and bring it home with her, and asked me if I had ever had that feeling. I assured her that I have had that feeling and the desire to keep it with me many times over.

Our conversation made me think of a book I had read years ago by Anne Morrow Lindbergh, called, *Gift from the Sea*. In her book she describes a day when she found a beautiful seashell on the beach. She picked it up, examined it, found it to be extraordinarily beautiful, and said, "I shall call you "Island Shell" and keep you with me when I return home." And that is just what she did. She concludes by saying, "You will remind me that unless I keep the island quality intact somewhere within me, I will have little to give my family or the world for that matter. You will remind me to relax and be still in the very midst of all of my many activities."

I wonder if you have had that experience while you have been on vacation. Have you been able to find a little piece of calm, quiet, and stillness that you can keep with you as you return home to your busy life? Jesus taught us that we always have access to such serenity if we just take the time to be still, notice the beauty around us, become aware of his presence in our life, and carry that peace and tranquility within us. Why not take some time right now to find your "Island Shell"?

June 3
Make Something Good

A young man who had been suffering terribly from depression went to visit with his grandmother. He thought it would be good for him to be with her because she was the most positive person he had ever met. They had a very close relationship. When he arrived at his grandmother's home he found her sitting on the front porch, convulsing with great big belly laughs. She was laughing so hard tears were streaming down her face.

"Grandma, what's so funny?" he asked.

"Oh, a friend sent me a story that just tickles me to death! And I was just thinking that I should give it to you to cheer you up."

"Grandma, I don't think a story will do it for me. It just seems that every day when I look in the mirror, I find more and more things I don't like about me," he said.

Grandma thought for a while and then said, "You just have to learn to take what you see and make something good come from it."

"Well, how could I ever do that? I'm really kind of hopeless, aren't I?" he asked.

"No, you are not at all hopeless; you just need to adjust how you look at things. Why, this story I'm thinking would be perfect for you will show you how one woman faced the stuff she saw in the mirror and enjoyed each day to the fullest. Here, read this story!"

Once upon a time a woman woke up one morning, looked in the mirror, and saw that she had only three hairs on her head. "Well," she said, "I think that today I might braid my hair." She did and she had a great day. The next morning she woke up, checked herself in the mirror, and discovered she only had two hairs on her head. "Hmm," she said, "Maybe I'll part my hair down the middle today." So she did and she had a fantastic day. The next morning she woke up, looked in the mirror and found that she had only one hair left on her head. "Well," she said, "Not to worry. Today I'll wear my hair in a pony tail." So she did and she had the best day. The next day she woke up, looked in the mirror and noticed that there wasn't one single hair on her head. "Hooray!" she exclaimed. "I don't have to do my hair today!"

When the young man finished reading the story he felt a smile cross his face, and as he heard his grandma begin to laugh, so did he. Grandma hugged her grandson and said, "Maybe you could try to deal with the tough things in your life as that lady dealt with her hair."

Are you able to take what you see and make something good come from it?

June 4
Learn to Whisper

At a retreat a woman got up and told a very interesting story, which has much to teach. I've been using this story each morning as a way to open my mind and heart to the day, as a monk I know once put it.

According to the story, there was a very holy man who was full of wisdom. He often shared that wisdom with his disciples by asking some simple questions. One day the saintly man turned to his disciples and asked, "Why do people who are angry shout at each other?"

After a little while, one disciple said, "Because we lose our calm. Then we shout."

"But why do you shout when the other person is right next to you? You can say what you have to say in a much softer manner, can't you?" asked the holy monk.

None of those gathered could give a good response. Then the holy man set out to explain his answer. Here is what he said:

"When two people are angry at each other, their hearts get further apart. To cover that distance, they have to shout to be able to hear each other. The angrier they become, the louder they must shout to be heard from what seems to be such a great distance."

The holy man let this wisdom settle within his disciples. He then smiled, and it wasn't too long before he asked them a new question.

"When two people fall in love, what happens? They talk softly to each other. Why? Because their hearts are very, very close and the distance between them is very small."

The disciples nodded in agreement. "That makes sense to us," they said.

The holy man paused for a moment, then concluded, "When two people's love grows even stronger, they only whisper because their hearts are so close.

In the end the love is so strong that they only need to look at each other. That is all. Take this wisdom to heart and learn to whisper."

June 5
Summer Time is God's Time

I often think of this story about the Buddha as the summer break comes around because I don't want to miss the opportunity the season offers to stop, take a break, and grow in my appreciation of life. Here's the story: One day the Buddha was sitting with all of his disciples gathered around him when a Heavenly spirit approached and said to him, "How long do you want to live? Ask for even a million years and they shall be granted to you."

Immediately, the Buddha gave his answer: "I want to live for eight years!" With that, the Heavenly spirit was gone.

Now, the Buddha's disciples were all quite taken aback, and rather shocked. They asked, "Master, why did you not ask for a million years? Just think of the many generations of people you could have influenced for good!" They were deeply troubled and even mystified.

The Buddha looked at them and with a smile, addressed their concerns. He said, "Now, if I were to live a million years, you and those who come after you would be more interested in extending your lives than in seeking wisdom. You would be more interested in merely surviving rather than truly experiencing all life has to offer. You would spend your time without having lived. When you allow the time around you to slow down, drink deeply and you will discover the real depth life has to offer."

These summer months are a great opportunity for us to allow our souls to catch up with our busy lives. This time of the year is truly God's time -- God's chance to get our attention. It's a time for us to stop the intensity that comes with just trying to survive, and slow down enough to become aware of what has been around us all year that we haven't noticed.

The slowing down that comes each summer is, I think, God's way of telling us there's so much more he wants us to experience. As you continue to enjoy this season, why not set some time aside to spend with God, to slow down and go deeper into the gift of your life?

Fr. Mark Burger

June 6
The Sound of Music

Here's a bit of a riddle for you: You cannot see it, feel it, touch it, or smell it. It weighs nothing and it disappears the split second it comes to you. It doesn't leave a trace of itself once it has left. While it is present it can give you much pleasure, much joy, and it can bring to mind some very wonderful and some not so wonderful memories. It has the power to make you happy or sad, and it can inspire you to do great things. It can change the atmosphere wherever it goes. What is it?

Have you come up with an answer? The answer to the riddle is -- music. It's a wonderful gift that most of us seldom take the time to appreciate. From the moment we awake in the morning and go sleep again at night, we are surrounded by music.

No matter where you go or what you are doing, chances are you will encounter music in some form. Whether it's on TV, radio, on a digital device, at an event, or in a public elevator, you just cannot get away from music. You'll hear it in malls, in church, in stadiums, in restaurants, while waiting on the phone, or even while having a medical test done. Music seems to be everywhere in our lives.

Where does it come from and how do we capture it? Some of the great classical composers have said they were overcome by the music that came to them, waiting to be written. Mozart said that his music came to him suddenly and in very large amounts. He had to rush to get all of it down on paper as fast as he could so he wouldn't miss or forget any of it. The composer Handel said that when he was writing *Messiah*, it was as if Heaven had opened its doors and the music just flowed down on him. Contemporary musicians speak in similar terms – the music just comes, almost sneaking into them until it demands to be heard. Music is everywhere.

I read the riddle above to some of our school kids. Some actually guessed what the answer was. One little girl said, "I think it might be music, but to me it sounds an awful lot like God." I think she's right, don't you?

June 7
Learning on the Job

A few years ago I was part of a men's fellowship group that met on a regular basis to discuss important spiritual things. It was a great group of guys from all walks of life, and I always found it really interesting to hear the different points of view these men brought to any discussion. At one of our meetings, each man was supposed to tell one thing they had learned from their job that has guided the way they chose to live their life. Each man at that meeting had wonderful insights.

One man, for example, was a police officer. He said that his job had taught him that, while a lot of the people he meets are criminals, he had met far more people who are truly good, caring, and hard working folks who quietly go about their business, doing good. He said, "In my line of work, you could easily get caught up in all of the evil stuff you see and conclude that life is not worth living. I have found an awful lot of good people mixed in among all of those bad ones I see, and the good far outnumber the bad."

My favorite comment came from a man who had spent the last thirty years as an undertaker. He said, "One thing my career has taught me is that when conflicts or disagreements with loved ones arise, I work to solve them quickly. I've seen many people who go off to work in the morning full of anger and resentment, that who never come home. I've learned to never assume that I can do tomorrow what ought to be done today. I tell myself and my family and friends, make sure to do what needs to be done. And I always add, don't just do it, do it *now*! You don't realize how soon time is gone."

In this season of graduations and completion of various school programs, it is important to take a few moments to consider not only the things we have learned in school but also those things that every day experiences teach us. What has your life and career taught you? If you were asked to give a talk about what your job has taught you about life, what would you speak about?

June 8
What Might God Be Up To?

I read something the other day at the library that got me thinking. In 1934 a traveling preacher came to Charlotte, North Carolina, to preach a kind of revival. The minister's name was Mordecai Ham. He set up a tent, called people together, and preached about salvation. He impressed on those gathered the importance of the meetings he would hold in their little town for the next couple of weeks.

One of the people in attendance was a farmer who heard the sermons and was moved by them. He called several of his friends together to pray for the success of the revival. One of them said they heard in prayer that God would do great things for the world if people came to the revival and responded the way God wanted them to respond. The farmer and his friends prayed very fervently that people would come and respond.

Some folks did, in fact, come to the revival and some seemed to respond, though there was no apparent outpouring of anything dramatic. There was one person at the revival who said he thought he felt something very strong moving in him, that he ought to do something for God and the world. He wasn't sure what it was he might do, but he knew something was happening within him. He hoped to respond to it and figure out what God might want from him.

The revival ended, and the Reverend Mordecai Ham moved on to other towns to continue his preaching ministry. The person who had felt something strong in him turned out to be the farmer's son. He did eventually do something about that inner movement of God's spirit. He became an evangelist, one who ended up preaching to millions of people about God's grace and love. What was his name? Billy Graham.

What struck me about this story is that at the time, no one could ever have known just how great an impact a farmer's son could have on so many people. He was just someone they knew, a face in a rather small, unimpressive crowd at a rather small tent revival. Who knew at the time that God had already chosen someone to carry a message to the world from the seemingly unimpressive, maybe even mediocre preaching of Mordecai Ham? Without much fanfare God had chosen one of the greatest preachers of our age.

It makes me wonder just what God is up to in our own little part of the world. There are, I'm sure, some among us whom God is calling to do great things for the kingdom. At the present moment he or she may appear to be just another face in the crowd. But just as that other "face in the crowd" back in 1934 had no idea what God had in store for him, we too may have little or no idea of what God might be moving us to do.

June 9
Take a Break

Recently I read about a man named Roger Moore who, as his wife put it, "hated being told what to do." Well, on one fateful occasion the man was given a speeding ticket. As the police officer was writing out the citation, he noticed that Mr. Moore's toddler was not properly secured in the car seat. When the cop brought that fact to his attention, Mr. Moore was not pleased and began to protest a bit, saying that the police officer should stop telling him what to do.

The policeman didn't say a word as he handed Mr. Moore a second ticket. Grudgingly, Moore properly strapped in his toddler and sped off. As he drove away, muttering to himself about how he hated being told what to do, he leaned over and put the two tickets in the glove compartment, growing more and more angry as he pressed the accelerator.

Twenty minutes later Roger Moore and his toddler were involved in a traffic accident. The little child sustained a few minor cuts, but because he was restrained in a car seat, those were the only injuries he had. Unfortunately, his father did not do so well. Although he had reluctantly obeyed the police officer and belted his son into the car seat, Mr. Moore failed to buckle his own seat belt. He was killed.

When I read that sad story I thought of just how easy it is for any one of us to drive ourselves into the arms of real pain and suffering because of our stubborn, willful desire to not be told what to do. One person's refusal to do the right thing can, in an instant, cause life-altering changes for those around us.

The Desert Fathers would advise their disciples to pay close attention to yourself that you not be so stiff-necked as to cause people pain and suffering.

The author of the Acts of the Apostles said a similar thing: "You stiff-necked people ... you are forever opposing the Holy Spirit, just as your ancestors used to do (7:51). This is pretty good advice given to us from many centuries back.

As we speed through our days with many things on our minds, and many minor and major stresses weighing us down, it might be good for us to take a break. A pause every now and then to pay close attention to ourselves would be something we all could use.

June 10
Emmanuel

I read recently about two college professors who were at the university president's home for a faculty party. One of the men was a professor of astronomy and the other man taught theology. These colleagues were chatting over cocktails when the discussion turned to their fields of expertise.

The astronomy professor, who had very little respect for faith or religion, began to make some rather cutting remarks about Christianity and its theology. He finished his comments by saying, "Well, I don't mean to insult you, but we all know that theology is a rather 'soft' subject and not a very challenging field of study. After all, it can all be distilled down to just one little concept called the Golden Rule; you know, love your neighbor as yourself. Isn't that so?"

The theology professor thought for a minute, then replied. "Well, John," he said, "I suppose it could be put that way, although there is certainly much more to Jesus' teaching than that. But let me make an analogy for you. To say that Jesus and his teaching can be summed up in only that one saying, "Love your neighbor as yourself," is like saying that all of astronomy can be summed up in another well-known saying."

"And what saying would that be?" asked the astronomy professor.

"Oh, that's an easy answer; it's one we all learned as little children: 'Twinkle, twinkle, little star....'"

I love that story because it can serve to remind us we cannot let the world try to trivialize or diminish the true meaning of our faith. We cannot let the world of those who do not believe define just who Jesus is. When we consider the life of Jesus, we are humbled by all that he did and does for us. He is not just some historical figure from the past. He is alive and with us still today.

Our 2,000-year tradition has a word to describe this: Emmanuel, meaning "God is with us." We have a God who loves us unconditionally and has entered completely into our lives. He will never abandon us.

June 11
Thirsty

With the temperatures rising this week I found myself getting so desperately thirsty that in a very short time I had used up all the bottled water I keep in my car. It seemed that I could not get enough cold water. My thirst reminded me of something I read a short time ago about our need for water.

Studies have shown that it takes less than a one percent deficiency in our body's water to make us thirsty. (I must have been really low on water!) Just a five percent deficiency in the body's water causes us to run a slight fever. Push that deficiency up to eight percent and our saliva glands stop producing saliva. Our skin color changes and takes on a bluish tinge. Once our body's water level reaches a ten percent deficiency you can no longer walk, and by twelve percent we are dead.

Water is certainly important isn't it? (Even as I write this I'm reaching for a drink of water!) I spent a day and a half this past week meditating on these facts, which led me to a few rather simple insights.

Our life depends on some very basic needs. When those needs aren't met properly, life becomes more and more fragile, and more difficult as well. Just think of it: a mere one percent deficiency makes us thirsty. Do you suppose there might be a similar effect in our spiritual life?

If we begin to let our prayer time slip, if we begin to drift away from Mass or other spiritual practices, how long do you think it will be until we notice it taking a toll on our life? It doesn't take too long for me to notice that my life gets more and more difficult if I try to go it alone or do it my loved ones, or myself, without God. If it only takes a twelve percent water deficiency to cause our body to succumb to death, what percentage of neglect of our spiritual life might bring about a similar result?

When you reach for a nice cool drink of water this week, think of the good thing you are doing for your body and the quality of your life. Then again, why not think about what you might need to do for your spiritual life as well?

June 12
A "Paying" Audience

I read about two people this week, and the combination of what they said gave me some material for my meditation time. The first person was George Burns. He was asked once what advice he would give to someone who wanted to be a stand-up comic.

Burns thought about it for a short time, then said, "Don't bother to perform for a non-paying audience. Not because you won't make any money, but because it's easier to make a paying audience laugh. You would think that a paying audience would be more critical because they had to pay for the performance. The opposite is true. A non-paying audience is much more critical. Paying customers, on the other hand, they get dressed up, they take a date, they might buy dinner, they get invested. They will look at what is good to prove to themselves that they had made a good investment with their money. Paying audiences always appreciate you more."

Research has shown that what George Burns discovered in his own career is actually quite true. I would bet that the same advice might apply to our relationship with Jesus. Those who have invested their life in following Jesus and have had to "pay" by enduring various forms of rejection or criticism are more apt to find the blessings in following Jesus.

Those folks, on the other hand, who are not invested, who have not taken Jesus seriously, are often quite critical of Jesus and his followers. These people not only see the flaws and weaknesses of Jesus' disciples, but they also make a point of looking for these. As George Burns put it, "We human beings tend to respect and honor what we have paid for."

The second person I read about this past week was Martin Luther. It is said that on one particular Sunday morning he went into a rage as he stood in the pulpit. Onlookers described him as purple-faced as he exploded at his congregation. He had found them to be "stingy givers" when it came to their faith. He was not just talking about tithing; he was talking about how open they were to the needs of those around them.

This is what he said: "You ungrateful beasts! You rotten filthy beasts! You are not worthy of the treasures of the Holy Gospels. If you do not improve, I will stop preaching here. I cannot cast the pearls of the Gospel before such swine!"

June 13
The Keys of the Kingdom

When I was on vacation recently I had a lot of time to read. One of the books I re-read was A.J. Cronin's novel, *The Keys of the Kingdom*. I particularly like a passage in which one of the main characters, Father Francis Chisholm, a missionary priest who has worked all of his life in China under terrible conditions, makes an important observation.

In the passage, Father Chisholm is trying to console a friend of his who is very depressed because his crop has been completely ruined by a horrible flood. The man is on the verge of despair and he begins to sob, saying, "My plantings are all lost. I can do nothing but to start all over again. It's the only way."

Father Chisholm puts his arm around the man and says, "But that's life my friend: to begin again when everything is lost." The man finds comfort in those words not because they are profound, but because Father Chisholm's own life of struggling to overcome disappointment after disappointment gives his quiet, caring words real depth.

The priest's words, combined with his witnesses of slogging through the difficulties of life with faith, become for his parishioners the real keys of the kingdom. Father Chisholm's people come to know the kingdom of God's love because they have come to know Father Chisholm.

Who are the people in your life who have been the keys to the kingdom for you, because through them you have come to know and love God?

June 14
Seeing God

I read a story recently about an artist who was on his deathbed. As he lay there, the painter's wife was yelling at him because she couldn't get him to confess his sins. "You foolish man!" she screamed, "You are about to meet your Maker and he could be very angry with you. You'd better wise up and confess your sins and tell him you are sorry or it will be hell for you!"

The painter was silent for a moment. He then spoke slowly and said, "My dear, why do you want to paint me such a monstrous image of God as I am so near to death? Don't forget the fact that I am a professional painter, and God is a professional forgiver. If he is half as good at his profession as I am at mine, I am sure that me and you and everyone else has very little to worry about. Why do you want to make such a monster of our loving God?"

The painter's wife realized that her husband was not afraid of God and that he was not confessing his sins because he didn't think he had any. She realized that her husband and God were truly good friends and she need not have been so worried about him. Just before death came the painter said to her, "I love you! And right now, as I go to meet him, I know he is twice the professional that I am. He will take me home. Don't make a monster of him. He loves me and you and he loves us all."

Today, take some time to consider how you see God. Do you know him as a loving, forgiving God or have you, like the painter's wife, made a monster of him? How we see God affects how we live and how we treat others. How do you see God?

June 15
Hitched Together

Back in the 1800s, when people were headed out West in covered wagons, one of the most dangerous points in the journey was crossing the Platte River. The current in the river was unpredictable and seemed to change so quickly that even the most experienced scouts found it really difficult to negotiate. Many wagons got stuck and eventually were overturned by the strong waters. People and their possessions often ended up in the water, and many died as a result of hidden pockets of quicksand, unseen drop-offs, and potholes. Even though strong teams of oxen were used on the wagons, they often lost their footing and disaster struck.

Eventually the problem was solved when one wagon train leader changed tactics. He would wait for all of the wagons to gather at river's edge. He then hitched together all of the oxen from all of the wagons to form a long line of teams to pull each of the families across the river, one at a time. Even if one team of oxen floundered in the long line, there would always be enough sure-footed oxen to keep the wagon on the move and help the floundering oxen find their footing. The wagon master knew that by hitching all the oxen together, the stronger ones could help the weaker ones. When the weaker oxen found their footing, then they could help the newly floundering ones.

Doesn't that sound like good advice when we find ourselves facing some difficult situation? Perhaps we might think about hitching ourselves together to help each other get through the troubled waters on our journey.

June 16
The Most Dangerous Animal

What animal that ever lived is the most dangerous to human beings? Throughout the centuries, scientists estimate that this creature has killed at least forty-five billion people. That's a lot of killing! So which animal has been responsible for such terrible carnage?

It's the female mosquito – and it's only the female that has done the deed since male mosquitoes only bite plants, not human beings. Mosquitoes carry more than a hundred potentially fatal diseases, everything from malaria to yellow fever, dengue fever, West Nile virus, encephalitis, and many other infections. Being bitten by a mosquito can be a life-threatening experience.

This information can serve as an interesting illustration of some "bites" that can occur in our spiritual lives. Just as there are very dangerous mosquitoes that can infect us in our bodies, so too there are spiritual mosquitoes that can bite our souls and infect us with deadly spiritual diseases.

We can be bitten by a way of looking at life that infects our souls with an attitude by which we only find faults in our family members. This can make our families sick with bickering, arguments, and bitterness. There are also those spiritual mosquitoes that can bite us and infect us with the disease of envy or jealousy. There may be a spiritual mosquito that infects us with an anger that boils over, and many people walk away from an encounter with us deeply wounded or offended. A spiritual mosquito of self-hatred, inferiority, and low self-esteem bites other folks. In short, there are many ways in which we can be spiritually infected.

The important thing to remember is that, just as there are both vaccines and treatments available when our bodies are infected by mosquito-born diseases, so too are there treatments for those maladies that result from the spiritual mosquitoes that have bitten us. Jesus is the healer of every ill and therefore is the perfect treatment and the best vaccine to protect us from the havoc that those spiritual bugs might try to inflict on us.

June 17
Being Wise

From time to time in parish ministry there are changes in personnel when the bishop assigns diocesan priests to particular parishes. Before this happens priests who are about to move to a new assignment go on a little trip around the diocese to look at what might be their next assignment.

This past week I've been getting calls from some of our priests who are interested in being parochial vicars – that is, assistant pastors – at our parish. When one of them called to see if he might be able to come out and talk with me, he added in an off-handed way, "I think it might be good for me to be with one of our more senior pastors." I guess that means I have become one of the "old guys" in the diocese (I have no idea how I got to be that!). Anyway, it got me thinking about my last few years in the seminary when I had a mentor who actually was old – he was eighty-eight when I knew him.

The priest was Father Gus Bernard and he taught me a lot. He had many wise sayings that even today I find myself going back to, over and over again. One of his wise sayings was this: "Every person has the power to make other people happy. One person can do that by entering a room, another does it by leaving the room. At any given moment you must decide which you must do to make others happy!"

Father Bernard also taught me about the importance of prayer in a priest's life. He would remind me often that prayer is the most important thing any priest, especially a pastor, ever does. When I asked him why he thought that, he smiled and said, "Mark, prayer is important for us priests because prayer may not change things for you, but it sure changes you for things." Each time he would give me that advice he would go on to remind me of how Saint Paul had prayed for God to remove the thorn in his side (2 Cor 12:7) – but God never did, no matter how often Paul prayed about it. What God *did* do was change Saint Paul.

Father Bernard would conclude by telling me there would be many times in my priesthood when I would come upon things that I would want God to change. Then he would remind me that I should not be surprised if I asked God to change something, and he didn't. If that happens, it will be because God is about to change me.

I learned so much from my very wise mentor, Father Bernard. With some of our younger priests beginning to see me as one of our senior pastors, I guess I'd better get my act together and start being wise, too!

June 18
Wasting Time

For some reason, I have spent more time this week with people who are at odds with each other over what they think are vitally important things. The truth of the matter, however, is that most of the fuss is over minor, unimportant differences – like this one.

A husband and wife were having a bit of an argument that seemed to be going nowhere. At one point in the argument the husband cleared his throat and said to his wife, "You have to admit at least this much; men have much better judgment than women do." "Oh, I can see how that's true," his wife replied.

That statement stopped the husband in his tracks, so he checked with her and said, "Do you really agree with me?" "Oh, you are definitely right about that. Men have better judgment than women. Why, just look at us; you chose to marry me, and I chose to marry you!"

The husband was a bit confused when that argument didn't come out the way he had hoped it would. He hadn't learned yet just how foolish most arguments truly are. It reminds me of another argument recounted by a hospital administrator at a recent conference.

The speaker had once worked in a hospital where a patient knocked over a cup of water, which spilled on the floor beside the patient's bed. The patient was afraid he might slip on the water if he got out of the bed, so he asked a nurse's aide to mop it up. The patient didn't know it, but the hospital policy said that small spills were the responsibility of the nurse's aides while large spills were to be mopped up by the hospital's housekeeping group.

The nurse's aide decided the spill was a large one and she called the housekeeping department. A housekeeper arrived and declared the spill a small one. An argument followed.

"It's not my responsibility," said the nurse's aide, "because it's a large puddle."

The housekeeper did not agree. "Well, it's not mine," she said, "the puddle is too small."

The exasperated patient listened for a time, then took a pitcher of water from his night table and poured the whole thing on the floor. "Is that a big enough puddle now for you two to decide?" he asked. That was the end of the argument.

Most arguments are about unimportant, foolish things. When you come right down to it, there is no bigger waste of time than arguing with someone over stupid things.

Have you been wasting any time lately?

June 19
Keep Your Family Out of Jail

All great spiritual leaders throughout history have given their disciples a two-word teaching: "Pay attention!" What do they mean by that? Well, they don't mean just pay attention in class or to a particular teacher, though that is important. What they really want us to do is pay closer attention to our life and the choices we make. Let me explain this a bit further.

I had a conversation a few months ago with someone I met when I was pastor up in West Chester. He is from Malaysia and was telling me about how things in his country are sometimes handled differently there than here in the United States. He said, "In my country, for example, if I were to get drunk and then drive home and were caught by the police, I would immediately be sent to jail."

I replied, "Well, that is what would happen here in the U.S. if you were stopped by the police and found to be drunk." He nodded at me and said, "I know, but you see, in my country, if I were driving drunk, I would certainly be thrown in jail for the offense, but in addition to that, my wife would also be thrown in jail."

"Your wife would be thrown in jail?" I asked. "If you were the one who is drunk, why would they throw her in jail too?"

"I'm not sure why it's that way; perhaps they assume that such a crime is a family problem. I am happy to be here, however, where one does one's own punishments," he said.

Although it may seem strange to us that someone can be thrown into jail for something a family member actually did, there is, I think, a very real way in which our choices and our "crimes" can throw our family members into a kind of jail. Have you ever had the experience of someone you love being in the hospital or maybe even in jail, and feeling as if you were right there with them? Isn't it true that when someone you love is hurting, you hurt with him or her too? Even if our nation does not throw people into jail for the crimes their loved ones may have committed, we do, in a way, throw ourselves there.

Now, if that's the case, then there is all the more reason for us to pay close attention to our behavior so our bad choices and bad behaviors don't land our loved ones in jail. Sometimes we may not be aware of just how much our attitudes and choices can badly affect our families, friends, and loved ones. We think our choices only affect us, yet that really is not the case. If we would just pay a little more attention to the choices we make in life, our loved ones could be spared the pain of being sentenced to some hard time behind bars.

Fr. Mark Burger

June 20
Weather Reports

"Every house is tested. Whether it is by fierce storms or by incredible cold or blazing heat, every house is tested. The difference is not in the weather; it is in the foundation to which the house is anchored."

This past week I was looking through some notes I had kept from a retreat I had made almost twenty years ago when I came upon the quotation above. It had been given to each of us on the retreat by the director of the retreat, with the instructions to use it in our prayer time. He directed all of us to spend time with those words, then examine our own lives to see just how our "houses of faith" were standing up to the "weather" life was throwing our way.

As I re-read that quote, I realized there has been a significant amount of weather thrown at my house in the twenty years since that retreat, some of it considerably more intense than any I had experienced before that retreat. I began to think it through, however, and realized that although I have been continually bombarded by life, I have continually been blessed by life as well. In addition, as I look back, I can see that I have never stopped making repairs to my house and shoring up its foundation. I think this is what a life of faith is all about. It's what we all have to find a way to do.

When I was pastor of St. Michael Church in Lower Price Hill, one of the parishioners, a woman from southern Kentucky, often talked about a man she knew years ago who lived in one of the isolated corners of the Blue Ridge Mountains. She said life was very hard for that man, and every day his little piece of land was at the mercy of drought, wind, cold, or horrendous storms. Yet he was about the most serene and deeply contented man she had ever known. She asked the old mountain man one day if he had ever had any troubles or spent any sleepless nights.

"Sure, I've had my troubles," he told her, "but no sleepless nights. When I go to bed I say, 'Lord, you have to sit up all night anyway. There's no point in both of us losing sleep. You look after things tonight, and when tomorrow comes, I'll do the best I can to help you.'"

My parishioner would end her story by saying that there was no storm that could blow down that old man's faith. I think she was right; that old mountain man's house had some pretty solid foundations.

How is your "house" holding up under the weather life has thrown your way?

June 21
Try Something New

A disciple came to his master for help with a problem. "What is the problem that troubles you?" asked the master. The disciple replied, "I have a terrible fear of making mistakes." The master thought for a moment, then said, "You must keep in mind this simple truth. Those who make no mistakes are making the biggest mistake of all: they are attempting nothing new."

I've been thinking about that little Zen story quite a bit lately because many of the people who have come to see me recently have been talking about their overwhelming fear of failure. Sometimes it's a fear of making even a simple little mistake. They all seem paralyzed and perhaps a bit bored, so I've been asking questions.

When was the last time you tried something new? Can you recall a time you boldly stepped out and attempted to do something you've never done before? In recent weeks I've been bugging people with questions like that, and the answers I've been getting are rather interesting. Most of the folks have to think long and hard to recall the last time they tried something new or did something they'd never done before. Many people said it was way back when they were in school that they were literally forced to try new things.

When I asked people why they thought it was so long ago since they tried something new, the answer was almost always the same: "Well, when I was in school it wasn't too hard, but now I'm afraid I would look foolish at my age trying something new." Or "I'm sure I'd make terrible mistakes and just end up not being very good at it. Then I'd feel like a failure, and I'd rather not."

It's amazing how the fear of failing has kept most people from experiencing some of the greatest joys of life. It's a shame that so many people are so afraid to try new things because there are so many new worlds life has to offer us. Every time we step out to try something new we are opening a door to one of those new worlds.

While on vacation I spoke with an older man who told me that once he retired he found himself sitting at home just "looking at the four walls, waiting for something to happen." He said for a year and a half he did nothing but sit in front of the TV and fall asleep watching terrible shows. Then one day a friend called and asked him if he would like to learn how to carve wood. "I immediately said no," he recalled, "because I had never done anything like that. But my friend asked me a second time, and I was about to launch into my reasons for why I wasn't interested when he said, 'Oh, so you're afraid to try something you might fail at?'"

Not wanting to look like he was afraid, the man agreed to go with his friend to a group of retired guys who did woodcarving. "Best thing I ever did," he said. "I had no idea I had that kind of talent. I wonder how many other things I'm good at that I never discovered because I was too afraid to try something new?"

When was the last time you tried something new? Is it time now to try?

JUNE 22
A Change of Focus

I had breakfast the other day with a man who was a graduate of West Point, and he had spent the majority of his adult years serving in the U.S. Army. In the course of our conversation I asked if there was one thing he recalled from his days at the academy that has stuck with him through his career in the military. He paused for a rather long time before he gave his answer.

The man said he had many great and not so great experiences at West Point, and all of those experiences taught him a lot. He went on to say there was a sign on the wall in the football locker room that he will always remember because it helped him get through some rough spots in his life. He said the sign was so important to him that he had one like it on his desk, and had even given one to each of his kids as they went off to college.

"What was on the sign?" I asked.

He said, "It simply reads: Do not let what you cannot do interfere with what you can do." He went on to tell me that throughout his life he had often found himself almost paralyzed by the overwhelming feeling that sometimes, there's nothing you can do about a particular situation. It was at those times that the little sign in the football locker room at West Point came back to him, and helped shift his focus from what he could not do to what he could do.

There's great wisdom in those words. In your life right now, are you feeling overwhelmed or paralyzed by the thought that there's nothing you can do about a particular situation? Perhaps a change of focus is in order.

June 23
Calling Forth a Masterpiece

Recently I've been reading about the famous artist, Michelangelo Buonarroti. Most of us know him simply as Michelangelo. One of his most famous works of art is his giant masterpiece, the statue of David. It stands over eighteen feet tall and is so finely crafted it appears as if David is truly alive. Its beauty overwhelms most folks who see it for the first time; many people expect to see it move. It truly is an amazing work of art.

What many people do not realize is that the beautiful stone from which this statue was made had been rejected as inferior by four other artists of Michelangelo's time. In fact, they declared that the marble was of such low quality that nothing of any value could be made from it. Michelangelo, on the other hand, looked at that very same slab of marble and was able to see "David" within it, struggling to be free. Five artists studied the same slab of marble; four declared it of little or no value. One saw the possibility of a masterpiece and brought it forth.

This is a great illustration of what can happen to each of us. Four people can look at us and declare that we are inferior, of little or no value. Sometimes when we are young, our classmates and friends make judgments about us and tell us we have no value. If we believe them and take that to heart, the best in us may never come out. But what if one person comes along, looks at us, and sees us with the same eyes that Michelangelo used when he studied that famous slab of marble? What if someone saw what was really in us: a great work of art? Our lives would be truly changed.

Take a few moments and consider the members of your family, or think about each of your friends. Can you see beneath the surface to discover in them the masterpiece that lies within? What do you think would happen if you were to help them see that side of themselves?

From time to time, each one of us is called to be a kind of Michelangelo for one another. The world is in need of some new great works of art. Maybe you are the one God is calling to bring them forth!

June 24
Finding a Bit of Peace and Quiet

A dad was talking with his young son as they sat in the car waiting at a traffic light. He asked the boy, "What does it mean when the light is red?" The boy didn't hesitate and said, "It means Stop!" The father then asked, "So, what does it mean when the light turns green?" The boy quickly said, "Go!" The boy's dad finally said, "Now this is a harder question. What does it mean when the light turns yellow?"

This time the young boy had to think a bit longer. After a rather long pause he said, "Oh, I know what it means: "Go faster!"

Smart kid, huh? He must have been a very observant child to notice what most people do when they see a yellow light – they speed up. You and I know, however, the purpose of the amber light is to warn us that the light is about to change, and we should prepare to slow down and safely stop.

Yet it's rare that someone actually slows down when they see a yellow light. Most of us do indeed speed up so we don't miss the light. And that illustrates what I see as a problem for all of us.

As I listen to people talk about the problems and various crises they face, I notice one thing that we all seem to have in common. It's the problem of speed. (No, I'm not talking about drugs!) We are all living at a faster and faster pace and rarely slow down enough to catch our breath, much less even notice what is happening to us. We rush ahead so we won't "miss the light," never realizing that a well-placed pause can do wonders for us.

Next time you come to a traffic light, pay closer attention to what the yellow light truly means: caution, slow down. Then ask yourself if you need to have a few more yellow lights in your life so you can catch your breath, and maybe find some time for God and a bit of peace and quiet.

June 25
Headed for Home

Many people are very troubled by death and what happens after it. As I spend time thinking and praying about it, I recall something I heard while visiting a Jewish seminary.

In a class that I audited the teacher spoke of an ancient Jewish parable about twin unborn children lying together in the womb. One believes there is a world beyond the womb where people walk upright, where there are mountains and oceans, and a sky filled with stars. The other unborn twin thinks his womb companion is a fool for even thinking such thoughts. He assumes his twin just made these things up because he is unhappy with life in the womb.

Suddenly the "believer" twin is forced through the birth canal, leaving behind the way of life he has known. All at once he is pushed out and is gone. The remaining unborn twin is saddened, convinced that a great catastrophe has befallen his companion. He begins to miss him and wonder where he has gone. Outside the womb, however, the parents are rejoicing. The new baby has found a new home. The twin still left behind thinks he has just witnessed death and utter destruction. In reality he has not seen death but rather, birth.

The teacher told the class that this idea is a classic view of the life beyond the grave. He said many people in the world believe death is a birth into a world that we on Earth can only try to imagine.

I certainly am one of those people who believe in the resurrection. As a Christian, I know that Jesus has, like that companion in the womb, gone ahead of us to a whole new world. Where Jesus has gone, we will follow. There's a whole new world that has been prepared for us from the beginning of time itself. One day he will come back to take us to that place so where he is we may also be.

This is what Jesus told his disciples he would do. Christians believe he will indeed come back again to take us all home. This is at the core of our beliefs as Christians. There is peace in knowing we are all headed for a real home.

Fr. Mark Burger

June 26
Are You Awake?

There was a hard-working foreman at a construction company who was conscientious, a team player, a good listener, and a man of much wisdom. All of those who worked under him admired him and always wanted to be on the jobs he led. Many of those workers wondered why upper management hadn't promoted him, and the workers often talked among themselves about how he deserved better treatment, higher pay, and a promotion.

One of the younger workers decided he would talk to the foreman about this, and asked why he continued to work for the company even though he had never been promoted. The foreman listened to the young worker and said, "Oh, you've noticed that, have you? Well. Let me tell you something. When I first started working here many years ago, when I was just about your age, I had a terrible argument with the owner of this company."

"What happened?" the young worker asked.

The foreman replied, "I won."

When I read that I was reminded of a famous adage about power, which states, Being powerful is like being a lady: If you have to tell people you are, then you aren't. The same is true for something as simple as kindness. If you have to tell people you are kind, perhaps you are not as kind as you think you are.

Sometimes we think we're getting somewhere by being important or full of our own authority. Some folks think this is what greatness or leadership is all about. The foreman learned over the years, I'm sure, that while it might have been important when he was young to win the argument with his boss, it may not have been worth it when it came to being promoted. As another adage suggests, one may win the battle and lose the war in the process. Through difficult years of experience, the foreman had learned the difference between being smart and being truly wise.

From time to time it's good for all of us to reconsider the purpose of our education. It's not just about the grades we earn, or the sports we play, or even about all of the other activities each academic year brings. The purpose of our education is our formation. Our education gives us the opportunity to ask ourselves a simple question: What am I becoming?

We must step back from time to time to see ourselves full in the face. Are we becoming kind, caring, truly Christ-like people? Are we becoming people who have true wisdom as opposed to people who merely know a collection of ideas or theories? Are we growing in our ability to relate well with others, to share real life and toil together for the good of others? These are all good questions to ask ourselves, and important that we follow up on them.

Whenever I think of my own formation over the years, I think of something I learned from a Hindu friend. She said that when she was young, she wanted people to think she was smart and thought the most important thing in life to be was "right." Then, as she matured and began to observe people and learn from them, she actually gained a little wisdom and realized that being right wasn't half as important as something else.

Trying to live life as a good Hindu, she began to realize that the most important thing in life is to be "awake." Being awake, she related, is how one grows in true wisdom. Paying attention to everything that is going on around you can teach you a lot.

Whether you are in a formal school situation or in the school of life, all of those experiences have the power to form us for good or bad. By staying awake, our formation can lead to real wisdom. One way to look at it is to realize that for each one of us, school is always in session.

Take some time to step back and see just what kind of person you are becoming. Is it someone who is fully awake?

June 27
Hooked

A few years ago I was in our school talking with one of the classes about Jesus in the desert as Satan was tempting him. One of the students, a fourth grader, asked me what I thought Satan did all day. I turned to the class and said, "So what do you think the Devil does all day?"

There was a pause that went on for a rather long period of time, and then one young girl said, "I think the Devil spends most of his time watching us."

"And why do you think he spends most of his time watching us?" I asked.

"I think he watches to see what we like to eat and stuff, and then when your mom or dad says you can't have that he tells us to go ahead and eat it when mom and dad aren't looking." She said all of that in one breath!

Another student chimed in, "I think he watches to see which one of us is going to do something that gets our mom really screaming and yelling and saying words I'm not allowed to say out loud." Everyone giggled.

Finally, one of the students said, "I think Satan tries to find out what you are like as a person and then he tries to ruin you!"

When the students had finished talking I held up a poster so they could all clearly see it. The poster showed two twelve-year-old boys baiting their hooks with night crawlers. The caption below the boys read, "Satan, like any good fisherman, baits his hook according to what the fish like to eat."

As the class read the words, they all started to laugh and talk to each other about what Satan would use to "catch" them. Already at ten years of age those children knew where they were the weakest. Do you? If Satan were to come fishing for you, what kind of bait would he use to hook you?

June 28
Continually Blessed

In 1860, the Lady Elgin shipwrecked off the coast of Evanston, Illinois. Over 300 people died in that disaster, but seventeen people were saved through the efforts of Edward Spencer, a student of Northwestern University. His heroic deeds left Spencer an invalid for the rest of his life. Yet when he was asked about the one thing that stood out in his mind from the incident, Spencer replied: "I remember that of the seventeen people I saved that day, not one of them ever came and thanked me." Although he had been given awards and was acknowledged by many for his heroism, those who had benefited most from Edward Spencer's brave actions – the people he saved from the shipwreck -- never took the time to be grateful.

In reading this story it occurred to me that each of us should take the time to be grateful. It would be good for each of us to first, thank God for the many blessings God has poured into our lives. It would be good too, for each of us to take some time to thank the people who bless our lives – family, friends, neighbors, colleagues, classmates, and so on –for the many ways they have been there for us.

When I was in high school, I read the book *Robinson Crusoe*, by Daniel Defoe. As the story goes, Crusoe finds himself on a deserted island following a shipwreck. Alone, scraping to pull together some tools and supplies from the shipwrecked boat to keep himself alive, he refers to that place as the "island of despair."

After a few days, when he had a chance to recover his bearings, Crusoe sat down to list the negative things about his situation. Across from each negative thing he wrote a positive thing about his situation. As Crusoe compared the two he concluded there was far more reason to be thankful than for despair. He realized there was no reason for him to be confined to an "island of despair" when there was so much for which to be truly grateful.

Why not take some time this week to list your problems and your blessings? Which list will be longer? When you have finished your lists, don't forget to come back and thank the one who has continually blessed your life.

June 29
Drop by Drop

One of the Desert Fathers, Abba Poemen, was assigned the task of teaching new disciples about conversion. He would begin his teaching by reading various verses of the Bible to them, especially the passages containing the teachings and warnings of the ancient prophets.

When one of the disciples asked him to sum up all of the various verses into one important teaching, Abba Poemen replied, "You must let the Lord change your hearts of stone." The disciple thought about that for a moment, then asked, "So how does that happen?"

Abba Poemen continued, "The nature of water is that it is soft and fluid; the nature of stone is that it is hard and seemingly unyielding. But if you were to hang a pail of water above a stone and allow just a drop of water at a time to drip down on a stone, drop by drop it would wear away the stone. So it is with the Lord."

"The Word of God, the Bible, is a bit like water in that it, too, is soft and fluid. Our hearts are often like stone, hard, unmoving, and seemingly resistant to change. Yet when a person begins to listen to the Word of God, drop by drop it wears away the hardness of the heart. Some of it even seeps into the heart and softens it until it experiences God's grace. From that time on, one is never the same."

Each day offers us a doorway into God's grace. Take some time this week to absorb the Word of God. If your heart is hardened by life, why not let the Bible seep into your heart, drop by drop?

June 30
What Do You "Know"?

Have you seen the commercial that's been running on TV lately for a paint company? In the ad there are two chameleons trying to choose a paint color for their living room walls. As each of them steps on a particular colored paint chip, the chameleon's skin changes to that color.

I love that commercial! It is cleverly done and has won several awards. The only problem with the ad is that it's based on a complete myth. The truth of the matter is that, while the paint being sold might be good paint, chameleons do not change color to match the background where they are standing. Most of us, including me, have always thought this was the case, that chameleons change colors to reflect their surroundings.

Biologists will tell you, however, that this is not true. They can change colors, but it has nothing to do with the color of their surroundings. They change color when they get scared. They change color if you pick one up, but that's probably because they are frightened. If a member of the opposite sex shows up, they change color then, too. They also change color when they are in a fight, or when it's too hot or too cold. Sometimes they change color because of the brightness or dimness of the light. The bottom line, however, is that most of us have believed a complete myth about chameleons.

It's really interesting that perhaps the only thing most people are sure they know about chameleons is wrong. This leads me to wonder just how many other things we are certain we know to be absolutely true are, in fact, not true. This could be a great reminder from God for each of us to check our facts when it comes to what we think we "know" about those we love. How often have we been wrong when we assume we know what a friend or loved one feels or thinks about something?

Our colorful chameleon friends have a lot to teach us about life, especially about making sure we don't jump to conclusions based on false information.

July

July 1
Invisible People

Who are the really important people in our world? If you ask someone who is the most important person in the United States, many folks would probably say it's the President. Although the President is a powerful person, I think there are others equally or even more important than him. Let me explain.

Back in 1981, an assassin shot President Reagan. The attempt on his life made the whole world hold its breath, yet our government continued to fully function. The nation did not collapse or begin to fall apart. In that same year, however, as President Reagan was recovering from his wounds, the garbage collectors in Philadelphia went on strike. No trash was collected for more than three weeks, and Philadelphia was brought to a standstill by the huge piles of refuse that filled the streets.

Although the President of the United States is a very important person, it was the trash collectors who proved to be indispensable. Those great heaps of trash made Philadelphia's streets impassable and the stench overwhelmed anyone who went outdoors. The strike had to be settled, and it wasn't too long before all sides came to an agreement. Our nation discovered that we could never take those good workers for granted. Until the trash collectors stopped doing their job, they were just about invisible to the average person. Probably very few people had ever even considered how important sanitation workers are to a city until the streets began to fill up.

Are there any invisible people in your life? Are there people you may be taking for granted who actually make a big difference in your life? Have you ever thanked those folks for the work they do on your behalf?

July 2
Free

A man was captured by his enemies and thrown into prison. The man knew that the next day, most certainly, he would be interrogated, tortured, and possibly even killed. He began to be filled with fear bordering on terror. He paced back and forth in his cell like a caged animal, tormented by his fearful thoughts.

Half way through the night, in middle of his pacing, a thought dawned on him. He recalled what his old spiritual teacher had taught him when he was rather young: "You don't have the past because it is finished. You have today. Tomorrow isn't real; only today." As soon as he recalled these thoughts, the man calmed down and fell into a very restful, peaceful sleep. The man was still in prison, still confined to a cell by his enemies, but he was free. He had remembered what his spiritual teachers had taught him long before, that the only thing real is now, and he was able to relax. He realized that the enemies of freedom are not just outside us, but inside us too.

On the Fourth of July we will take the day off to celebrate the birth of our nation. As we remember the great events that have lead to our independence and recall all those who have sacrificed in its cause, it is important for us to remember our own responsibility in preserving our freedom -- the freedom we enjoy on the outside, but also that freedom we are offered by God that is in our hearts and souls.

God made us to be free, free as a nation and free as individuals. Why not take time this Fourth of July to thank God for the freedom you enjoy?

July 3
Wounded Hearts

A farmer was trying to sign up for health insurance. In the process of filling out the appropriate forms, the insurance agent began to ask the farmer a series of questions. "Have you had any accidents recently?" the agent asked. The farmer thought about that for a minute or two, then replied, "Well, no, not really. But I guess there was that time the mule kicked in two of my ribs. And there was that time a few months back when a rattlesnake bit me. And I also remember about a year ago when the bull caught me off guard, hit me with his horns, and threw me head-first over that fence over there. But I guess I'd have to say that I haven't really had any accidents at all."

The insurance agent said, "My goodness, Mister, don't you think those things were accidents?"

"No" said the farmer "I don't think any of them did it on accident; they done it on purpose!"

Although that story makes me laugh, it also makes me take a few minutes of quiet time. Recently, in the middle of some marriage counseling I was doing, a husband broke down and began to cry. He said that what had hurt him the most in his marriage is that his wife appeared to be hurting his feelings, as he said, "on purpose." Before I could say anything, his wife began to cry and whispered, "In my whole life I have never tried to hurt you on purpose. I would never do that! If I hurt you, it was certainly not on purpose. It was simply my own weakness and insensitivity and stupidity!"

There was a long period of silence as both quietly wept. Then the husband said in a very gentle voice, "I could endure anything else on earth except the idea that you, the one person I love more than anyone else, would purposely try to hurt me. You don't know how big a burden you just lifted from my heart."

As I listened to them it reminded me there is probably no deeper wound one can endure in this life than to feel or know that someone we love deeply has purposely tried to hurt us. There are many among us who have, in fact, experienced such deep wounds. Recovery from such a wound screams for God's help.

Jesus came among us as the healer of our every wound. Has anyone wounded you that deeply? Are you in need of his healing love? Let Jesus heal your burdened and wounded heart.

July 4
A Second Look

There's a poem I remember from college days that I think of often, because it illustrates what most of us find ourselves doing. The poem is called *Muckers*, and it's about a crew of workers who are digging a ditch for a gas main. It describes the workers covered in the ditch with the pipeline, mud gushing over their boots. The job is very difficult, dirty, and dangerous.

As they continue to dig and slog their way along, they begin to complain about what a hell of a job they have to do. Meanwhile, above them, outside of the hole in the ground, are a bunch of men who are out of work, unable to support their families. While the men in the ditch are complaining about their terrible job, those above it are saying, "I wish I had that job!"

Isn't that what happens to many of us? We have a good job or are in a good situation but we find reasons to complain about it. Others who don't have what we have long to have the very thing we are complaining about. Sometimes the things in life we complain to God about are in reality the very gift God is giving us to take care of ourselves.

If you are in a "mucker" kind of job and find yourself complaining and griping about it, is a second look perhaps in order?

July 5
Feeling Pain

A man wasn't feeling very well, so he went and made an appointment to see his doctor. "Doctor," he complained, "I'm hurting all over; everywhere I touch it seems to really hurt. I don't know if I'm just getting older, or maybe my mind is off or I'm just senile. If I push on my knees here, I hurt. If I poke here on my stomach, it hurts like crazy! If I press on my head right here by my temple I find that hurts too! What's going on?"

The doctor called for a full body X-ray and other scans. Two hours passed, and after evaluating the X-rays carefully, the doctor returned. Stroking his chin, the doctor slowly began, "I think I've found the reason why everything hurts." "Well, tell me!" the man anxiously replied.

Fr. Mark Burger

The doctor pointed to the X-ray. "Your body is fine; it's your finger -- it's broken."

I laughed when I first read that story. But as I got to thinking about it, I began to see how that story could be a kind of parable about pain. How often in your life have you found yourself in some kind of pain and immediately you began to look for its cause?

It's fairly easy to get confused about the pain we may have in life. So often we can think that one person or a particular situation is the cause of our pain, when in reality the pain may have its source in another, unexpected place. Very often we want to blame someone or something for the pain we are enduring, only to find out later that the source of our pain is not there but, in fact, may well be from within us.

When Saint Anthony of the Desert was asked to heal someone, he would reply, "First, let us look for the source of your pain and suffering. Then you and I can make our way to the God who is the healer of every illness and every pain, sorrow, or suffering." As the patient above discovered, his pain was not in the other parts of his body; it was in his finger. If his finger were healed, he would no longer feel the pain in his body!

July 6
What Difference?

Recently at a Sunday Mass, a missionary made an appeal to the congregation for funds to support the work of his mission. After Mass, as people were greeting one another on the way out, one parishioner came up to the missionary and asked, "Just give me one good reason why I should give you money?" I listened to see what the priest would say in response. What he said impressed me.

"Well, sir," the missionary said. "I want to tell you about a man in my mission. All of this man's family had been instructed by me and by some of our lay catechists, and everyone had asked to be baptized – everyone except for the man I am talking about. This man absolutely refused to be baptized; in fact, he was angrily opposed to it. One year went by, then two, then three. Finally, after four years, the man came and asked to be baptized."

"When I asked him what had changed his mind, he told me this: 'When my family and many of my friends were baptized, I didn't trust it. I wanted to wait and see if being baptized made any difference in the way they lived. I wondered whether or not it would change the way they treated me, or thought of themselves or others. I wanted to see if they treated their enemies differently after they got baptized. Now, four years later, I know it is a powerful thing to be baptized. I want to do so for myself because of what it did for my family and for my friends. Thank you for coming to my village and giving us such a great gift!'" The missionary then said, "The reason you should give to my mission is so that I can continue to travel through my mission, baptizing our people and changing the world."

I don't know if the parishioner gave the missionary any money. I know I did. And once I did give, I asked myself a simple question, "What difference has my baptism made in my life?" What difference has *your* baptism made in your life?

July 7
Now What?

When I was living as a hermit in the desert in Israel, I studied the writings of the ancient Desert Fathers. One of them told the story about something from his own younger days, when he first went into the desert.

On a trip into a nearby village for supplies, the young hermit saw a man with only one leg going by. Then he saw a mother begging for food for her starving child. Finally, he saw a man who had been a victim of a severe beating.

Seeing these unfortunate people parading before him, the monk turned to God in prayer and asked, "Oh Great Lord, how can you, such a loving and merciful God, see so much suffering and do nothing about it?" A few minutes later the holy monk heard God's voice down deep in his heart. "I have done something about it – I made sure that you saw them! Now, what will you do in response to their suffering?"

Fr. Mark Burger

July 8
Around the Corner

When I was in the seminary there was a man there who taught Spanish. In addition to teaching Spanish, he was also a translator for several large corporations who did labor negotiations in Central and South America. He used to tell us how much stress he felt trying to accurately translate each person's words so that he would not inadvertently change what someone was trying to communicate. He told us that the subtle use of phrasing can change the meaning of what is said in negotiations, and he did not want to be the cause of negotiations falling apart because of inaccuracies in his translations.

Our teacher said that one difficult job he had was trying to translate the word "comfort" in a way that those who did not speak English would understand. As he was thinking this over, a man from Mexico who was at the meeting was talking about how he needed the next day off because his uncle had died, and he wanted to be with his aunt at this difficult time. He said, "May I have the day off tomorrow so I can go be with my poor aunt and help her heart around the corner?

When the Spanish teacher heard that phrase, he knew exactly now how to translate the word "comfort" so that all would know what he meant.

Isn't that a great way to describe the process of working through grief? Is there anything in your life that has become a real heartache to you? Perhaps there is someone to whom you can reach out to help you get your own heart around the corner.

July 9
Among the Ruins

The famous cathedral in London, St. Paul's, was designed and built by a young and brilliant architect named Christopher Wren. He was asked to build this new cathedral because the old one had been completely destroyed in the great fire of 1666. It took Christopher Wren thirty-five years to finish his work. The result is a real masterpiece, and many throughout the ages have come to marvel at its beauty, grace, and grandeur.

It's been said that when Christopher Wren was kicking through the ruins of the old cathedral, he picked up a stone that had a Latin inscription on it. When he read it he felt as if God had chosen him for a special task. The inscription on that charred piece of stone was rather prophetic, and the translation of the Latin words was this: "I shall rise again." Wren then knew he would be the instrument through which God's house of prayer would indeed rise again.

In your life right now there may be some things that are lying in ruin. Things may have fallen apart in your marriage, or at work or school or in an important relationship, and you may feel that all is lost. Just kick through the ruins for a bit, and remember what Christopher Wren found among the ruins of the old cathedral: "I shall rise again." For a believer, one thing is certain: God cares for us and will always be with us among the ruins to make the next rising possible.

July 10
Your Choice

The owner of a rather large dog franticly called a local veterinarian early on Christmas morning. "Doc, it's our dog, Sam! You've got to see him today; it's really bad!"

The vet patiently listened to the man and said, "What's wrong with your dog?"

"Well, when I went to take him out this morning, I noticed that he has this terrible, ugly swelling in the corner of his mouth. I don't think he had it yesterday, but it's rather big and I'm really worried. Can you see him today?"

There was a long pause, then the vet replied, "You know it's Christmas; can't this wait until tomorrow?"

"I don't know, Doc, this swelling seems to be getting worse. I'm really worried," the man said, with a hint of desperation in his voice.

The veterinarian agreed to see the dog that morning. When the dog arrived with its owner a few minutes later, the vet made a thorough examination. "Hmmm," he murmured as poked at the swelling in the corner of the dog's mouth. He turned and asked the dog's owner, "Do you have any children?"

"Good Heavens," the man replied, "is it contagious?"

"No," said the vet. "It's bubble gum."

Have you ever had an experience like that in which you were worried sick, thinking the worst possible thing is about to happen only to find out everything was just fine? Fearing the worst is a very common human experience, yet each one of us has the freedom to frame our day by choosing how we look at things.

We can choose to see life as a gift that offers us new and exciting opportunities each day, trusting in God that things will work out fine. Or we can choose to see things from another perspective, letting fear and anxiety creep into our lives. If we allow fear to get a foothold in our hearts, in a short time we will be certain that the worst is about to happen. In other words, when we let fear get into us, it isn't long before we are seeing the "bubble gum" of our life as some dreaded, contagious disease that will kill off our children.

We have the power to choose how we see the world. We can choose to trust in God and see everything from that perspective, or we can let those little nagging, gnat-like voices of fear make us imagine only the worst. It really is our choice.

July 11
The Gift of Days

A woman who lived in an assisted living facility was celebrating her ninety-ninth birthday. Many special guests came to celebrate with her, one of whom was her pastor. After cake and ice cream had been served and a rousing chorus of "Happy Birthday" sung, people began to leave the party. One of those making their way out was the old woman's pastor. As he shook her hand, he said to her, "Now, Mrs. Smith, I hope that one year from this very day, I will be able to come here and celebrate your one hundredth birthday with you."

Mrs. Smith looked carefully at him, thought about it for a few minutes, then said, "Well, I don't see why you couldn't. You look fairly healthy to me!"

Isn't it amazing how many assumptions we make about people, and even life itself? I'm sure that pastor thought he was right in assuming that Mrs.

Smith might not be alive in a year. Yet in her own way Mrs. Smith let him know something the Bible tells us, that we do not know the number of our days. We often make plans about the future and do so without thinking too much about whether or not we will be alive to complete those plans. Many of us just assume we have all the time in the world, when, in fact, we do not. Each day is a gift.

Consider this: If time is a gift and if time is limited, just how are we using that gift? Most of us assume we have plenty of time to let people know we love them, but do we ever get around to saying so? Are there other important things you plan to do some time yet have put off to another day, assuming you have an unlimited amount of days? Perhaps this can serve as a friendly reminder to use your gift of days wisely.

July 12
Check Your Commas

Someone recently wrote me a letter about how he and his wife were having troubles in their marriage. It seems they keep misunderstanding each other, and end up hurting each other's feelings. In reply I sent him a little story someone had given me a few years ago.

According to the story, a woman went on a vacation to Europe with her friends while her husband, who had to work, stayed home with the kids. As she traveled through France she would send her husband telegrams letting him know what she was doing and seeing. When she got to Paris she saw a wonderful bracelet that she wanted to buy, so she sent her husband another telegram. "I have found the most wonderful bracelet I have ever seen in a shop here in Paris. It's exactly what I have been looking for my whole life. Do you think it's OK for me to buy it? It costs only $7,500."

Her husband issued a rather short but firm reply, "No, price too high!" then signed his name.

But in the transmission of the telegram the comma was inadvertently left out, so the message his wife received was this: "No price too high!" His wife was thrilled that he loved her so much there was "no price too high."

I don't know what happened when she got back home with her new bracelet, but I bet there was a lively discussion. Isn't it amazing how one, little, left-out comma can change the entire meaning of a message? It makes one wonder if, at some time or other in our relationships, we all have inadvertently left out a comma and thereby communicated something we did not intend to.

It might be good for us to pause long enough and make an effort to "check our commas." That way we can make sure what we intend to communicate to someone is actually being communicated.

July 13
Heat or Light?

There was a guy who had some serious domestic troubles. He just did not get along with his wife. Not only that, he couldn't get along with his mother-in-law, either.

One day, after a particularly frustrating argument with his wife, the man went on a long walk to sort out his feelings. As he was walking home, he came to a street corner and saw a long black hearse stopped at the red light. There was a casket in the back of the hearse, and a mean-looking dog sitting next to it. Behind that hearse was a second hearse with a casket in the back of it, and behind the second hearse there was a group of about sixty men walking in kind of a procession.

The man was very curious as to what was going on, so he walked up to the first hearse and knocked on the glass. The driver rolled down the window. "Yes?" he asked.

The man said, "What's going on here with these two hearses?"

The driver replied, "Well, in this casket is my wife. In the casket in the other hearse is my mother-in-law. This big, mean-looking dog killed them both."

"This dog killed both your wife and your mother-in-law?" the man asked.

"That's what happened," was the reply.

Then the man asked, "Can I borrow that dog?"

The man inside the hearse replied, "Get in line with the rest of those guys back there!"

Although that story can make you laugh, family fights are no laughing matter. Domestic difficulties account for a lot of human suffering. Differences between people who love each other often boil over into some rather nasty fights in which some very hurtful things get said. It can be quite a painful ordeal to go through.

I think it was Thomas Aquinas who said that most arguments between family members create more "heat" than "light." He concluded that if people listened more than they talk, real arguments that seek to heal differences would, in fact, create more light than heat. Then people will find themselves living in greater harmony.

In your family, when disagreements arise and discussion follows, do those arguments create heat or light?

July 14
Grass

Are you a happy person? Are you able to find reasons to be joyful and satisfied no matter where you find yourself? I've been thinking about this because of something I saw recently while driving out in the country.

The scene that caught my eye and got me to thinking was of four horses eating some tasty grass, near each other in a huge pasture. Two of the horses were on one side of a fence, and the other two were on the other side. What amused me was that they all had their heads poking through the fence, and they were eating the grass on the other side! They seemed just a like a lot of people who are never quite happy with what they have already.

Does the grass on the other side of the fence always look better to you than the grass you find yourself in? Why do you suppose that is? Are you able to find blessings right where you are or does it seem they are always on someone else's land?

July 15
Good Neighbors

Sitting in the waiting room of a doctor's office recently, I was browsing through some ancient magazines when I came upon an article on the longest fence in the world. According to the article that fence, which is in Queensland, Australia, is 3,500 miles long and six feet high. The fence was built to protect sheep and cattle from a wild dog the Australians call a "dingo." These wild dogs prey on the herds of local farmers, who asked the government to help them combat the dingo menace. The government's solution was to erect this long fence and hire inspectors whose job it is to tend the fence and make sure the dingoes can't penetrate it.

This has turned out to be a very successful solution to a problem that has plagued the Queensland farming community for a long time. The farmers remarked that the fences, combined with the ever-present fence tenders, created a healthy, safe environment for their livestock. The fence has made all the difference.

As I read about that very long fence, I recalled a poem by Robert Frost that I had first come in contact with when I was in college. The poem is called *Mending Wall*, and it's the story of two New England farmers who go out each spring to mend the rock fences that have fallen down over the winter. They do it every spring, in the belief that "good fences make good neighbors."

But one spring, one of the farmers begins to question that long-held assumption. As they work on their respective sides of the fence, wearing their fingers raw with the rocks, he begins to think about things.

> He is all pine and I am apple orchard.
> My apple trees will never get across
> And eat the cones under his pines, I tell him.
> He only says, "Good fences make good neighbors."

Then the other farmer says this:

> "Before I built a wall, I'd ask to know
> What I am walling in or walling out,
> And to whom I am like to give offense
> Something there is that doesn't love a wall,
> That wants it down."

The man begins to wonder if tending to the wall still makes sense. He wonders if the wall still has a good purpose.

I really like that poem because it forces me to look to any "walls" or "long fences" I may have put up in my life over the years. Those walls and fences may need some tending; then again, they may not even be needed. I have to think on that, and see whether or not these walls and fences make "good neighbors." Whether they do or don't, I must then determine just what I might do next about them.

Are there walls or long fences in your life? Do they make good neighbors? Do you need to tend them?

July 16
Drying Wells

Recently, I was listening to a parishioner pour out a very sad story about her son, whom she was terrified was headed for an early death. I recalled something I had read about coping with those times when we feel utterly powerless, a little article about facing the hurdles life often puts in front of us. In the article, the author stated that at some time or other, everyone realizes they are completely overwhelmed. This happens, the writer explained, because we often rely solely on our own inner strength, which eventually runs out.

That thought took me to a quote from the book, *Springs in the Valley*, written over sixty years ago by a missionary named Lettie B. Cowman: "A drying well will often lead to the river that flows from the throne of God." What she meant by that, I think, is when the well of our own strength has finally dried up and we realize we have nothing left in us, it is then that many of us turn to God. It is then we discover a rushing river of God's love and strength that can fill our dried-up inner wells. It is when we come to God and say, "Lord, I'm at my wit's end. I am lost. I can do nothing," that our dry wells begin to fill with the waters of God's love.

Are you feeling overwhelmed by life? Does it feel like your inner well is drying up? Perhaps now is the time to open your heart to that great healing river of God's love. No matter how deep we think the well of our strength is, the day will come when it dries up. If we rely solely on our own strength we will be drawing on a drying well. Why not let your drying well lead to that great river that flows from the throne of God?

July 17
Squeeze Play

There's a story about a local fitness center that was offering $1,000 to anyone who could demonstrate they were stronger than the owner of the place. Here's how it worked. This muscle man would squeeze a lemon until all the juice ran into a glass, then hand the lemon to the next challenger. Anyone who could squeeze out just one more drop of juice would win the money.

Many people tried over time, other weightlifters, construction workers, even professional wrestlers, but nobody could do it. One day, a short, skinny guy came in and signed up for the contest. After the laughter died down, the owner grabbed a lemon and squeezed away. Then he handed the wrinkled remains to the little man.

The crowd's laughter turned to silence as the man clenched his fist around the lemon, and six drops fell into the glass. As the crowd cheered, the manager paid out the winning prize and asked the short guy what he did for a living. "Are you a lumberjack, a weightlifter, or what?"

The man replied, "I work for the IRS."

That story makes almost everyone laugh because the IRS has such a strong reputation of squeezing money out of people. They seem to know just the right kind of pressure to use to get out of people exactly what they want.

There's a lesson here for each of us, and it's simply this: "What does it take to get you to do the things you are supposed to do? Take a moment to think about this. How many times must a family member ask you to do something for them before you actually do it? What does it take to "squeeze" a donation to charity out of you? When someone at work or school or church asks for volunteers, do they have to twist your arm to get you to help out?

Do kindness, generosity, and charity flow freely from your heart or does some pressure have to be applied?

July 18
Do You Know Someone Who Needs a Sandwich?

I recently read about a man who had survived the Nazi concentration camps of World War II. He had entered one of the labor camps when he was fifteen. Conditions in those camps were horrible, and food was so scarce that over time his weight dropped to eighty pounds. He was terribly weak, and was slowly starving to death.

Over the years he was transferred from one camp to another, and each time his situation seemed to get worse. In one labor camp, he was sent to work in a textile factory. German women worked in that textile factory, but they were forbidden to speak to prisoners like him. They were not even allowed to look them in the eye. But it was here that his situation began to change.

One day a German woman pointed, motioning for him to go to another part of the room. He waited until no one was looking, then went to the spot she had picked out. She pointed to a crate and walked away. He lifted the crate and found a sandwich. He couldn't believe his eyes: right there in front of him was a precious sandwich. How he had taken such riches for granted in the past! He quickly ate the sandwich while no one was looking.

Every day for two months the woman left a sandwich under that crate. She risked her life for him; her sandwiches probably saved his life.

Not long after that, the war ended and he was set free. He believes that God used this woman's heroically kind act to save him so that today he can tell others his story, and the story of millions of unfortunate people who were executed by the Nazis.

Very few of us have had such extremely horrible experiences as the man above, but we do have our own very difficult times. It's been my experience in listening to people tell their stories that, for most people, someone comes along at an unexpected time and in an unexpected way to deliver a "sandwich" or two that keeps them going. I believe God will always send someone to feed us whatever we need to survive and even begin to thrive.

If you were to look back over the difficult times of your life, can you recognize the presence of people who were there for you? You may not have known it at the time, but as you look back you may very well discover

God did send you a version of that kind lady with a sandwich. You survived because someone heroically arrived for you.

Why not pause right now to give thanks for such folks? In addition, perhaps this would also be a good time for each of us to consider whether God might be calling us to care for someone else. Is there someone in your life who needs a sandwich?

July 19
The Long Race

While on a walk the other day, I recalled something I had read earlier in the week about an athlete from Tanzania who was competing in the Olympics. This particular athlete was a marathoner, and in the Olympic race he was the unfortunate one to come in last. He limped into the stadium after most of the day's drama had already been played out and most of the spectators were gone.

But as he told it, "My race was still going on, so I had to keep at it to the very final steps." As he finished the race, both knees were bleeding from falls along the way. He looked half-dead. When those who were still seated in the stands saw him, they jumped to their feet and began to cheer him home. He finally made it to the finish line.

The man was asked why he had stayed in the race and endured such pain when he knew he couldn't win. He simply said, "My country didn't send me 7,000 miles away to start the race. They sent me 7,000 miles to finish it. I did."

As I was finishing my walk, I wondered how many "races" I had been in where I wanted to quit before I got to the finish line. I began to think about how easily we all can quit something as soon as it gets to be more of a burden than we thought it would be. Then I recalled how Saint Paul had written about finishing the race and fighting the good fight (2 Timothy 4:7).

It occurred to me that God the Father didn't send his Son just to start the race. The Father sent him to finish the race for us. And even though on Good Friday it looked like Jesus might finish the race, the truth of the matter is that he did. On Easter Sunday, Jesus not only finished the race – he won it! Because of that win, you and I have a tomorrow that will never end.

Are you in a long and difficult race right now? Are you engaged in fighting the good fight? At this very moment, perhaps God is in the half-empty stadium seats, on his feet cheering for you and urging you on to the finish. Remember, you and I do have a tomorrow that will never end!

July 20
Don't Forget to Remember

Here we are in July, and I bet you probably are not thinking about Christmas. Yet for some odd reason my prayer recently has turned to thoughts about that great feast, and I was reminded of a story.

At the dinner table one night a few days before Christmas, a father asked his three children what they were doing at school to celebrate Christmas. The oldest son said, "We're making Christmas cards for our parents, for the other school teachers, and for some old people who don't get out very often."

The boy's younger sister said, "Our class is making paper chains that we can take home and put on our Christmas trees. They're made of red and green paper loops that we glue together. It's really fun to do."

Finally, the youngest spoke up and said, "We're practicing our songs so we can sing in church on Christmas Eve."

"What songs are you singing?" the dad asked his youngest.

"My favorite one is the one we sing as a group, and then there's one part where we each take turns singing the refrain."

"And what is the refrain that you get to sing?" the little one's mother asked.

He replied, "Mom, it's that one that goes like this: 'O come let us ignore him, O come let us ignore him, O come let us ignore him, Christ the Lord!'"

We may smile when we hear a little child make a mistake in singing that famous Christmas Carol, but he may very well be pointing out a truth that we all need to be reminded of. In that great time of the year, there is one person who often gets ignored: Jesus.

Have you ever noticed just how rare it is to hear anything on TV or in any advertisement or in a news program about what the Christmas holidays are really celebrating? If they say anything at all it is usually some vague reference to Christmas being the season of giving. They never seem to mention this is when we celebrate the birth of Jesus Christ, Savior of the World.

Now, I know it's the middle of summer and you may very well be wiping the sweat from your brow. But why not take a few minutes right now to remember who Jesus is and what he means to you? If we forget who is at the heart of Christmas at Christmas time, how much more are we likely to forget who Jesus is in the middle of the lazy days of summer?

Whether it's in the midst of winter or summer, hopefully none of us will be singing, "O come let us ignore him"!

July 21
Mind Your Manners

Consider the last time you and your family gathered at the dinner table for a good meal. As you were enjoying your dinner, was there anyone at the table who seemed to have bad manners?

A few years ago, while I was at dinner at a parishioner's home, one of the children at the table stood on his chair to reach for the gravy. Immediately his mother told him in no uncertain terms that he was being impolite and had forgotten his manners. The boy's father ordered him to sit at once. There was an uneasy, silent pause. Then the child turned to me and said, "Does your mom make you use good manners at the table?" When I told the boy that my mom does, he replied, "Don't you just hate it?" At that point everyone laughed and we went on with our dinner.

The incident made me think about why we have such things as manners, and reminded me of a story about Queen Victoria. According to the story, the Queen was once at a diplomatic reception in London where the guest of honor was an African chieftain. All went well during the meal until finger bowls were served, at the end of the meal.

The guest of honor had never seen a British finger bowl, and no one had thought to brief him beforehand about its purpose. So he took the finger bowl in his two hands, lifted it to his mouth, and drank its contents down to the very last drop! For an instant there was breathless silence among the British upper crust, then they began to whisper to one another. No one knew quite what to do, and the murmuring continued to grow louder.

All that stopped in the next instant as the Queen, Victoria, silently took her finger bowl in her two hands, lifted it, and drank its contents! A moment later 500 surprised British ladies and gentlemen simultaneously drank the contents of their own fingerbowls. A silence followed. Then the queen said to the person sitting beside her, "Manners were meant to remove barriers between people, not impose them."

When I first read that story I thought about how manners and being a good follower of Jesus have something in common. Being a good Christian most often means simply that each day, we try to do some simple kindness to help to remove the barriers that separate folks from one another. Jesus came to help us all become bridge-builders, healers, and peacemakers. Perhaps today would be a good day to be just that by minding our manners!

July 22
Tissue Paper Horses

I once had a conversation with a Jesuit missionary working in Nepal, and I have never forgotten it. We had been talking about praying for others and how important those prayers are. He told me that whenever he begins to pray for others he thinks of paper horses. When he saw the look on my face he said he would explain.

In his years as a missionary in both India and Nepal, he became friends with many Tibetan monks. Those monks had a wonderful custom. When there was stormy weather, they would cut out tissue paper horses. Then taking them up on the roof of their monastery, they would release those horses into the wind. They did this with a prayer that God would turn those paper horses into real horses and send them to anyone who was in great distress, to deliver them from danger and harm.

The missionary went on to tell me that whenever he begins his prayers for others, he often thinks of tissue paper horses. He imagines himself writing the name of each person for whom he is praying on a tissue paper horse. "It's a way of visualizing what I am asking God to do for them," he said.

I love that image. All this past week, I've been seeing tissue paper horses in my mind and imagining the names of those I love being written on each of those horses. Isn't that a great way to pray? This week I would like to invite you to send out a few tissue paper horses of your own.

JULY 23
Granted

It is reported that in the late 1860s, President Ulysses S. Grant gave a cigar to Horace Norton, philanthropist and founder of Norton College. Because of his respect for the President, Norton chose to keep the cigar rather than smoke it. After all, he thought, how many people have been given a cigar by the President of the United States? He kept it on his desk where he could admire it.

Upon Norton's death, the cigar passed to his son, and later it was bequeathed to his grandson. It was Horace Norton's grandson who, in 1932, chose to light the cigar during a speech at Norton College's seventieth anniversary celebration. At a dramatic moment in his speech, Norton showed his audience his grandfather's cigar, lit it, and began to smoke it. He then proceeded to extol the many virtues of Grant until... Boom! The renowned cigar exploded.

Norton's grandfather had never known that, as a practical joke, Grant had given him a loaded cigar. The result was that it eventually made a fool of his friend's grandson!

As I read that story I couldn't help but think of all those famous pictures of Grant in which he looks so serious and so stern. You would not assume from them that he had a sense of humor. I suppose it can serve as a reminder to be careful of the judgments we might make about people. You never can tell just what kind of surprises may come from the folks you think you know so well.

Today might be a good day to give the folks you know and love – as well as some folks you may not know much at all – a second look. Perhaps by looking again you may discover some wonderful things about the folks right around you. Maybe we should all resolve to (forgive me for this one!) not take it "for *Grant*ed" that we really know each other.

July 24
Organic Christianity

In one of the art classes I took back in college, I learned that the famous American architect Frank Lloyd Wright had an idea he called "organic architecture." This idea reflected his belief that buildings should blend into the surrounding natural environment. In other words, you should not be able to tell where the landscape stopped and the building began. Wright believed buildings should form a seamless reality.

Maybe Frank Lloyd Wright was on to something. If we did for our faith what Wright did for architecture, maybe we could start talking of organic Christianity. If you look at the life of Jesus, you see no sharp line of separation between his religious life and his everyday life; they blend and mesh together. Shouldn't it be that way for you and for me?

If we practiced an organic Christianity, our faith would no longer be just a Sunday kind of faith that consisted of going to church once a week or just saying prayers. It would not be a matter of keeping rules, but something that shaped our life in such a way that when we talked with someone or laughed with someone or listened to someone, it would be shaped by Jesus' influence. His life and love would permeate our lives in such a way that we would never have to mention him by name; our actions would preach the Gospel.

Are you living an organic Christianity? Does your faith and life blend together in such a way that you cannot tell where one ends and the other begins?

July 25
Eyes Wide Open

In his letter to the Romans, Saint Paul says a remarkable thing. He says we should all have our eyes wide open to the mercies of God. Isn't that a marvelous phrase? I love what Paul says because it is quite easy for each of us to go through life with our eyes either half-open or closed all together to the wonderful ways of God. Every day, in countless ways, God is active on our behalf. Yet so many of us are completely unaware of this. At least, most of us are unaware until we take some time to look back over our past.

A study was done some years ago in which elderly people were asked what they wished they had done differently in their lives. Almost every person in the study responded the same way: They wished that they had paid more attention to life. Many felt they had missed out on some of life's greatest blessings simply because they didn't even notice the goodness right around them.

One woman commented, "I just wished I had paid attention to things like the beauty of the colors of so many flowers, or the shades of blue you find in the oceans or the sky." Another person said, "I wished I had paid more attention to the things my kids and grandkids would get so excited to show me. They were little people with very big eyes who saw things that I didn't see. I know now I really missed out on a lot of life. I was always so busy and so adult that I missed the simple and most beautiful things only an innocent child can find."

One elderly man noted that one of the things he has begun to see as he looks back over his life are those events in which God has provided the right people doing the right things and saying the right things that get us through rough times. He also notes, things he had prayed for that didn't come through are really a mercy from God, saving him from some unforeseen thing that may have been devastating. "These were all mercies extended by God," the man said.

That leads me back to good old Saint Paul and his words to those Christians in Rome. Just as he advised the people of his day to keep their eyes wide open to the mercies of God, I am sure he would pass on the same advice to us in our time.

This week I've been doing a kind of "mercy inventory." I've been keeping a list of the "mercies" God has given to me over the years, trying to keep my eyes wide open to God's goodness in my life. It has been a good experience, and I recommend it to you. Why not take some time in the next few days and weeks to compile a list of God's mercies that have been poured into your life? I assure you that you will certainly be amazed at the many blessings and mercies God has given you throughout the years.

July 26
There's No Better Time

Sir Isaac Newton had a dog, named Diamond, who was his constant companion. According to Newton, the dog did something that cost the scientist a lot – but also gave him much, as well.

For about eight years, Newton had been writing a very important book. One morning he came into his study to find that Diamond had knocked over a candle, and set fire to the pages of the book that Newton had spent eight years writing. The book was completely destroyed. Eight years of work was ruined and lost, but Newton's friends and family marveled at how he handled the disaster.

Isaac Newton put it this way: "Diamond, little do you know the labor and the trouble you have caused your master. I had thought you robbed me of eight years of my life and work, but now I see you have shown me that I had been preparing for eight years to start over again. You have given me, perhaps forced me, to make a fresh start. For that I thank you. There is no better time than now to get to it."

Today is as good time as any to consider if there are areas in our life that have fallen into such a state, the only thing we can do is let them fall apart and move to make a fresh start. Jesus came to teach us that our God is the God of second chances, the God of new beginnings. Do you need a second chance? Do you need to make a new, fresh start? There is no better time than right now to get to it!

July 27
Taking Time to Check In

During these quiet days of summer, I've been able to do a little reading. One of the things I read was a description of the difficulties encountered during the Apollo space missions to the moon. I remember watching the progress of those missions on television, and thinking things always seemed to be going well.

My reading confirmed that my impressions were very wrong; those missions were far from perfect. It was only the quick thinking, highly intelligent engineers who saved the day on numerous occasions. One fact that is amazing and startling at the same time is that the navigation systems of the spacecrafts were less than stellar. According to NASA, during the Apollo missions, the spacecrafts were off course more than ninety percent of the time!

I wonder how many of the astronauts would have signed on to the Apollo program if they had been told they would be off course more than ninety percent of the time? It was only through constant contact with mission control that the astronauts were able to steer the correct course to the moon and back.

When I read that description of the Apollo missions, it occurred to me we are like those trusting astronauts, putting our lives and their direction into the hands of those at our "mission control." By constantly checking in with God each day we can ensure that, even if we veer off course, the Lord will give us the direction we need so we can find our way safely home. It may have been Saint John Vianney, who lived long before there was anything like the Apollo missions, who said that if he used Jesus' simple teachings as his compass, he would surely find his way to Heaven.

If you are feeling that maybe your life has kind of gone off course, why not take some quiet time right now to simply check in with God?

July 28
What Are You Doing with Them?

I love to read the writings of the famous American author, Mark Twain. Whenever he gave a speech, his audiences always went home laughing and quite satisfied that he had improved their lot in life.

One of my favorite anecdotes about Twain tells of the time he was giving a speech in which he talked about some of the difficult times he had been through, and how he had overcome some failures. He told the crowd that he had made many mistakes in his life and had learned a great deal from them. Twain went on to say, "I've also made a few blunders in my day and am still working at overcoming them."

Someone in the crowd asked, "Mr. Twain, just what is the difference between a mistake and a blunder?"

Mark Twain paused for a few minutes to collect his thoughts, then replied, "If you walk into a restaurant and walk out with someone's silk umbrella, leaving your own cotton one, that's a mistake. But if you pick up someone's cotton umbrella instead of your own silk one, my friend, that's a blunder."

If you look back over some of the difficult times in your life, have you made a lot of mistakes or have you made some real blunders? I'm sure you, like most folks, have had your share of both. Mark Twain taught his audiences that making mistakes is part of being a human being. The important thing is not how many mistakes or even blunders we have made, but rather what we do with them that makes all of the difference.

July 29
Peaceful Waters

In 1520, Ferdinand Magellan did everything he could to find a passage around South America. There, at the very tip of the continent in ice cold waters, he encountered some of the worst weather anywhere on earth. Raging seas, huge ice floes, and a crew that was ready to mutiny at any moment plagued his efforts.

When he finally made his way through those straits (which today are called the Straits of Magellan), he entered into the great body of water that lay beyond. He and his men then realized they had found the way through, and they gave thanks to God. As Magellan looked at the huge seas that lay before him and saw how peaceful the waters looked, he named the new ocean "The Peaceful One." Today we call it the Pacific Ocean."

Does it feel like you may be in your very own "straits of Magellan" right now? Do you feel that you are facing rough waters, huge ice floes, a mutinous crew, and seemingly certain failure or death? Sometimes life can feel like that. Even if it does, Jesus taught us to not be afraid. He promised to be with us in every situation.

If our life is presenting us with stormy seas, Jesus reminds us that even as we pass through them, he will take us to a peaceful, even pacific, place. Peace is the gift Jesus gave to his disciples. He told us he would give us a peace the world cannot give. He didn't say there wouldn't be rough seas in our lives.

What he did say was that he would be with us as we work our way through dire straits, to calmer waters.

As you, like Magellan, try to navigate your way through life, know that you will eventually find your way through it all to peaceful waters.

July 30
How Big Is Your Fear?

There is probably no one on the face of the earth who has not had to deal with fear. I've been thinking about that this past week because while I was sitting on a bench at a local Creamy Whip, eating an ice cream cone, a man sat down next to me. He quietly ate his ice cream cone, then said, "I guess you are wondering why, of all the many places there are to sit here, I chose to sit on this bench with you." I said, "I wasn't really thinking about it, but I bet you're going to tell me, aren't you?" He laughed, and then went on to tell me.

"I'm sitting here," he said, "because that woman over there is feeding her German Shepherd dog a dish of ice cream."

"What's that got to do with you sitting here?" I asked.

"Well, that dog is eating its ice cream right next to the door of my car. I'm terrified of big dogs. That dog might as well be a full-grown vicious wolf as far as I'm concerned. It's big, and I'm sure it doesn't like me!"

Before I could say anything in reply, the man went on. "You sure look a lot less threatening to me than that lady's dog! I'll just sit here with you, if that's OK, and wait for the mongrel to finish his ice cream."

I was amazed at how much the poor guy was paralyzed by the sight of that dog eating a bowl of ice cream. It made me think of how frightened I was as a child when any dog came around me. I was always sure any dog that came near me was going to bite me and give me a fatal case of rabies. I told the man on the bench with me about that. He laughed at me and said, "Fine help you are! Maybe I should have sat with someone who looks more threatening!"

That whole episode made me think of how fears can truly hold us captive. It reminds me of a parable I once read. According to the story, there was a little boy who was running as fast as he could from a witch who had turned herself into a cat. As the boy ran, he kept glancing over his shoulder.

Falling Awake

The first time he looked back, the cat was the size of a calf. The boy screamed in fear but kept running as fast as his little legs would carry him. The next time he looked, it had grown as big as an elephant! Then the boy fell, and was unable to go farther. Scared as he was, he got up and faced the pursuing horror. It stopped, so he took a step toward it. It backed away. As he continued to advance toward it, it began to shrink in size as it retreated from him. Finally, it changed into a mouse and ran under the door of the witch's cottage, and was never seen again.

The moral is clear: If you run from your fears, they will only get bigger and bigger. When you face your fears they can be overcome. Are you dealing with fears right now? Perhaps it's time to stop, turn around, and knock them down to size. Having a little ice cream might help too.

July 31
Widening the Borders

Some years ago, at a conference for writers, reporters were walking among the writers asking them about their art and the craft of using words. One journalist asked Carl Sandburg, "What is the ugliest word in the English language?" After thinking for a few minutes he replied, "Exclusive."

As the reporter listened to Sandburg he realized just how right the poet was. "Exclusive" is a word that conjures up the idea there are those folks who should be excluded, separated, or kicked out. It's a word that says there are some people who will never fit in, never be accepted, and never be welcomed. Of course, the ugliness of exclusive depends on whether we are among the included or the excluded. If we are among the included everything is fine; if, however, we are among the unwelcomed then that is another story.

This week I had a conversation with a guy about where he was going on vacation. He kept saying, "We are going to a very exclusive resort that has all the amenities you could ever want. Most importantly, there will be no 'riff-raff' there. There are only restaurants, golf clubs, and beaches that are quite private and spa facilities that are only for club members. It will all be very exclusive."

If we pride ourselves on being members of elite clubs, living in exclusive neighborhoods, dining at exclusive restaurants, vacationing at exclusive resorts, or even belonging to exclusive churches, we may not notice that we might be buying into a philosophy contrary to the Gospels. Being an insider carries with it a sense of pride and security. Most of us, however, have been excluded often enough to agree that "exclusive" truly is an ugly word. When we, for some reason, find ourselves among the marginalized, the rejected, or the left out, all of a sudden we realize how much it hurts to be an outsider.

Jesus came to the outsiders and the marginalized, to teach us that in God's heart there are no outsiders. No one is excluded. He has invited us all to follow him and always be working to widen the borders of our love.

August

AUGUST 1
The Next Step Closer

A man brought his boss home for dinner. The boss was a very arrogant, blustery, and self-absorbed kind of person who dominated the conversation and gave his opinion on just about everyone and everything.

The youngest child in the family, a little boy, kept staring at his father's boss for most of the evening but didn't say anything at all. He just kept looking at the boss as if he was the most fascinating person he had ever seen. Finally, the boss, thinking he had impressed the young boy, leaned over and spoke to him.

"Hey there," he said. "Do you know your dad works for me?"

The little boy looked at him with wide eyes and said, "Yes, my daddy told me. He said that you are a self-made man."

The bossed loved hearing that, and replied, "Well, that is exactly true."

The boy then said, "Well, if you're a self-made man, why did you make yourself like that?"

I like that story because it gives each of us the opportunity to ask ourselves the question, "What am I making of myself?" Are you aware of the things you are allowing to shape you? Do you ever stop to consider just who you are becoming, with all the various activities, decisions, and opportunities you have chosen to be a part of your life?

Saint Ignatius said it is vitally important for each of us to ask ourselves a very simple question from time to time. He said that every so often, we should look back over the past few months and examine how we have been living our lives. Then you must ask yourself this question: "What am I becoming?"

Ignatius said, asking that question will take you the next step closer to God. Why not ask yourself that question now, and take the next step closer?

August 2
Take a Hike!

A woman was experiencing some depression because she didn't feel appreciated at work, and she dreaded going into work each morning. She felt that the environment was almost toxic to her because most of her co-workers seemed so negative and hypercritical. She decided to take a personal day to get some perspective on what she had been feeling.

The woman decided that the best therapy she could get was to take a walk through a local forest. She began her day in nature by following along one of the many trails that she had often hiked in the past. It wasn't long before she noticed an unfamiliar plant along the trail. Strikingly beautiful, it had large, variegated leaves and was covered with some fairly big red flowers.

Further down the path, in the gravel, was another plant with four small leaves misshapen from being stepped on. Their color was concealed completely by mud. As she looked closer she was surprised to discover it was the same kind of plant whose beauty had caught her attention earlier. She felt sorry that this little plant had sprouted in such a hostile spot.

Then she thought to herself, "Nature does not give seeds a choice about where they are planted. A plant will suffer malnutrition if it grows in rocky soil, or if it is bruised and broken by passersby. A plant in inhospitable surroundings has no power to move to a more favorable spot. Unlike plants, though, people can make choices that affect their growth. People can either leave that hostile environment to find a more enriching one, or in some way change their environment to make it more livable."

When she finished her hike, the woman had come to a decision. She decided that she couldn't just spend her time complaining about her work environment -- she would purposefully try to change it in some small way to try to bring out the best in others. She also decided that, after six months, if there was no change brought about by her efforts, then it would be time to seek out a new environment. She would quit her job and start over somewhere else.

Happy with her decision, she concluded her thoughts by saying, "I always find it consoling how God uses a walk in the woods to lead me to the next steps in my life." Would a walk in the woods right now be of use to you in understanding the next steps God may be asking you to take?

August 3
The One Who Lives

In the last few weeks I have been seeing, in many different places, copies of a print of Danny Haltom's painting, with the title "Reunion." The painting shows Jesus wrapping his arms around a man who has apparently just arrived in Heaven. There is a dove hovering over the two embracing figures, and there are two hands coming out of the clouds. The painting is meant to remind us that the Father, the Son, and the Holy Spirit will be there to welcome us when our journey on earth is at an end. The look on Jesus' face is one of great joy, and it is obvious that the man is receiving a joyful welcome home.

I saw this picture just this past Monday, when a woman who attends my Lunch with the Lord Scripture series came up to show me a holy card from her son's funeral. She said, "The man in this painting, the one being hugged by Jesus, looks just like my son! This little holy card helped me find some peace after my son died. He died very suddenly, and it felt like he was ripped right out of my life and my heart went with him. I could not be consoled. Then a good friend gave me this little holy card. When I saw that painting with the man who looked like my son being embraced, why, I felt a great, warm healing run right through my body and soul! I can go on now because this painting has shown me just what happened to my son after he died. He is with the One who lives, Jesus."

That woman's words, "He is with the One who lives," have stayed with me all week. I keep thinking about what that poor mother went through and how she found comfort. The comfort she found is what Christianity is all about.

The One who lives is among us, and he has gone before us to prepare a place for us. One day each of us will find our life's journey at an end. We, like the man in that painting, can look forward to the day when we shall be welcomed home to the place God has prepared for us. There will be great rejoicing that day, as we are welcomed and embraced by the One who lives.

August 4
A Life Worth Living

Over the years I have read a lot of biographies. I enjoy them because I find it fascinating how people get through the ups and downs of life.

A short time ago, I read a biography about Benjamin Franklin, which told of a practice he followed daily, based on a teaching of Socrates. Through his study of philosophy, Franklin had learned that Socrates had warned his students to not be stupid, and told them, "An unexamined life is not worth living."

Ben Franklin thought that over, and from his days as a young man vowed that he would not be stupid; he would watch carefully over how he was choosing to live. And so he began the practice of asking himself two questions each day. Before the sun rose each morning, he would ask, "What good shall I do today?" He would spend half an hour thinking about that, then plan his day.

Franklin reserved his second question for when he went to bed at night. Before he would fall off to sleep, he would ask himself this: "What good have I done today?" He would spend his last moments before falling into sleep thinking about that. In this way, Franklin attempted to live an examined life so that, in the end, he would have what Socrates had called a "life worth living."

Are you living such a life?

August 5
A Few Ruined Trees

The other day, a friend of mine was telling me about his present difficulties in life. As he talked, I noticed that he kept saying, "I guess my past is finally catching up to me." After he had said those words several times, I finally asked him what he meant.

He said that when he was a kid, his dad used to tell him bad behavior always catches up to you. I asked him how those words affected him. He thought about it for a moment, then said, "Those words have always scared me and haunted me. I keep expecting my past to sneak up on me and do me in. Do you have any ideas as to how I can deal with the things in my past that I'm not so proud of?"

I thought about that for a minute or two. Then I recalled something from a sermon I had read in an old book someone had given me. I remembered that the sermon was from an unknown itinerant country preacher, and it was the best sermon in that book. I related part of it to my worried friend.

In the sermon, the preacher told about a thunderstorm that swept through southern Kentucky, and hit the farm where his family had lived for six generations. The wind knocked over an old pear tree that had been in the orchard for as long as anybody could remember. The reverend's grandfather was quite upset to lose the tree on which he had climbed as a boy, and whose fruit he had eaten all his life.

As they were looking at the downed tree, a neighbor came by and said, "Doc, I'm so sorry to see your pear tree blown down like that."

His grandfather replied, "I'm sorry too. That tree has been a big part of my past. This is a sad day for me to see it in such a state."

The neighbor asked, "So what will you do now with this wrecked old tree?"

"Well," said the grandfather as he let out a long breath of air, "I'm going to pick the fruit and burn the rest of it."

In his sermon, that old preacher concluded by saying, "That's pretty good way to deal with many things in our past. We need to learn their lessons, enjoy their pleasures, then go on with the present and the future."

When I had finished relating this story to my friend, he said, "So, I'm supposed to take what I've learned from the stupid stuff I did in the past, use it for some kind of good, and then just forget about all the rest? Is that it?"

"That about sums it up," I said.

"It sounds too neat, too simple to me," he said.

Fr. Mark Burger

"Look," I replied, "everybody has a few ruined trees in their lives. The important thing is to make sure you take the good fruit and use it for good. In some way or other, burn the bad stuff and let it go."

Carrying around a lot of dead wood doesn't do anybody any good. Use the fruit, and let the rest go.

AUGUST 6
New Worlds

Do you like to travel? I think most people do because it literally opens new worlds to us. I've been thinking about this lately because I came upon a little book about Marco Polo, who was one of history's greatest travelers. Polo wrote a book about his many journeys to and around China. In his day there was no one who traveled as far as he did, and he was able to do so safely because he had been befriended by the great leader, Kublai Khan.

In 1260, Marco Polo's father and his uncle left Venice on what was for them a rather common trip to the Crimea to do some business. When they got there, to their horror, a war had broken out between two Mongol rulers. They were held there for three long years.

A Mongolian diplomat noticed the two stranded merchants and thought that the military leader, Kublai Khan, might want to see them. It turned out that Kublai Khan did want to see the merchants, and insisted they stay at his court for a whole year so he could learn from these men from the West. At the end of that year, he sent them home with a request that the Pope send him 100 European scholars who could teach him the wisdom of the Western world.

In 1271, the two merchants went back to China with the 100 scholars. Also in the company was Marco Polo himself. The Khan took a great liking to Marco Polo, and sent him on journeys all over China so he could learn the wisdom of the Eastern world. The Polo family stayed in China for over seventeen years and then returned to Italy.

When Marco Polo returned home he wrote a book about his travels, and it became one of the most popular books in medieval Europe. As he reflected back on all the places he had visited and all the things he had seen, Marco Polo wrote these words: "I believe it was God's will that I should come back, so men might know the things that are in the world, since no other man, Christian or Saracen, Mongol or pagan, has explored so much of the world as did Marco Polo, son of Nicolo Polo, great and noble citizen of the city of Venice."

Through his accounts of his travels, Marco Polo opened the world to many people.

Have you ever considered what worlds have been opened to you by your travels? How has your traveling shaped who you are? Has your worldview been broadened by other travelers who have shared their experiences with you?

Just as physically traveling around the earth can open new worlds to us, so too can various life experiences reveal new worlds to us. Think for a moment about the experiences that have changed you. For some people, going off to college is a life changing experience that opens up new worlds. For other folks, it was the experience of falling in love, or becoming a parent, or even surviving the loss of a loved one that brought the dawn of a new world.

Take some time right now to consider your own personal journey through life so far. What new worlds have you been able to enter over the years that have shaped who you are today? Is there a new journey coming soon that seems to be opening before you?

August 7
That Kind of Attention

A few years ago, the Harry S. Truman Presidential Library made public 1,300 recently discovered letters that the late President had written to his wife, Bess, over the course of their lives. Harry Truman had a habit of writing to his wife every day they were apart. He said he simply missed talking with her, so he wrote her a letter as a kind of substitute. He followed this rule whenever he was away on official business, or whenever Bess left Washington to visit her beloved home of Independence, Missouri.

Scholars are examining the letters for any new light they may throw on political and diplomatic history. I don't know if they've discovered any kind of new light, but I do know I'm impressed with one thing. Every day he was away, the President of the United States took time out from dealing with the world's most complicated problems, and conversations with the world's most powerful leaders, to sit down and write a letter to his wife.

When Harry Truman was asked why he did that, his reply was, "When you love someone as much as I love her, you pay attention to him or her. She's always been first in my heart. That's all there is to it."

Is there anyone in your life you love as much as Harry Truman loved his wife, Bess? Is there anyone in your life who deserves that kind of attention from you?

August 8
Too Heavy

I was attending a conference on prayer and healing when an extraordinary thing happened. Just as a scheduled speaker was about to begin his lecture, a man in the audience stood up and said he was just overwhelmed by life. He could not see how he could go on living. "I'm so tired; I'm spent and worn out. I cannot go on!" he said as he sobbed. Several people rushed up to the man, put their arms around him, and led him out of the room as they spoke consoling words to him. He continued to cry uncontrollably.

As the audience sat in a stunned silence, the man who was scheduled to speak took his lecture papers and put them in his briefcase. He cleared his throat, straightened up, approached the microphone, and began telling us the following story.

Once there was an eagle that hovered over a lake. One day it suddenly swooped down and caught a two-foot-long fish in its talons. Slowly, the bird rose with its ten-pound catch, but when it reached about 1,000 feet, it began to descend until it splashed into the water. Later, both the bird and fish were found dead. Apparently, the fish was too heavy for the eagle, but its talons were embedded in the flesh of the fish. The great eagle could not let go of its heavy burden. The truth is, often what we cannot let go of will end up doing grave harm to us.

When the speaker had finished the story, he simply asked all of us to consider whether we too were heavily burdened, like the eagle and the man who had been escorted out of the room. He said that perhaps this incident was God's invitation for each of us to lay down our burdens and let them go.

Is there something in your life you are holding on to that is dragging you down? Are you carrying something that's much too heavy for you to handle? Is there something God is asking you to let go of so you can fly free? Perhaps today is the day to let go of those burdens.

AUGUST 9
Remembering Teddy's Words

Teddy Roosevelt would often tell people that the greatness and beauty of nature, and the vastness of the universe, overwhelmed him. When he was at home at Sagamore Hill, he would invite friends to stay with him for a weekend or even an entire week. In the evenings he would have dinner with his guests and tell them stories of his adventures in the wilderness, and of the many things he had seen on safari.

After an evening of talk, he would take his guests out on the lawn and search the skies for a certain spot of star-like light near the lower left-hand corner of the Great Square of Pegasus. Then Roosevelt would recite: "That is the Spiral Galaxy in Andromeda. It is as large as our Milky Way. It is one of a hundred million galaxies, and consists of one hundred billion suns, each larger than our sun."

Then Teddy Roosevelt would grin and say, "Now, I think we're small enough! And I think the God who made all of that is certainly big enough to take care of us. We can certainly trust God enough to rest for a spell without worry. Let's go to bed."

If your life gets to be too much for you to handle, perhaps you, like Teddy Roosevelt, might want to go out tonight on your front lawn and look up. Look at the stars and remember Teddy's words.

AUGUST 10
Unexpected Irritations

I read about a man who decided to walk from New York City to San Francisco to promote a cause that was very important to him. He asked people to support his cause by pledging a certain amount of money for each leg of the trip he completed. Can you imagine all the difficulties involved in completing such a long walk? I find it hard to even think about all of the things that could go wrong in that long distance between New York City and San Francisco. It seems like such an impossible thing to do.

After almost an entire year of walking, the man finished his trip. He was obviously exhausted by the whole thing, but not defeated. In fact, he was elated that he had been able to do what he had set out to do. He almost had given up many times, but he held out to the very end and finished his long walk.

The news media was all over the man's story. There were numerous requests for interviews, and he agreed to be interviewed by as many folks as had asked him. There was one question that almost every reporter asked in the course of their conversations with him: "What was the most difficult part of your journey? Was it the weather conditions? Was it the terrain, or was it just pure physical exhaustion?"

He said, the toughest part of the trip wasn't traversing the steep slopes of the mountains or crossing hot, dry, barren stretches of desert. Instead, "The thing that almost did me in and came closest to defeating me was something really simple, yet it was a terrible thing to endure. It was the sand in my shoes. It was the one thing I had not counted on, something I had not even given a thought to. Yet it was what almost ended the whole damned thing. I learned that the most important thing to pay attention to is the unexpected little irritations that can wreck your life."

If you were to take a few minutes to trace the source of the unhappiness that sometimes fills your days, what do you think that source would be? Are there unexpected little irritations wrecking your life today?

August 11
Cut Flowers

A woman regularly welcomed her three grandchildren to her home for the weekend. She loved to have them, and they really enjoyed being with her. One of the activities she looked forward to doing with them was to have them help in the garden. Over the years she taught them how to weed, how to plant little seedlings, how to properly water the plants, and how to recognize the various kinds of flowers.

On this particular weekend a remarkable thing happened with her little ones. When they arrived, she hugged them and asked them to go out to the garden and look at the flowers they had planted the last time they had visited. As the children arrived in the garden, they noticed that the plants were now in full flower. "Let's make a little bouquet for grandma!" one of the grandchildren suggested. Immediately each of them went and picked three or four of grandma's newly blooming flowers. They were so excited they ran as fast as they could back into the house to surprise grandma with the flowers.

The look on grandma's face was all the children needed to see to know they had made a terrible mistake. Grandma was not happy in the least. The little ones stopped in their tracks and said, "Its okay, grandma, we'll just go put 'em back where we got them!" This was probably the first time, though I'm sure not the last, these little children realized some things cannot be put back the way they were found.

Way back in the third century some holy men and women, known as the Desert Fathers and Mothers, taught this very same thing to their disciples. They said, "There are three things that can never be taken back: a spent, wounding arrow; a cruel, mean-spirited word spoken to a loved one; and an opportunity missed." They advised their students to be sure to avoid the terrible pain that can come from not paying close attention to the decisions life may bring. They warned those with whom they worked there is nothing quite as devastating as the realization that one has brought about an irrevocable though maybe entirely unintended consequence that causes others pain or sorrow. They would conclude their teaching with a simple warning: "pay attention!"

August 12
No Time Like Now

I want to tell you a story about Buddhist monk who was visiting New York. His Western host was taking him to visit Central Park, and said they could save ten minutes by making a complex transfer in the subway at Grand Central Station.

When they emerged from the subway in Central Park, the monk quietly sat down on a bench, closed his eyes, and began to breathe deeply. His host was a bit annoyed and wanted to know what the heck he was doing.

The monk opened his eyes and replied, "I thought we should enjoy the ten minutes!"

How long has it been since you've stopped for ten minutes simply to take a break, to observe your surroundings and take in the wonder of the world around you or enjoy the time you have? Ten minutes may not seem like a very long time, but I've discovered over the years it can be just enough time to ponder the simple gifts that enrich our lives. I like to think of them as mini-vacations from the hectic pace of life.

Do you need a mini-vacation? There's no time like now.

August 13
Need a Monk?

What would it take right now for you to be happy? What would it take for you to know true peace of heart and mind? As I've been thinking about this recently I remembered something from the time when I lived as a hermit in the desert of Israel. I was looking out into the barren desert one day when an image came to mind, that of a monk walking along, talking to someone. Then it came to me.

There's an ancient story about a well-known holy monk who found a precious stone. This truly was a very valuable jewel. When the holy man looked at the stone and saw it reflected the light in such a wonderful way, he couldn't help but marvel that such a beautiful thing had fallen into his life.

A short time later, the monk met a traveler who said he was hungry. He asked the holy man if he would share some of his food with him. At once the monk said yes and added, "Let's look in my bag here to see what God has provided for me and you." When the monk opened his bag, the traveler saw the precious stone and, on an impulse, asked if he could have it. Without hesitation the monk gave the traveler the stone.

The traveler departed quickly, overjoyed with his new possession. In just a few days, however, he came back, looking everywhere for the monk. He returned the stone to the holy man and made a request: "Please give me something more valuable, more precious than this stone."

"What is it you want from me that is more valuable than this beautiful stone?" the holy man asked.

"Please give me that peace of heart which enabled you to give me this precious stone!" the traveler replied.

Are you in need of a monk in your life? What would make it possible for you to have peace of heart and mind right now? Is there a monk or holy person in your life who could reveal the secret to you?

August 14
A Walk Through the Day

Perhaps one of the holiest and most universally loved people in the history of the church was a young man named Francis. One day that man, whom we now refer to as Saint Francis of Assisi, invited an aspiring monk to join him on a trip into town to preach. The young monk in training was so honored to get such an invitation from the well-known Francis that he quickly accepted. All day long he and Francis walked through the streets and byways, alleys and suburbs, and they rubbed shoulders with hundreds of people.

At the end of the day, the two headed back home. However, the young monk realized that not even once had Francis addressed a crowd, nor had he talked to anyone about the gospel. He was greatly disappointed, and said to Francis, "I thought we were going into town to preach? We did everything but preach."

Saint Francis responded, "My son, we have preached all day long. We were preaching while we were walking. Many saw us, and our behavior was closely watched. It is of no use to walk anywhere to preach unless we preach everywhere as we walk! The gospel was indeed preached today."

If people were to simply observe you as you walk through your day today, would the gospel be preached to them?

AUGUST 15
It Will Come

"When did you get your calling?" That question was put to me during a retreat I was leading for a group of farmers and their sons. My response to the young man who asked the question was to ask him a question. "When did you know that you wanted to be a farmer?" He thought for a moment and then said, "It's been building up in me since I was a little boy. Then one day, not too long ago, I was out in the field. All at once I had this inner voice say, 'This is where you belong; you were born for this!'"

I used that young man's question and his answer to launch into a teaching about the call we all receive from God. One never knows how or when the call will come, but it comes. My sister told me that when she was a very small child and she looked at babies, she knew even then that all she wanted to be was a mom. She received her calling at quite a young age. She still loves being a mom and a grandma.

You never know when or where God's invitation will come. If you flip through the pages of the Bible you will see people "getting called" at different times and places. Abraham, for example, was sitting at home. Moses was out in the wilderness when he saw a burning bush. Isaiah, on the other hand, was praying during a worship service. Mary of Nazareth was simply at home, alone when the call came. Peter, James, and John were finishing up a day's work. Matthew too was at work, although he was probably cheating people.

The woman caught in adultery was, well, caught in adultery and about to be stoned to death. Then, of course, there was Saint Paul, who was on his way to kill Christians when his call came. The bottom line is that it doesn't matter where you are or in what situation; God will find you. He will let you know what his plan is for you.

Has your call come yet? If so, when and how did it come? If it hasn't come yet, the Bible shows us over and over again, it will come.

August 16
New Oceans

    A young man had signed up to be part of a college program based in Europe, and he was getting ready to leave. He had never been overseas; for that matter, he had been pretty much of a homebody all his life. Realizing how scared the young man was, his grandfather invited him to lunch.

    When they were comfortably seated at a table in a quiet corner of the restaurant, the grandfather spoke. "I know you're probably scared to death right now. You're taking a big step in your life and I'm very proud of you. You're showing real courage in choosing to go so far away from all that is familiar to you. You're starting an exciting journey, but let me be the first to warn you, this will be the hardest thing you have ever done. I think this will either make you or break you."

    The young man sat in silence for a minute and then said, "What do you mean by 'make or break you'?"

    "When I was your age," grandpa said, "I didn't go off to college, I went to the Navy. The moment I arrived at boot camp I knew I had done something that was either going to destroy me or make me into something. At first I was upset and wanted more than anything to go home. Of course, I didn't want to look weak so I stayed put. It was hard, really hard, but I stuck it out."

    "How did you do it, grandpa?" the young man asked.

    "Well, I guess it was a week or two later when I got a letter from my grandpa. He had been in the Navy too and he wanted to encourage me. He sent me two little postcards with some important words on them." Grandpa reached into his pocket and brought out two little postcards and handed them to his grandson.

    His grandson looked at them. The first one had these words on it:" You cannot discover new oceans unless you have the courage to truly leave home and lose sight of the shore." The second card read: "A calm sea does not produce a skilled sailor."

    Before the young man could say anything, his grandfather said, "Those two sayings got me through boot camp and all my years in the Navy. I ended up loving the Navy and never regretted my decision to join up. It made me the man I am today. Now, as you go to Europe, you take these two cards. They will get you through the rough times ahead. You will not regret taking this big adventure. If you are going to grow, you have to let go and move forward."

Are you at a point in your life where you have to step out in courage to discover new oceans?

August 17
The Deepest Loneliness

The Bible warns us that the love of money is the root of all evil, and that it can easily change the way a person sees the world around him or her. It can literally lead to a kind of blindness. Here is a little story that is often used by rabbis as they teach young folks how to negotiate the challenges of daily life.

One day a certain rich man who was very lonely visited his rabbi. The rabbi took the rich man by the hand and led him to a window. "Look out there," he said. The rich man looked into the street. "What do you see?" asked the rabbi.

"I see men, women, and children," answered the rich man.

Again the rabbi took him by the hand, and this time led him to a mirror. "Now what do you see?" he asked.

"Now I see myself," the rich man replied.

Then the rabbi said, "Behold, in the window there is a glass, and in the mirror there is a glass. But the glass of the mirror is covered with a little silver, and no sooner is the silver added than you cease to see others, and you see only yourself."

For the rabbi, one of the most dangerous things one can do is to be too worried about adding a little silver to one's life. He was truly a wise man who knew well how the often-subtle allure of wealth could lead to greed.

Greed can lead to a blindness that isolates us from the needs of our brothers and sisters. It is that kind of blindness that leads to this world's deepest sort of loneliness.

AUGUST 18
A New World Coming

A friend of mine who was going through a terrible divorce told me over lunch the other day that she felt like Noah. I asked her what she meant by this. This is what she told me.

According to the Book of Genesis, after the flood destroyed the world, poor Noah was left alone with his family and all those animals. There were endless days on the Ark, days and days of waiting and hoping for the water to clear. In every direction Noah could see only water.

She went on to tell me that getting through her divorce made her feel totally isolated, and that time just dragged on. She said she looked in all directions but only felt lost and like a failure. Her world had fallen apart. She could see no future. Then she continued her story about Noah, from the Book of Genesis.

One day, in faith, Noah decided to release a dove to search for land. The Bible says the dove "found no place to set her foot" and returned. Noah's ark was still floating. He had to wait a while longer. He waited with faith and in hope. He sent out a dove a second time, and it returned with a sprig of fresh olive leaves in its beak. Noah could not see the land yet, but he knew it was there. It was time for him to get ready and start the world all over again. Soon land began to appear out of the waters, and worst was over.

My friend concluded by saying she realized that new world was possible for her and that new world was coming. She was getting a chance to start over.

Have you ever been like Noah, floating over a world that has fallen apart, just waiting for some dry land to appear so that you can start over? One thing Jesus taught is that there is always a chance for a new beginning when we put our lives in God's hands. Like Noah, we may have to wait a while for things to settle down, but a new world is coming.

Fr. Mark Burger

AUGUST 19
A Deep Pool

There is a saying by a famous Quaker named George Fox that I have always liked. I write a shortened version of it on the top of each page of my calendar as a little reminder for my spiritual growth. There are only six words in this abbreviated quotation, but those six words really did change my life, maybe even my temperament.

By keeping these few words close to my heart and in my mind, my experience of God's presence and his love for me became concretely real. Here are the six words: "Carry some quiet around inside you." These six words helped me face the big and little storms and difficulties that life can sometimes foist on us.

Each morning when I wake up I try to find a quiet place to sit for a moment or two. I have found over the years that quietness is like a deep pool of water. I can skim the surface or plunge into its depths -- it's up to me.

Whether I plumb the depths of quietness or merely float on the surface, each morning I take some of that quietness and purposefully carry it with me in my heart so that when some storm or difficulty springs up during the day or night, I will find calm waters within as a place of refuge and true peace.

AUGUST 20
Throwing Stones

One of the most powerful stories in the Gospels is the story of that woman who had been caught in the act of adultery. I always marvel at how Jesus handled that large crowd of "righteous" people. They stood around the woman, stones in their hands, ready to stone her to death.

When they kept questioning him about what they should do, Jesus straightened up and said to them, "Let anyone among you who is without sin be the first to throw a stone at her" (John 8:7). This certainly changed the tone of the whole situation. One by one each righteous person dropped their stones and walked away.

There's an old story I remember from my days in seminary, when I was learning about preaching. According to the story, a Baptist pastor fresh out of seminary was assigned to a small church in the hills of Kentucky. The young man was excited about preaching the gospel, so in his very first sermon, he ranted and raved and then finally condemned gambling, especially betting on the horses.

To his chagrin the sermon was not well received. "You see, Reverend," a parishioner explained, "this whole area is known for its fine horses. Lots of our members make their living breeding racehorses. I wouldn't put such a high priority on preaching about that sort of thing."

The next Sunday the young preacher spoke on the evils of smoking, and once again to his amazement, his sermon was not well received. It turned out that many of his parishioners also grew tobacco. The third week the young pastor thought it would be good to preach on the evils of drinking, only to be told afterwards that a major distillery was one of the town's largest employers.

After that third poorly received sermon, the frustrated pastor exclaimed, "Well, then, what can I preach about?" A kindly, older woman spoke up and said, "Pastor, preach against those godless Chinese communists. Why, there isn't a Chinese communist within 4,000 miles of here!"

Ever notice how most folks love to hear sermons that condemn people for doing bad things, as long as those "bad things" aren't their bad things?

August 21
What is God Doing?

During the Second World War, six Navy pilots left their aircraft carrier on a mission to find some Nazi U-boats that had been sinking American ships. After searching the seas for enemy submarines, they began to return to their ship shortly after dark. But they could not locate the aircraft carrier because the captain had ordered a blackout of all lights on the ship.

Over and over the frantic pilots radioed, asking for just one light so they could see to land. But the pilots were told that the blackout could not be lifted. After several appeals and denials of their request, the ship's operator simply turned off the switch to break radio contact, and the pilots were forced to ditch their planes in the ocean.

Can you imagine how those young pilots felt as they frantically searched for their aircraft carrier? They were running low on fuel, completely in the dark, and seemingly without hope. They had been ordered on a mission, yet when they returned from the mission, the same person who sent them out there didn't seem to care enough to give them some light to find their way home. Those six Navy pilots must have felt a boatload of anger, resentment, and fear.

As I thought about those six pilots, I remembered so many people whom I have counseled as they dealt with divorce, or a sick child, or cancer, or so many other tragedies or crises. They often expressed feelings not unlike those the Navy pilots must have felt. You go through life living the way you think God wants you to live, and then the bottom falls out and you are facing something terrible. You feel lost in the dark, begging God to simply turn on a single light to help you find your way. Why would God seem to abandon us when we need him the most? Well, maybe the story of those six fliers can shed some light here.

The truth of the matter is that the very captain they thought had abandoned them eventually rescued all six of those pilots. Although the pilots had to ditch their aircraft, all of them were able to swim away from their planes. As the light of dawn approached, the captain was able to locate each of them.

The captain would not light up the aircraft carrier because he knew enemy aircraft were nearby and could have easily sunk the ship had the lights been turned on. From the very beginning, the captain intended to rescue his pilots, but he could not rescue them if he allowed the enemy to sink his carrier. The captain had to work to save not only those six pilots but every other person on his ship, as well. He truly never abandoned anyone.

When life puts us in the dark and we feel that God is not sending us the light we need to find our way, it may be he is up to something much bigger than what we can see at present. It may well take the coming of the dawn before we discover just what God has been up to all along.

August 22
Before the Alarm

Have you ever noticed that you often wake up in the morning just before your alarm goes off? It's a very common experience. There are various theories about why this happens, but generally it's thought to be the work of the subconscious.

The theory is, waking up is a stress-inducing event that, when coupled with a loud, startling noise is even more stress inducing. So the subconscious, in an effort to spare us the stress of being startled awake, wakes us up before the alarm goes off. This is meant to provide a calmer, more peaceful wake-up call.

Those more peaceful wake-up calls are wonderful, but not all of life's wake-up calls turn out to be as pleasant. Sometimes a series of poor judgment on our part can lead us into an utter and complete disaster that creates pain, heartache, and suffering for us and those around us. These kinds of experiences are, in a very real sense, truly startling wake-up calls. They remind us to pay close attention to our choices because they will have consequences.

I wonder: is there a kind of subconscious alarm for our daily life that can wake us up before our life goes off track? Probably the best thing to help us stay on track is a daily period of quiet reflection during which we do an inventory of our thoughts and actions. This can gently wake us up to the choices we are making, and thereby help us avoid those disastrous startling alarms.

August 23
Clay in the Potter's Hands

A few years ago I went on a retreat with a group of pastors from various churches and denominations. Some folks who practiced Zen Buddhism, as well as two young Hindus, joined us. A nun who wanted to bring people of faith together to "listen to God" organized the group. There were folks there who were ready to teach us a variety of forms of meditation, yoga, and other spiritual practices.

Fr. Mark Burger

One of my favorite experiences of the retreat was what the nun who led us called "a group dialogue with God." The group sat in a circle around a jar filled with folded pieces of paper, and we began the session with what the Buddhists called a "sitting meditation." We sat in silence, emptying our minds and opening ourselves to God in the quiet stillness that descended on us. We sat for a full half-hour, not moving or speaking but simply breathing quietly. It was very peaceful.

When the quiet was almost palpable, the nun reached into the jar, retrieved a folded piece of paper, opened it, and said: "Hear these words taken from the Hebrew Scriptures, from the Book of the Prophet Jeremiah: 'So I went down to the potter's house, and there he was working at his wheel. The vessel he was making of clay was spoiled in the potter's hand, and he reworked it into another vessel, as seemed good to him'" (Jer.18:3-4).

Each of us in that circle of peace drank in those words. There was more silence. Finally, someone said, "Here we are in the potter's hands; will each of us allow ourselves to be reworked into whatever the potter wants, as it seems good to the potter to do?" As we took that question within ourselves, we could feel God's presence among us. Each of us set about answering that simple question.

Sit in quiet today, and imagine yourself as clay in God's hands. What would you like God the potter to do with the clay of your life? Can you trust God enough to allow him to rework you, as it seems good to him to do?

AUGUST 24
Do You Need a Grandma?

In a high school introduction to business class, the teacher wanted to impress on his students how some of the world's well-known businessmen became successful. He began by telling them about Charles Schwab.

Schwab was one of the few men before World War II who was paid a salary of one million dollars per year. Schwab, who was a steel executive, was once asked what made him worth so much. He replied, "It's not that I know more about steel than anybody else. The greatest asset I possess is my ability to arouse enthusiasm among people. I have learned that people respond best to appreciation and encouragement. People may respond to threats or bribery, but neither their respect nor affection is won. However, if people are affirmed and thanked and encouraged, their hearts will cause them to respond enthusiastically, willingly, and creatively."

As the students were listening to their teacher, one student raised her hand and said, "If what Charles Schwab said is true, I think my grandma would have been a great steel executive."

"Why do you say that?" the teacher asked.

"I don't know any human being who is more kind and more encouraging than my grandma. She can spot a talent, or at least find what you do best, better than anyone. She always finds something good to say about you, and she never puts you down. The best thing about my grandma is that she loves me even when I screw up!"

The teacher looked at his student and asked, "Do you think your grandma is worth a million dollars a year?"

Is there someone in your life who needs you to be his or her grandma? Is there someone who needs you to help them find their talents, or at least what they do best? Do *you* need a grandma right now?

August 25
Undone

Did you know that the month of July, the seventh month, was named after Julius Caesar? Historians of that era tell the story that, after Julius Caesar's assassination, the Emperor Augustus, not to be outdone, insisted the eighth month should be called August after himself. Since that month had only thirty days at the time, he ordered that a day be borrowed from February and added to August, just to make sure his month would not be inferior to Julius Caesar's month. He was a very jealous emperor, and would have no one appear to be greater than he was.

Theologians teach that there is an important distinction between jealousy and envy. To envy is to want something that belongs to another person. Simply put, they have it and you do not, and that fact preoccupies you until you find a way to get it. Envy can be consuming.

Jealousy, on the other hand, is the fear that something we possess will be taken away by another person. Although jealousy can apply to our jobs, our possessions, or our reputations, the word more often indicates an anxiety that comes when we are afraid the affections of loved ones might be lost to a rival.

Scholars say that when we are jealous, we fear our mates, or perhaps our children, will be lured away by some other person who, when compared to us, seems to be more attractive, capable, or even successful. Augustus was certainly a jealous person. He was, without a doubt, one of the most powerful people in the world at that time, yet he was undone not so much by any worldly power but by his own insecurity.

Even though you may not be as powerful and important as any one of those ancient Caesars, do you have a spirit of envy or jealousy that could get into your heart, consume your thoughts, and be your undoing?

August 26
A God Diet

There are very few people who have not, at one time or another, gone on some kind of diet. I think there are about as many diet plans as there are people, each one claiming to be the best diet ever. Recently someone sent me the newest technique for losing weight. It came in a fancy envelope with instructions on how to open it. When you open the letter, here's what it says: "Did you know that moving your head from side to side can make you lose weight? The best time to do it is when someone offers you food."

I love that! I've been laughing all day thinking about it. What I love about that little gag is it points to an important truth not only about diets, but also about life itself. In the end, with diets as with life itself, it all comes down to the same bottom line; we have to say no to the things that are not good for us, and yes to the things that are. It couldn't be any clearer.

If you compare your spiritual life to going on a diet, a kind of "God Diet," are you saying no to those things that are not good for you and could lead you away from God? Just as important, are you saying yes to those things that are good for you and could lead you to God?

August 27
Are You Able?

Do you have the courage to admit when you have made a mistake or simply been wrong in choosing to do something? I've been thinking about this for a week or so ever since I observed a married couple arguing at a local restaurant. Their argument ended in silence when the wife, finally exasperated, said, "George, you just don't have it in you to admit when you are wrong!"

That comment made me think of something I learned about Abraham Lincoln. The story is told that when he was president, Lincoln once got caught in a situation where he wanted to please a politician, so he issued a command to transfer certain regiments from one location to another. He didn't think it made that much of a difference, and the transfer would certainly make him a political friend. He thought it was a win-win situation.

Well, when the secretary of war, Edwin Stanton, received the order, he absolutely refused to carry it out. He was so upset that he actually said the President was a fool!

It wasn't too long before Lincoln was told what Stanton had said. Lincoln thought for a moment and he replied, "If Stanton said I'm a fool, and then I must be, for he is nearly always right. I'll see for myself and talk it over with him." As the two men talked, the President quickly realized that his decision was a serious mistake, and without hesitation he withdrew it.

Do you think you have the same kind of courage and the humility to do what President Lincoln did? Are you able to admit it when you have made a poor judgment or made a terrible mistake?

August 28
Newton's Vision

Isaac Newton once did an experiment in which he stared at an image of the sun reflected in a mirror. The brightness burned into his retina, and he suffered temporary blindness. Even after he had shut himself up in a dark room for three days, still the bright spot would not fade from his vision. "I used all means to divert my imagination from the sun," he writes, "but that bright spot was still in my eye though I was in the dark."

Newton was afraid he would never know happiness again if the sun had stolen his ability to see the beauty of the world around him. If he had fixed his eyes on that bright reflection a few minutes longer, Newton might have permanently lost all vision. His experiment showed that the chemical receptors that govern eyesight couldn't withstand the full force of unfiltered sunlight.

I'm sure Isaac Newton was terrified that the bright spot in his eye, which was keeping him from seeing anything else, would never leave. He worried he had caused himself permanent injury, and the prospect of losing his vision almost paralyzed him.

Can you imagine losing your sight? It would certainly be a devastating experience that would completely change your life. Our eyes, our sight is truly a precious gift that we could easily take for granted. When it is threatened in any way that fact is brought home to us. If you lost your sight, could you know happiness again?

We have another way of "seeing" that is not connected directly to our physical ability to see, but has to do with our ability to choose how we see, how we look at life. We can, for example, choose to look at our world and see all the beautiful things that make up the world of nature. Just looking out over a field of flowers, noticing the clouds in the sky, the way the sunlight filters through those clouds and the way a gentle breeze makes the tall grass look like flowing water, can frame the how you see all of life. You can conclude the world is beautiful place filled with natural wonders that can take your breath away.

On the other hand, someone who works among highly critical colleagues who are always looking to find fault or catch someone in a mistake, who seldom compliment anyone and are more likely to pick a fight with someone than become a friend to them, that person may see the world in an entirely different light. They may find their world to be a hostile, scary place. The frustration of living and working among highly critical people may blind them to the beauty of nature that is right outside their window. Like Isaac Newton alone in the dark after he had injured his eye, they may fear they will never see happiness again.

One of the most important experiments we might do is take some time to consider just how we choose to look at life. As Isaac Newton realized, the way he chose to look at the sun could have blinded him to all the world has to offer. So too we must realize that the way we choose to look at life will certainly affect what we see.

AUGUST 29
Heading Back Home

During the summer months many families make a point to get away from it all and head out on vacation. Spending a few days or a couple of weeks away can be so much fun and is often so relaxing that many folks find it difficult to return home. Even with the best vacations, however, there's a point when being away from home gets a bit tedious. Even though we might say we don't want to go home, inside of us there may be a secret desire to get back to normal and the comfort of sleeping in one's own bed. Whereas getting away for a while may be very enjoyable, there is something to be said for coming home again as well.

Earlier this summer I took a few days off to relax. Those few days away gave me more time to read, and in the course of my reading, I came across a story from China about the importance of home.

As the story goes, at the base of a mountain in China lived a father and his three sons. They were a simple and loving family. The father noticed that travelers came from afar eager to climb the dangerous mountain. But not one of them ever returned! His three sons noticed this as well, but they also heard stories that the mountain was made of gold and silver. Despite their father's warnings to stay away from the mountain, they could not resist venturing up it.

One day they left home and made their way up the mountain. Along the way, under a tree, sat a beggar, but the sons did not speak to him or give him anything. They ignored him. One by one, the sons disappeared up the mountain, the first to a house of rich food, the second to a house of fine wine, the third to a house of gambling. Each became enslaved to his desire, and in a short time forgot his home. Meanwhile, their father was heartbroken. He missed them terribly. "As dangerous as it is," he said, "I must find my sons."

Once he scaled the mountain, the father found that indeed the rocks were gold and the streams silver. But he hardly noticed. He only wanted to reach his sons and help them remember the life of love they once knew. On the way down, having failed to find them, the father noticed the beggar under the tree and asked for his advice.

"The mountain will give your sons back," said the beggar, "only if you bring something from home to cause them to remember the love of their family."

The father raced home, brought back a bowl full of rice that he cooked himself, and gave the beggar some as thanks for his wisdom. He then found his sons, one at a time, and carefully placed a grain of home-cooked rice on the tongue of each of them. At that moment, the sons recognized their foolhardiness. Their real life was now apparent to them. They returned home with their father and rejoined the rest of the family, and as one, loving family lived happily ever after.

The Chinese sages taught that even though we all have a taste for fun and adventure, at some point in our wanderings another taste would develop within us. They remind all who will listen that we will never be truly happy if we do not pay attention to the desire for home and family.

AUGUST 30
The Way of Love

A group of people commonly known as Bedouins lives in the deserts of the Middle East. I learned about these people when I lived as a hermit in Israel. The word "Bedouin" is the Aramaic name for "desert dwellers." The Bedouins still live pretty much like the people described in the pages of the Old Testament. Their culture imposes strict laws on just about every facet of life.

A rather famous story that comes out of Bedouin folklore is meant to be a parable for living. I like the story because it reminds me of the way Jesus taught us to be.

During a heated argument, according to this story, a young Bedouin struck and killed a friend of his. Knowing the ancient, inflexible customs of his people, which call for "an eye for an eye," the young man quickly left, running across the desert under the cover of darkness, looking for protection.

The young man knew he had to find his way to the black tent of the tribal chief in order to seek his help and protection. The old chief took the young man in, and assured him that he would be safe until the law could settle the whole affair.

The next day, the young man's pursuers arrived, demanding the murderer be turned over to them. They would see that justice would prevail in their own way. "But I have given my word," protested the chief, "and I cannot turn him over to you."

"But you don't know whom he killed!" they countered.

"I have given my word," the chief repeated.

"He killed your son!" one of them blurted out.

The chief was deeply and visibly shaken with his news. He stood there, not saying a word.

The accused and the accusers, as well as curious onlookers, waited to see what the tribal chief would do. Would he let them do what they wanted with the young man? Finally the old man raised his head. "Then he shall become my son," he informed them, "and everything I have will one day be his."

Doesn't that story sound like something Jesus would use to teach us the way of love? Thankfully most of us do not have to deal with the kind of heartbreak endured by the tribal chief. Most of us, however, are faced with heartbreaks of one kind or other. Whether they are big or little, Jesus would ask that we deal with them according to that way of love. Perhaps this would be a good time to ask ourselves how well we are following the way.

August 31
Learning to Savor

There is a famous Jewish tale about a holy man named Shalom Aleichem. It seems that Shalom was a man who experienced every misfortune imaginable, but nevertheless went about his life returning good for evil. No matter what terrible things happened to him, he would always seem to bounce back and continue to enjoy life. He was a man much like Job, whose story we know from the Bible.

Shalom was so well known for being such a good man that when he finally died and arrived in Heaven, all the angels and the Lord himself were present to greet him. The Lord told old Shalom that whatever he might wish for would be granted him. And what do you suppose that holy old man asked of the Lord? It was something quite simple, yet something he dearly loved.

All Shalom wanted was that each day in Heaven would begin with a hot, buttered roll. He said that would mean he was home. The angels and even the Lord wept at the beauty of the simple thing he requested.

The rabbis taught that this story is a reminder that God is found in the most simple yet incredibly rich experiences of daily life. Hot buttered rolls were a contemplative experience for old Shalom. The taste of a hot butter roll had taught him to savor all of life even in the midst of misfortune and troubles. For him, God was not very far away if he had a hot buttered roll to call him to mind.

September

SEPTEMBER 1
The Main Thing

I spent some time this past week with a friend of mine who, in the middle of our conversation, turned to me and said, "I think my life has gone off track." When I asked him what he meant by that he simply said, "I guess I just don't know where I'm headed anymore."

Have you ever felt that way? I know lots of folks who have found themselves feeling that way. As I said that to my friend I began to think of something I had read the night before, an article about success that quoted one of Yogi Berra's famous sayings. Berra was a New York Yankees catcher back in the 1950s and '60s who had a way of saying things that made everyone laugh. Almost all of his sayings were really funny, but sometimes he actually said some very profound things. When he was asked how a player could learn to stay focused, he paused to think about it, then said, "If you ask me, the main thing is to keep the main thing the main thing."

As silly as that sounds, Yogi Berra was saying the same thing Jesus said to his disciples when he told them not to be so worried about life and all its burdens. Jesus was concerned that his disciples were being distracted by unimportant concerns; they were losing their way. When he explained this to his disciples he put it this way: "Seek first the kingdom of God and his righteousness and all these things (the things you are so worried about) will be provided for you" (Matthew 6:33). In other words, Jesus was reminding his friends that if you put first things first, you would not lose your way.

Is there a "main thing" in your own life right now that you've let slip away from being the main thing? Have you given your spouse or children or other folks the attention they deserve? When it comes to the main things in your life, just where does your relationship with God rate? Is God a main thing in your life?

How differently would you be living your life right now if you lived by the motto, "First things first"?

September 2
Feeling God's Presence

A well-known Catholic theologian and author once spent an extended time at a monastery, writing and praying. During his time in residence he noticed there was one particular monk who looked completely at peace. That monk was actually one of the lay brothers of the community, whose job it was to work in the kitchen cleaning pots and pans and sweeping the floor. He spent long hours each day making sure the kitchen was spotless.

The theologian noticed that if that monk was not in the kitchen, he was certainly in the chapel. The one thing that made the brother stand out was that no matter how hard the man was working, no matter how much time he spent in the chapel, the man's face just exuded peace, serenity, and a sense of calmness.

One day he asked the brother, "What do you do when you spend time in the chapel, and even when you work in the kitchen, that brings you so much peace?"

The brother replied, "I just look up at God and exhale so I can empty my lungs. I say to God, 'O beloved one, I release to you all that is in me that gets between me and you.' Then as I inhale I say, 'Beloved one, come and fill me with your presence, and bring peace and serenity and calmness with you.'"

On hearing those words the theologian felt a rush of peace and serenity surround him, and he began to weep. The scholar said, "I've spent years studying about God and felt very little, but as that man spoke about his love of God, I suddenly felt God's presence and knew I was loved."

Have you ever felt that presence?

SEPTEMBER 3
Letting It Go

A holy man from the fourth century told his disciples, "It's most often the little things in life that have the greatest power over us. Don't be so much afraid of the big things: beware of the little things!" I think this Desert Father was talking about resentment. One of the most important things I've learned from studying the teachings of the Desert Fathers is the danger resentment can pose to our happiness.

Recently, I gave a presentation at a conference in which I spoke about how easily resentment can take over our lives if we are not careful. I described how very happy people could become bitter, angry people in a very short time if they let resentment build up in them. The folks at the conference listened attentively; you could feel that many of them were wrestling with the subject.

After I had given my talk, a woman approached me and said she would like to send me something that would illustrate what I had just been talking about. Later that night I opened an email from her that contained the following account:

"A lady took my seat in church the other day. She's really very nice, a good friend. In fact, I can sit any place in the church. It's no big deal. But I like my seat. It's on the right as you enter the sanctuary. I can rest my arm on the end. It's a good seat, but I wouldn't raise a fuss over just a seat. I never hold a grudge. Actually, it was three months ago that she took it and I really don't know why. I've never done anything to her, never taken her seat. I suppose I'll have to come an hour early now to get my seat."

"I think she took it because it's one of the best seats in the house. You know, she had no business taking it, and I'm not going to church two hours early to get what's rightfully mine! This is the way great social injustices begin: abusive people taking other people's seats! It's the way seeds of revolution are sown. A person can only stand so much, you know. Where's it all going to end? If someone doesn't stand up and be counted, nobody's seat will be safe. People will sit just where they please, and next they'll take my parking place, then my home. World order will be in a shambles!"

Isn't that a great illustration of just what that fourth-century holy man warned his disciples about? He knew, probably from his own life experience, how a seemingly unimportant event could become a resentment that can eat away at us until we're at our wit's end.

Is there resentment in your life, even one that stems from some little thing, that is stealing your peace? Perhaps today is the day you could begin the process of letting it go.

September 4
The "Eyes" Have It!

During my prayer time this past week I realized the card I had used to mark my place in my Bible was a postcard from the previous day's mail. I had not looked at the card when I originally put it there, but when I read it I saw it was a notice from my eye doctor, telling me it was time for my routine exam. The card reminded me that my vision is important.

It's not only important to see clearly with our eyes, it's also very important to clearly see our lives. How we look at life makes all the difference. Two examples came to me in my morning meditation. Here's the first one.

The leadership team of a shoe manufacturer decided to build a new factory in Africa. The first step in getting the project off the ground was to send two sales reps to the new and undeveloped territory to investigate the market potential. One salesman sent his report: "Prospect here nil. No one wears shoes." The other salesman reported enthusiastically, "Market potential terrific! Everyone is barefooted."

Both sales reps investigated the same territory and talked with many of the same people, yet each saw the situation differently. How each of them looked at things would, I am sure, determine their attitudes about working in that territory. How we look at life shapes how we deal with life.

The second example that came to me concerns something one of our parishioners told me about a former boss. He said he loved his old boss because he was a good man who always tried to see things from the most positive point of view. He said his boss taught him that to be a good person you must choose to look for and cultivate goodness.

The man said his boss was asked to write a letter of recommendation for a really lazy employee. The boss didn't want to say anything bad about the employee, but he also wanted to be honest – and help the employee get the new job so he would leave the company. And so the boss wrote a wonderful letter that ended with these words: "If you get John to work for you, you will be extremely fortunate. Yours truly."

I concluded my prayer by promising myself I would make an appointment to get my eyes examined. I also decided to take an inventory as to how I am looking at life these days. By the way, when was the last time have you had your "eyes" checked

SEPTEMBER 5
God Close By

Can you remember the last time you saw something extraordinary? Recently, someone invited me into their garden, made me sit in a particular chair, then made me promise to sit completely still and be absolutely quiet. It was then I saw something extraordinary.

As I sat there in silence, I began to hear a kind of fluttering sound. It sounded as if it was getting closer, and the sound seemed to become more intense. All at once, out of the corner of my eye I noticed the rapid movement of what I thought were large insects, but as I looked more closely I saw they were hummingbirds. They were darting back and forth near various flowers, then toward a hummingbird feeder. I couldn't believe the number of them! They were moving in all directions, and it appeared to be almost a ballet of ten to twenty birds moving around.

As I watched, my friend spoke in hushed tones about what I was seeing. She said there are over 300 species of hummingbirds, but they are only found in North America. She continued, "If you watch you will see that they not only fly forward, but they are the only bird that can fly both backward and even upside down!" She went on to tell me that they can hover in mid-air because of the rapid movement of their wings, which have been timed at over eighty beats per second! In addition to that, hummingbirds flap their wings entirely different than other birds. Whereas all other birds flap their wings up and down, hummingbirds flap their wings forward and backward.

As we sat there watching the birds, my friend leaned over and said to me, "When I want to feel close to God, I come out here and sit and watch that extraordinary group of tiny birds fly around. It makes me wonder what Heaven must be like!"

Do you have a place like that where you can go and observe something extraordinary that makes you feel God is close by? When was the last time you were there?

SEPTEMBER 6
No Pipe Dreams

As a pastor I am often invited to be part of the events that take place in some of our local schools. On one occasion I was a guest at an all school assembly that had been called to open a new school year. During the assembly, the principal of a rather exclusive high school rose to address the students. In her remarks she encouraged her students to, as she forcefully said, "study hard because your education can make your dreams come true." She paused to let those words sink in, then added, "If you do not take your education seriously your dreams may never be realized, and they will just be mere pipe dreams."

Hearing those words got me thinking about the difference between having a dream and mere pipe dreams. I researched the term "pipe dream." It turns out it means a desire that is not attainable, just mere fantasy and an unrealistic hope. The term came from the "dreams" experienced by opium smokers who inhaled the drug through a pipe, vivid hallucinations that seemed very real at the time. Users would say that when the smoke cleared and they came back down to earth, in reality once again, they began to realize those hallucinations were "from the pipe" and had no substance.

What are your dreams, your plans for your life? Are they based in reality or do they come "from the pipe"? Are you working to make those dreams and plans a reality? Most of us forget that God, too, has dreams and plans for each one of us. Jeremiah the prophet shared that truth when he wrote, "For surely I know the plans I have for you, says the Lord, plans for your welfare and not for harm, to give you a future with hope" (Jer 29:11).

God's plans for us are not mere pipe dreams; rather, they are from the mind and heart of the one who created us and loves us dearly. Those dreams and plans will lead to a bright future.

September 7
Shortsighted

One of my favorite people in history is George Washington, and I often think about one incident in particular from his time as a commanding general. It took place a short time after the fighting that ended the American Revolution, but before peace had been negotiated.

Washington was with his troops in Newburgh, New York, and they had been through a lot together. As the fighting began to wind down, however, some of the troops grew restless and agitated because they hadn't been paid. Washington had begged the Continental Congress to do what they said they would do and pay the soldiers, but they refused. The General was frustrated, and weary of all the difficulties he had endured.

Well, some of the officers began to organize a rebellion; they were fed up, and they were going to do something about it. They talked about marching on Philadelphia, which at the time was the seat of the reigning national government, overthrowing that government, and setting up an army to rule the nation.

Washington become aware of their grumbling, and with the fate of America in the balance, he made a surprise appearance before the officers. After praising them for their service and thanking them for their sacrifice, he pulled from his pocket a copy of a speech he wished to read to them. He fumbled with the paper, and finally reached for a set of reading glasses. None of his men had ever seen General Washington wear glasses before.

With his glasses on, Washington looked around the room and made this simple statement: "I have already grown grey in the service of my country, and now I am going blind." The officers were stunned into silence. Seeing that Washington had endured all the hardships they had and even more, they realized what the revolution had cost the General. All plans for a rebellion were abandoned.

I like that story because it illustrates how George Washington was truly a great leader. By fumbling with his eyeglasses he subtly yet profoundly taught his officers that they were looking at things in the wrong way. He showed them that they were being shortsighted, only concerned about their own needs. He made them see the bigger picture, and what the suffering they had endured was really all about.

Fr. Mark Burger

Take a few moments right now and try to picture George Washington as he was talking with his officers. Picture him looking at each of them through his eyeglasses, then ask yourself this question: In your life right now, are you seeing the whole picture or are you being a bit shortsighted, concerned with only your own needs and your own welfare?

SEPTEMBER 8
A Unique Perspective

In 1799 some French soldiers stationed in the Nile Delta discovered a black stone slab near the village of Rosetta. On the stone were three rows of inscriptions written in something called "demotic," which is a kind of cursive hieroglyphics used during a period in Egyptian history. The inscriptions on that stone were a great find for historians because they led to an understanding of how to translate the written language of Egypt.

One of the scholars who studied the Rosetta stone, as it came to be known, was a young French student by the name of Jean-Francois Champollion. From the early days of his childhood, Jean-Francois had an easy time with languages. He mastered Latin, Greek, and Hebrew by the age of thirteen, then went on to master Arabic, Syriac, Chaldean, Coptic, and Chinese. By the age of seventeen he had also learned Sanskrit and Persian. Although he had mastered all of those languages, the one language he was obsessed with was hieroglyphics.

When he learned of the discovery of the Rosetta stone, he had to see it. Champollion realized that what the other scholars who had studied the Rosetta stone before him had theorized about the writings was wrong. Those scholars believed that hieroglyphics were "picture writing," whereas Jean-Francois discovered they were phonetic symbols.

This knowledge enabled him to translate the hieroglyphic writings on the stone and open a doorway into Egypt's ancient history, which up to his time had been hidden to the world. Little did Champollion know that his own fascination with languages would one day help the world better understand itself. He probably thought of himself as some insignificant, unimportant person, yet he contributed much to our understanding of the world, and in particular, ancient Egypt.

There is a great teaching here for each of us. Sometimes we may think we have very little to offer humanity. Yet the truth of the matter is that God has given each of us an ability to see and look at things from our own unique perspective. Every now and then throughout history, someone comes along whose insight into the world leads to a new way of seeing things, which can lead to great discoveries. Your own unique perspective may very well have the potential to change the world.

SEPTEMBER 9
Time

A few years ago I attended a directed retreat. My director met with me each morning and each evening to discuss what God might be doing in my life. At each session he would ask three or four questions for me to consider, and then we would discuss them. When our discussions were over, my director would hand me an envelope containing some Scripture passages he wanted me to pray about or consider.

After one of our sessions he handed me a sheet of paper and said, "Spend some time with this." Here is what he gave me to consider.

"If you had a bank that credited your account each morning with $86,000 that carried over no balance from day to day, allowed you to keep no cash in your account, and every evening cancelled whatever part of the amount you failed to use during the day, what would you do? Draw out every cent every day, of course, and use it to your advantage!"

"Well, you have such a bank, and its name is TIME! Every morning it credits you with 86,400 seconds. Every night it marks off as lost whatever of this you failed to invest to good purpose. Time carries over no balances or allows any overdrafts. Each day it opens a new account with you. If you fail to use the day's deposits, the loss is yours. There is no going back. There is no drawing against tomorrow."

When my director and I met the next time, he smiled at me and said, "I have just one question for you. What are you doing with the precious gift of time God has given you?" We had a very long conversation about time and how it can easily get away from us. That conversation was the best one of the entire retreat.

How well are you making use of your time? Spend some time with the retreat director's description of time, then took a few minutes to look at your own life right now and see.

September 10
Today

As you awoke yesterday morning, what was your plan for the day? How many different things did you hope to accomplish? How many of those things did you actually end up doing? As you went to bed last night did you feel good about what you were able to get done during the day?

As I think of yesterday and all I had wanted to get done but didn't, I think of something that Henry Ford once said: "A weakness of all human beings is trying to do too many things at once. That scatters effort and destroys direction. It makes for haste, and haste makes waste."

There are many mornings when I wake up and think of ten or more things I want to get done that day, knowing full well I will probably not be able to do so. Henry Ford was asked if he ever woke up in the morning with a dozen or so things to do on his mind. When he admitted that it happened to him quite regularly, he described what he did about it in this way. "I go out and trot around the house. While I'm running off the excess energy that wants to do too much, my mind clears and I see what can be done and should be done first."

Ford said the problem that develops when you want to do too many things in a day is you try to do them all at once. That means you will do all of them poorly. His advice was to do the most important one as if it was the only thing you had to do that day, then move on to the next and act the same way with that one as well.

What one thing would you like to accomplish today?

September 11
A Purposeful Pause

I had lunch recently with a friend from another parish, and during lunch he told me about something that happened at work the day before. He said,

"While I was sitting in my company van on the street yesterday, a woman from the car ahead of me came over and asked if I had a hammer she could borrow. I reached over to my toolbox, got a hammer, and handed it to her. She thanked me and said she would be right back."

"She then proceeded to smash out the driver's side window of her car. Having cleared away the broken glass, she reached through her now broken window, took out the keys, and waved them at me with a triumphant grin. She walked back to my van, handed me the hammer, and said, 'You've been a big help, thanks!'"

As my friend finished his story we laughed because we both knew something she didn't. My friend is a locksmith! As he put it, "If only she had looked at the side of my van and saw the name of my company, she would have known I'm a locksmith! It would have been a very simple thing for me to fix."

Isn't it amazing how in trying to "fix" things we often act on impulse and end up making things a lot worse than they may have been in the first place? It happens to all of us at one time or another. We grew up learning that if something is wrong we need to fix it, so we forge full-steam ahead to make things right.

One of the ancient Desert Fathers taught his disciples that the most important thing anyone can do in the face of some crisis or difficulty is to practice the art of purposeful pausing. By that he meant, one of the best responses to any crisis, big or small, is to first take some time to be quiet in front of it. He said it is within the quietness of that purposeful pause that solutions or possible courses of action will surface. He would conclude his teaching by saying, "Now you must remember to always keep in mind that, after a pause, right action usually follows."

The next time you are confronted with a crisis, be it large or small, remember the importance of the purposeful pause before you try to fix anything.

SEPTEMBER 12
What Do You Say?

In the seventeenth chapter of Luke's gospel, you'll find the story of Jesus healing ten lepers. It's an important story about how easily we fall into a dull world of our own making in which we think only of what we want or need.

Luke tells us that one day, Jesus, filled with loving compassion, reached out and healed ten suffering lepers. Once healed, the lepers dash off to claim the life that has up to this time been denied them. Luke goes on to tell us that only one leper came back to give thanks. Ten were healed, but only the Samaritan came back. If any of those leper's mothers had been there, I'm sure they would have said to the nine, "Have you forgotten something?" or "What do you say?"

Do you remember one of those questions being addressed to you as a child when someone gave you something? How often as a little one were you reminded to thank people for the kindnesses they showed you? Those questions were perhaps our first instructions about the role of gratitude in our lives. Those little reminders that our parents gave us as we matured were truly important because they formed in us a grateful heart. They taught us that all of life and its experiences are a gift to us.

If we are appreciative of all the many gifts that come our way, it is because someone showed us that gifts are reminders of the giver. Gifts remind us that someone thought enough of us, loved us enough to reach out to us. And, of course, the ultimate gift giver is the God who never stops pouring gifts into our lives.

This leads me to ask you a question. As you think of all God has done for you, of all that your family and friends have done for you, as you think of life itself, what do you say?

SEPTEMBER 13
The Wisdom that Comes from Experience

One of the most famous scientists in history is Sir Isaac Newton. Just about anyone who ever took a basic science course knows that Newton is said to have discovered the law of gravity by watching an apple fall from a tree. Some even surmise he discovered this law when an apple fell from a tree and hit him in the head.

While Isaac Newton may have observed the law of gravity that day, it was almost twenty years before he could really interpret the results of his observations. He had at first tried to demonstrate that the same force that keeps planets in orbit and the moon in orbit around the earth also makes the apple fall from a tree. His experiments were inconclusive, so he dropped them to study what he thought were more interesting things like light and optics.

It wasn't until the late 1600s that he actually returned to his apple experiments. It was then, with years of experience under his belt, he was able to demonstrate that gravity is a universal force that applies to all objects in the universe.

Why did it take so long for Newton to complete his work on gravity? Perhaps when, as a young person, he observed the apple falling he didn't have the necessary wisdom that years of experience often bring to situations. As we get older we begin to see that book knowledge isn't always enough to lead us to real wisdom. Sometimes it takes the knowledge that comes from living through the difficulties life can bring to help us see things in context.

Are you finding it difficult to make all the pieces of your life fit together in such a way that they make sense to you? Perhaps you need to see them from a wider perspective before any real wisdom becomes apparent to you. Ask yourself this: What has my life experience taught me about handling the difficulties life has given me? Would I respond to a crisis today in the same way I did when I was younger?

Your life experience may have given you a new appreciation for working things out that you may not have had at an earlier time in your life. Although Isaac Newton may have known about gravity when he was much younger, it took years of experience before he could truly understand its universal applications.

September 14
A Door to New Worlds

While I was on retreat with some friends, one of the speakers gathered us together in a room and asked us to sit in silence for about twenty minutes. As we sat quietly a kind of peace descended on us. When the time was up, our speaker rose to his feet and slowly walked around the room looking directly into our faces. It was a bit uncomfortable as he stared at us. Finally he said, "I want you to answer a question. How does it look to you?"

Most of us were taken aback by the question. "How does *what* look?" we all wondered. We looked around the room and at each other. Finally, the speaker said, "Listen to this story, and consider my question again." Here is the story:

One day a young Buddhist on his journey home came to the banks of a wide river. Staring hopelessly at the great obstacle in front of him, he pondered for hours on how to cross such a wide barrier. Just as he was about to give up and stop his journey home, he saw a great teacher on the other side of the river. The young Buddhist yelled over to the teacher, "Oh wise one, can you tell me how to get to the other side of this river"?

The teacher pondered for a moment, looked up and down the river, then yelled back, "My son, you *are* on the other side."

After giving us some time to reflect on the story, our speaker stood up. "A first and very important spiritual principle you must understand if you wish to grow is that we see the world from a particular point of view. True wisdom is to realize there are other points of view as well. Perhaps we can try these on for size to discover a new perspective on our own point of view. This may broaden our horizons and show us whole new worlds." After a long pause, he said, "I'll leave you all to discover some new worlds."

Why not take some time yourself right now to reflect on the story of the young Buddhist. Maybe you too will discover a new perspective, and perhaps even open a door to new worlds.

SEPTEMBER 15
Craving Air

A young man came to a spiritual master to ask him for a favor. "Holy One," he asked, "how can I become closer to God? I know God exists, but I do not feel close to him. I have spoken to the parish priest and he has agreed to teach me. I think I shall learn faster if I study with both you and the parish priest. What do you think of this?"

The holy man paused to consider what the young man had asked, then said, "I have two stories to tell you, and they will give you your answer. The first story is called, 'The Tale of Two Rabbits.'"

A martial arts student approached his teacher with a question. "I'd like to improve my knowledge of the martial arts. In addition to learning from you, I'd like to study with another teacher in order to learn another style. What do you think of this idea?"

The master answered, "The hunter who chases two rabbits catches neither one."

When the holy man finished the story he said to the young man, "Do you understand the meaning of this famous story?"

The young man replied, "Yes, Father, I think I understand your meaning."

The holy man went on, "The second story I want you to hear is about the exact thing you seek. It will teach you what such a quest entails. The second story I give you is called 'Wanting God,' and here it is:

A hermit was meditating by a river when a young man interrupted him. "Master, I wish to become your disciple," said the man. "Why?" replied the hermit. The young man thought for a moment, then said, "Because I want to find God."

The master jumped up, grabbed him by the scruff of his neck, dragged him into the river, and plunged his head under water. After holding him there for a minute, with him kicking and struggling to free himself, the master finally pulled him up out of the river. The young man coughed up water and gasped to get his breath.

When he eventually quieted down, the master spoke. "Tell me what you wanted most of all when you were under water."

"Air!" answered the man.

"Very well," said the master. "Go home and come back to me when you want God as much as you just wanted air."

The holy man concluded, "If you want to walk with God, seek one master to keep you on course and then crave God as much you crave the air you breathe."

SEPTEMBER 16
Someday

The Desert Fathers would often refer their disciples to basic spiritual principles. One such principle or axiom was called "the Law of the Echo." The Fathers taught that the Law of the Echo is quite simple and can be summed up in one sentence: "What you send out will come back to you." Those holy men would tell their disciples to be very careful of their attitudes and the way they treated others because those very attitudes and behaviors would one day come back to them.

Whenever I think of the Law of the Echo, I think of the following story a monk once gave me. A farmer grew so old that he couldn't work the fields anymore, and he would spend the day just sitting on the porch. His son, still working the farm, would look up from time to time and see his father sitting there. "He's of no use any more," the son thought to himself. "He doesn't do anything!"

The son became so angry and frustrated by this that one day he built a wood coffin, dragged it over to the porch, and told his father to get in. Without saying anything, the father climbed inside. After closing the lid, the son dragged the coffin to the edge of the farm where there was a high cliff.

As the son approached the drop, he heard a light tapping on the lid from inside the coffin. He opened it up. Still lying there peacefully, the father looked up at his son. "I know you're going to throw me over the cliff, but before you do, may I suggest something?"

"What is it?" replied the son.

"Throw me over the cliff, if you like," said the father, "but save this good wood coffin. Your children will surely need to use it someday."

September 17
Truly Blessed

There was a sixth-grade teacher who liked to test her students' ability to use math to figure out solutions to real life problems. She said to her students, "I'm going to give you a math problem that comes from real life. I want you to listen to the situation I will describe for you, then I want you to think about your answer. When you have thought about it for a while, tell me what you think the answer is."

She then posed the following problem: "A wealthy man dies and leaves ten million dollars. One fifth is to go to his wife, one fifth is to go to his son, one-sixth to his butler, and the remainder is to be given to charity. Now, after you think this through, what does each one get?" After a very long silence while the students scratched their heads and thought long and hard about it, a boy named Michael raised his hand. The teacher called on him for his answer, and with complete sincerity, Michael said, "A lawyer!"

Although it's a funny answer, it's also, in a way, a very sad answer in that our children are aware enough to realize that when money is involved, people often greedily look out for their own best interests. It's as if they cannot enjoy the spontaneity of a gift freely given.

This is so unlike what Jesus taught his friends and disciples about the joy of living. He taught that all of life is a gift freely given to us by a loving father – no strings attached, no contracts to ink or sign. Life is simply God's love freely poured out to us. So much of the simple joy of living can be lost when we lose our perspective. Are you aware of how truly blessed you are?

September 18
I'm Worried about You

Have you ever been worried about someone you love and are a bit uneasy about what to do about it? Have you ever found yourself stewing about that person, thinking to yourself, "I'm certain there's something wrong with him or her?" Perhaps the following incident may shed a bit of light on this situation and help you check if you are clearly seeing the problem.

Fr. Mark Burger

A man feared his wife wasn't hearing as well as she used to, and he thought she might need a hearing aid. Not quite sure how to approach her, he called the family doctor to discuss the problem. The doctor told him there was a simple, informal test the husband could perform to give the doctor a better idea about her hearing loss.

"Here's what you do," said the doctor. "Stand about forty feet away from your wife, and ask her a question in a normal, conversational tone to see if she hears you. If not, go to thirty feet, then twenty, and so on until you get a response."

That evening, the wife was in the kitchen cooking dinner while the man was in the den. He said to himself, "I'm about forty feet away; let's see what happens." Then in a normal tone he asks, "Honey, what's for dinner?" No response.

So the husband moves to closer to the kitchen, about thirty feet from his wife and repeats, "Honey, what's for dinner?" Still no response. Next he moves into the dining room, where he is about twenty feet from his wife, and asks, "Honey, what's for dinner?" Again he gets no response. He walks up to the kitchen door, about ten feet away, and says, "Honey, what's for dinner?" Again there is no response.

The man then walks right up behind his wife and says, "Honey, what's for dinner?"

She turns around, looks him in the face, and says, "Jim, for the fifth time, I said we're having chicken!

September 19
The Trouble with Comfort Inns

I read about an inn that's built on the side of a mountain in the French Alps. The little hotel has a very strange name; it's called the Mediocre Inn. As I read the name I wondered, who would want to stay in a "mediocre" inn? I then learned it's called that because of where it is located. "Mediocre" in French means "half way," and that is exactly where the Mediocre Inn is situated, half way up the mountain.

The inn does a great business, as I'm sure you can imagine. Just think of what it would be like climbing up a very icy and windy mountain, feeling more and more the kind of fatigue where every muscle in your body is aching and you are beginning to have second thoughts about making the climb. All at once the Mediocre Inn comes into view! At the Mediocre Inn, you find a hot meal and a warm bed, a good stiff drink, and a place to relax and find rest. It isn't long before you are really cozy and comfortable.

Those who stay at the Mediocre Inn absolutely love it. The owners of the Inn say that most folks stay for about two or three days. They also say that about eighty percent of climbers never go any farther than the Mediocre Inn. Once they've had a day or two of rest and comfort, they turn around and descend the mountain, never reaching the Alps' highest peak. The coziness of the inn has stolen their zeal for the climb.

If you stop to think of it, have you ever stayed in a kind of "mediocre inn"? I don't mean that place in the French Alps. What I mean is, have you ever set out toward a certain goal and as you are working at it, things get tougher and tougher and you begin to wear out? You may get just about half way to your goal then say to yourself, "this is just too difficult," and you look for some safe, comfortable place to go for relief. It's an easy and understandable thing to do.

This can happen to married couples who get worn out by the hard work that maintaining a relationship requires. Not trying seems easier than trying, so progress stops. This happens often with parents as well when they try to raise their children. Parenting can be a huge mountain to climb, and it is so easy to find a "Mediocre Inn," a half-measure, "I'll be your friend rather than your parent" kind of place in which to hide.

Mountain climbing is not an easy thing to do. Whether it is climbing an actual mountain in the French Alps or climbing the mountains of personal growth, getting to the top is never easy. The biggest threat to getting to the top is that half way point, the choice that will eventually present itself: "Do I keep climbing or do I check in at the Mediocre Inn?"

September 20
He Hears

When veteran journalist Bill Moyers was press secretary and special assistant to President Lyndon B. Johnson, he was asked to say grace before

Fr. Mark Burger

a meal in the family quarters of the White House. The President had asked him to lead the prayer because he knew that Moyers had been a Baptist pastor.

As the meal was about to start, everyone in the room bowed their head and became quiet. Moyers began praying softly, but the President interrupted him, saying, "Speak up, Bill! Speak up!" But Moyers continued to pray in a hushed voice. Just as the President was about to ask Moyers to speak louder, the former Baptist minister from east Texas stopped in mid-sentence, and without looking up replied steadily, "I wasn't addressing you, Mr. President."

In the Old Testament there's a passage in which God says something remarkable to the Prophet Jeremiah. God says, "When you call out to me and come to me in prayer, I will hear your prayers." Jeremiah truly needed to hear these words because his was not an easy life, nor was it an easy thing God had called him to do. In the midst of his difficulties, when his world was crashing in on him, he had worried about whether God heard his prayers or not. Then God lovingly says those calming and reassuring words, "I will hear your prayers."

When you are in difficulty or when your world appears to be crashing in on you, are you afraid that God, like President Johnson, has somehow not heard your prayers? If you are, remember the words God so lovingly spoke to Jeremiah, and know that he speaks those very same words to you as well.

SEPTEMBER 21
How Some Blessings Find Us

Very early one morning, before the sun had even come up, I was sitting in church praying. A woman tapped me on the shoulder and said, "Here is a story you need to take to your prayer; I have found that it has blessed my life." She handed me a piece of paper and walked away. Here is that story.

A ship was wrecked during a storm at sea, and only two of the men on it were able to swim to a small, desert-like island. The two survivors, frightened to death and not knowing what else to do, finally agreed they had better pray to God for help.

To pass the time and conquer their boredom they challenged each other to find out whose prayer was more powerful. They agreed to divide the island in half, and stay on opposite sides of the island.

The first thing they prayed for was food. Behold, the next morning, one of the men saw a fruit-bearing tree on his side of the island, and he was able to eat its fruit. The other man's side of the island had no such tree and no fruit.

After a week, the first man began to realize that he was lonely, and he decided to pray for a wife. Behold, the next day, another ship was wrecked, and the only survivor was a woman who swam to a part of the shore that was on his side of the island. On the other side of the island, there was nothing.

It wasn't long before the first man realized he needed more; so he prayed for a house, clothes, and even more food. Behold, the very next morning, as if by magic, all of these were given to him. However, the second man still had nothing.

Finally, the first man prayed for a ship, so that he and his wife could leave the island. Behold, in the morning, he found a ship docked at his side of the island. The first man boarded the ship with his wife and decided to leave the second man on the island. He wondered why the other man's prayer never got answered. The first man said to himself, "I guess God thinks he is unworthy to receive God's blessings, since none of his prayers were answered."

As the ship was about to leave, the first man heard a voice from Heaven booming, "Why are you leaving your companion all alone on the island?"

"Lord, I prayed and you granted my requests. My blessings are mine alone, since I was the one who prayed for them," the first man answered.

Then God spoke, "I answered the prayers of you both. You think his prayers were all unanswered and so he does not deserve anything. You are mistaken!" God said. Then God went on, "He had only one prayer, which I answered. If not for that, you would not have received any of my blessings."

"Tell me," the first man asked God, "What did he pray for that I should owe him anything?"

"He prayed that all your prayers be answered."

When I came to the end of the story, I noticed something the women had written across the bottom of the page. It read, "Even though we know who the source of our blessings may be, we may not know through whose intercession they have come to us."

Both the story and that woman's comment are great food for meditation.

Fr. Mark Burger

SEPTEMBER 22
A Terrible Sadness

Being a parish priest brings with it at times a terrible sadness. Because we often spend time with people when the worst possible things happen, we are sometimes plunged into unimaginable grief and sorrow. Jesus himself was moved with the deepest emotions as he ministered to the suffering, the grieving, and the dying. But there are days when the sadness is very strong and deep because we witness a kind of pain and suffering that doesn't have to happen. It's the kind of suffering that occurs when loved ones hurt each other.

A lot of folks endure a terrible loneliness because their family members are at odds with them or with each other over some past hurts. When people begin to describe their feelings, or when I witness families at each other's throats, I am often reminded of something I read when I was in seminary studying philosophy.

A German philosopher, Schopenhauer, compared the human race to a bunch of porcupines huddling together on a cold winter's night. He said, "The colder it gets outside, the more we huddle together for warmth; but the closer we get to one another, the more we hurt one another with our sharp quills. And in the lonely night of earth's winter eventually we begin to drift apart and wander out on our own and freeze to death in our loneliness."

In my work as a pastor I have been with many people who are in the process of freezing to death because of some very hurtful wounds inflicted by various family members. Sometimes words spoken in anger or even words spoken without any ill will at all have been taken to heart and interpreted as utter rejection. Family members begin to avoid each other, to speak with one another less and less, until they finally wander away from each other out into the cold.

Sometimes when we have been hurt we take to wearing "sharp quills" to keep loved ones at bay so they cannot hurt us again. That brings with it a terrible sadness, because we don't really have to live that way. Jesus came to show us a different way – the way of forgiving each other from the heart.

If only a spirit of forgiveness could warm our hearts, perhaps the beginning of a great family thaw would take place. Then as each person starts to forgive, and each person takes steps to drop those sharp quills, perhaps then we could reach out to embrace each other. Then there would be an end to the coldness and that terrible sadness.

SEPTEMBER 23
A New Direction

Have you ever felt like you were in a rut when it comes to life? Have you ever felt that you needed to do something different? Perhaps you may recognize yourself in the following fable.

A man who lived in the desert would wake up every morning and follow his shadow. As the sun moved across the sky from east to west, the man essentially walked in a large oval. At sundown he ended up where he had started, and he would be so disappointed that he had wasted the whole day. Unfortunately, this continued for years. The man walked in circles day after day, following his shadow.

Then one very special night the man heard God speak to him in a dream. The Lord God told him to stop following his shadow. Instead, God encouraged him to, "Follow the sun. Do this and you will experience life as you have never dreamed it could be."

The man thought for many days about his vision of God while he continued to walk around in circles in the desert. But one day he mustered up enough courage to break away from his shadow. Little by little, step-by-step, the man began to follow the sun. In doing so, he discovered a world that, heretofore, had been way beyond his wildest dreams and imagination.

Have you been walking around in circles? Is it time for you to do what God told the man in the fable to do? Perhaps today is the day you turn away from the dead-end, walking in a rut existence you've been in for some time. Is today the day for you to move in a new direction?

SEPTEMBER 24
The Way We Are Made

One summer night during a severe thunderstorm, a mother was tucking her small son into bed. She was about to turn off the light when he asked in a trembling voice, "Mommy, will you stay with me all night?" Wanting her son to find some courage, the mother gave him a warm, reassuring hug and said tenderly, "I can't dear. I have to go sleep with Daddy." After a long silence, the boy's shaky voice was heard saying, "The big sissy!"

There is probably no more difficult thing to endure than to face a frightening time alone. That's why I love that story. It can serve as a reminder to us of a truth articulated in the Book of Genesis, when God says, "It is not good for human beings to be alone." We were not meant to face life alone. One of our most basic human needs is loving companionship.

We all need the reassurance that comes from the people who love us. In addition, our love needs to express itself in reaching out to others. So, it's a sure thing that when the severe thunderstorms of life come our way perhaps the very best thing we can do is to reach out to a loved one. It's the way God made us. We truly need each other.

September 25
Living Trust

This past week I spent some time with friends who are teachers. A new principal had been hired at the school where they worked, and the teachers were talking about the challenges they would face with that situation. "A new principal means that everybody has to adjust!" said one of the teachers.

That reminded me of a story I had heard about a new principal who was starting work at a school in New York. According to the story, the principal was walking through the school on the first day. Passing the stockroom, he was startled to see the door wide open and teachers going in and out, carrying off books and supplies.

The previous school where the principal worked had a checkout policy that mandated all teachers must indicate what supplies they had obtained. Curious about the practice here he approached the member of the faculty with the most years of service in the school. "Do you think it's wise to keep the stockroom unlocked and let the teachers take things without asking?"

That wise old teacher said, "You sound like you're not a very trusting person. Well, now, you think about it for a minute or two." She paused for a few minutes to let him to ponder a bit, then said, "We trust them with the children, don't we? I think, then, that they are worthy of your trust when it comes to supplies. One of the best gifts we give each other is our trust. Trust is a way of life. Your teachers will do wonders for you and the students if they know they have your trust."

Are there people in your life who need your trust?

SEPTEMBER 26
Blinded

Do you remember the famous myth of old King Midas, who loved the sight and sound and feel of gold? His love of gold had made him a greedy man. The king was convinced that enough gold would bring meaning to his life, and begged the gods to grant him his wish that everything he touched would be changed into gold. Old King Midas thought this would make him the happiest man on the face of the earth.

The god Dionysus had promised to grant him any wish he desired, but at the same time warned Midas to think his wish through. Dionysus warned King Midas that his wish might not be as great a thing as he thought it would be, yet Midas still insisted that he wanted everything he touched to turn to gold.

Midas' wish was granted, but his golden world came with some unforeseen disastrous consequences. He soon discovered he couldn't eat because his food would turn to gold as it touched his lips. He couldn't embrace his young daughter because that would turn her to gold. Yet he did, and she was turned into a golden statue. As long as he had the Midas touch, the king could not have life or love.

Midas soon realized that his greed and love of gold was in fact a curse of death, and begged to have it removed so he could once again enjoy the true blessings life offered – blessings that had nothing to do with gold or wealth. Despairing and fearful, he raised his arms and prayed to Dionysus to take this curse from him.

The god heard Midas and felt sorry for him. Dionysus told Midas to go to river Pactolus and wash his hands. Midas did so: he ran to the river and was astonished to see gold flowing from his hands. When he went home, everything Midas had touched had become normal again.

Midas hugged his daughter in full happiness, and decided to share his great fortune with his people. He had learned that his greed had blinded him to the real beauty of life. Once he discovered where his true riches lay, he gave up his greedy ways and became a better person, a man who was very generous and grateful for all of the true blessings of his life. King Midas was a new man, and his people loved him.

Is there anything in your life that has blinded you and kept you from discovering the real blessings of life?

September 27
Wounded Healers

In an article I read recently, a professor of psychiatry from Harvard Medical School said that when Sigmund Freud died at the age of 83, he had become a bitter and disillusioned man. The professor went on to say this influential thinker had a very low opinion of the ordinary person. In fact, the professor said that Freud had little or no compassion for the common person's suffering.

Freud himself expressed it in these words: "I have found little that is good about human beings on the whole. In my experience most of them are trash, no matter whether they publicly subscribe to this or that ethical doctrine or to none at all." The end of Freud's life was bitter. He died friendless because he had even broken contact with his followers.

I find it very sad when a person succumbs to such bitterness over the hurts of life that they end up dying of bitterness itself. With all of our imperfections, sins, mistakes, blemishes, and utter failings, we human beings can do remarkable things and be instruments of tremendous healing if we don't let our sufferings isolate us. Because we have suffered, we can learn to be compassionate.

A Catholic priest and theologian by the name of Henri Nouwen described Christians as people who are called to be full of compassion for the human race. In fact, he described Christians as people who know suffering well, and because they do, they can become what he called "wounded healers." He said wounded people know what it means to suffer and they know that pain can isolate us. Because of this, they also know how important it is to suffer with those who are suffering. That, by the way, is what the word compassion means – to suffer with.

The disillusioned Sigmund Freud was a person with little or no compassion. He could not suffer with anyone. He died in bitterness because he saw most human beings as trash.

Henri Nouwen, who suffered greatly in life from a deep and dark depression, did not die a bitter man because he saw human beings as fellow sufferers who were his brothers and sisters. Freud ended life alone, bitter, and friendless. Nouwen ended life as a wound healer who was much loved by many brothers and sisters.

SEPTEMBER 28
A Tale from the Fourth Grade

Are you a happy person? Are you satisfied with who you are and what you are doing with your life? I ask the question because I often find myself listening to people who seem to be so very unhappy. I try to listen and understand. And so when I was in our parish school this past week, I was so surprised to hear our fourth graders talk about a little story they had read that taught them about being happy. Here's the story:

There was a wonderful crow living in a forest, flying about from tree branch to tree branch. When it had settled down and was resting for a moment or two, the bird began to think about how happy he was. Just then, the crow looked over at the lake and saw a very beautiful swan. "This swan is so white," he thought, "and I am just ugly and black. This swan must be the happiest bird in the world. I wish I was like him!"

The crow flew over to the swan and expressed his thoughts to the beautiful bird. The swan thanked him for his compliment, but then added, "Actually, I was feeling that I was the happiest bird around until I saw that parrot over there, which has two colors. I now think the parrot is the happiest bird in creation."

The crow just had to go talk to the parrot. The parrot explained, "I lived a very happy life until I saw a peacock. I have only two colors, but the peacock has hundreds of colors."

Fr. Mark Burger

The crow then visited a peacock at the zoo, and saw that hundreds of people had gathered just to look at him. Once the people had gone home, the crow spoke to the peacock. "Dear peacock," the crow said, "you are so beautiful. Every day thousands of people come to see you. When people see me, they immediately shoo me away because they are annoyed by me. I think you must be the happiest bird anywhere."

"Oh, how wrong you are," the peacock replied. "I always thought that I was the most beautiful and happy bird on the planet. But because of my beauty, I have been locked up here in this zoo. I have seen every part of this zoo, and I have realized that the crow is the only bird not kept in a cage here. Crows can fly in and fly right on out. So for past few days I have been thinking that if I were only a crow, I would be able to fly in and out just like them, and then I would be the happiest bird anywhere in the whole world."

Having read this tale from the fourth grade, are you happy being the person you are?

SEPTEMBER 29
An Angry Letter

Abraham Lincoln was well accustomed to people's foibles and shortcomings. He knew human nature quite well, and there are many stories about him that illustrate his deeper insight into people's souls.

One of these stories tells about the time Lincoln's secretary of war, Edwin Stanton, came storming into his office. Stanton was angered because an army officer had accused him of favoritism, and he went on and on, blustering and complaining. Lincoln knew Secretary Stanton quite well and hated to see him so upset, so he suggested Stanton write the officer a very sharp letter.

Stanton wrote the letter as Lincoln had suggested, and showed the strongly worded missive to the president. "What are you going to do with it?" Lincoln inquired. Surprised, Stanton replied, "Well, damn, I'm going to send it!"

Lincoln shook his head. "You don't want to send that letter," he said. "Put it in the stove and let it burn. That's what I do when I have written a letter while I am angry. It's a good letter and you had a good time writing it, and I'm sure you feel better. Now burn it, and write the kind of letter we both know you should write. Be kind and understanding as you would with a child who has had their feelings hurt."

Is there an angry letter inside you that needs to be written but not really sent?

SEPTEMBER 30
Spiders

There is a famous story from Tibet about a meditation student. One day, while meditating in his room, the student believed he saw a spider descending in front of him. Each day after, the horrible creature would return, and each day it grew larger and larger.

So frightened was the student that he went to his teacher to report his concern. His teacher asked him what he planned to do about the menacing creature. The student said he planned to place a knife in his lap during meditation, so when the spider appeared he could kill it. The teacher advised him against this plan. He suggested that instead of the knife he should bring a piece of chalk to meditation, and when the beastly spider appeared, mark an "X" on its belly. Then report back.

The student returned to his meditation. When the spider again appeared, he resisted the urge to attack it, and instead did just what the master suggested. When he later reported back to the master, the teacher told him to lift up his shirt and look at his own belly. To his astonishment, right there in the center of his belly was the "X".

When you take the time to pray and meditate, are there any "spiders" that descend in front of you? These creatures can steal your peace and your concentration, and leave you worried, terribly distracted, and afraid. When you lay down at night to sleep, are there any spiders that descend on you and keep you tossing and turning all night? Where do you think they come from?

October

October 1
Tending Your Fire

The Greeks held a unique race in their Olympic games, where each runner had to carry a flaming torch. The winner was not the runner who finished first, but the runner who finished with his torch still lit. To win, runners had to be sure they balanced their running skills with tending to the fragile flame they were carrying.

Isn't that a great illustration for life today? The pace of life too often seems so swift that one can hardly catch one's breath. On top of that, life often requires we care for and tend to some very fragile and painful situations, while meeting the demands of work or school or other commitments. Many folks caught up in the rat race of life can keep the fast pace going strong for quite a while, only to find that when they have reached the finish line, the flame of their marriage or their relationships with their children, friends, or even with God has long ago flickered out.

Fragile people and painful situations, much like the flickering flame carried by a runner, call for us to slow down the pace so we can tend to those needs. For a time, it may require that we stop running altogether. You cannot truly win the race if your fire has gone out.

October 2
Reassuring Words

There's a story told of a famous Hassidic rabbi from the early twentieth century who was riding in a horse-drawn carriage along a country road. The man who was driving the rabbi's coach looked and saw an apple orchard to the side of the road. The driver quickly stopped the coach, jumped out, and began to pick some apples.

The rabbi saw what the driver was doing and cried out, "You are being watched! You are being watched!" The coachman quickly got out of there, jumped back in the carriage, and drove the horses as fast as he could.

After a while, when they were a considerable distance away, he stopped and said to the rabbi, "But I did not see anybody watching! Who did you see watching me?"

The rabbi replied, "God was watching you."

"Do you think God was watching me because he now hates me for eating these apples?"

"No," the rabbi replied. "God was watching over you because he loves you dearly. He watches over you to protect you. God watches you and sees what you are doing. God then watches me and says to me, 'Sol, what are you doing there watching him? Tell him to get out of that orchard!' Then God said, 'And don't be too harsh because he's one of my favorites!'"

"Did God really say that to you, rabbi?" the man asked.

"Yes, he did, and he said if you asked me, that I was to tell you in exactly those words – 'He is one of my favorites!'" said the rabbi.

Wouldn't it be wonderful to have such reassuring words spoken to you?

October 3
Steady!

Take a moment right now to consider how you deal with worrisome thoughts, fears, or distractions. Then take another moment and read this Zen story.

There once was a young and rather boastful archery champion who had met no one person who even came close to him in his chosen sport of archery. One day he heard there was an old Zen master who was reputed to be a great archer. The young archer decided to challenge the Zen master to a contest, and the Zen master accepted.

When the contest began, the young man demonstrated remarkable technical proficiency when he hit a distant bull's eye on his first try. Then, to everyone's amazement, he split that arrow with his second shot. "There," he said to the old man, "see if you can match that!" Everyone turned and looked at the Zen master. A hush fell over the vast crowd.

Undisturbed by the young man's display of skill, the master did not draw his bow, but rather motioned for the young archer to follow him up the mountain. The crowd followed. Curious about the old fellow's intentions, the champion continued following him high into the mountain until they reached a deep chasm spanned by a rather flimsy and shaky log bridge. It was a poor excuse for a bridge, to say the least.

Calmly stepping out into the middle of the unsteady and certainly perilous bridge, the old master picked a far away tree as a target, pointed at the tree, drew his bow, and fired a clean, direct hit.

"Now it is your turn," he said to the young archer, as he gracefully stepped back onto the safe ground.

Staring with terror into the seemingly bottomless abyss below, the young man discovered that he could not force himself to step out onto the log, no less shoot at the target. With one foot on the ground and one foot on the shaky bridge, the young man could do nothing.

"You have much skill with your bow," the master said, sensing his challenger's predicament. "But you have little skill with the mind that lets loose the shot."

Are you standing with one foot on solid ground and one foot on the edge of an abyss? What will give you the confidence, the strength, and the steadiness that the old Zen master certainly possessed? What is the source of your confidence and strength?

October 4
Unmoved

Another famous Zen story, like yesterday's account, can give us some insight into the source of our strength. Consider the following tale.

Long ago, during the civil wars in feudal Japan, there was a powerful general who led an invading army into a small town and announced he was taking control of things. The fear among the townspeople was so intense that everyone fled for their lives just before the army arrived. Only the Zen master remained behind, undisturbed in his temple.

Curious that the Zen master had stayed and not fled like the rest of the town, the general went to the temple to see what kind of man this Zen master was. As he entered the temple, the general saw the Zen master standing quietly, watching and waiting. The master did not make a move as the general approached, but stared straight ahead at the general.

The general was taken aback because he wasn't being treated with the deference and submissiveness to which he was accustomed, so he burst into a rage of intense anger. "You fool," he shouted as he reached for his sword, "don't you realize you are standing before a man who could run you through and kill you without blinking an eye?"

Despite the threat, the master was unmoved. "And do you realize," the master replied calmly, "that you are standing before a man who can be run through and killed without blinking an eye?"

What is your response to other folk's fits of anger or rage? Do they frighten you and paralyze you or cause you to surrender who you are? Why do you suppose that is the case?

October 5
Unaware

The parishioners at St. Thomas Church were becoming disappointed with their organist. They didn't like the music he played, and they complained loudly to each other that they wanted him to play the music they had always heard in the church.

Evidently the musician did not hear their loud complaining, so the parishioners went to complain to the pastor. He tried to reassure them that the organist was a fine musician who knew what he was doing, but the parishioners would hear none of it. They demanded their pastor speak to the organist and order him to play only the music the parishioners knew and liked to sing. The pastor said he would speak to the organist, but it was to no avail. The musician continued to play what he chose, and that was that. The parishioners were not happy.

Eventually the organist died, and a new musician replaced him. The previous organist's music was no longer played at the church, and the parishioners were pleased to be singing "the good old songs" once again.

What the people of St. Thomas Church did not know was that their former organist was not just an ordinary church musician. He was a very gifted man whose name was Johann Sebastian Bach. We know him today as one of the greatest musical masters of all time, yet the folks in his parish didn't realize that. The strange and innovative music that the people of St. Thomas Church complained about was what Bach wrote for the choir and organ each Sunday. Each piece was a gift to the parishioners, but they refused to receive it. They were unaware that a talented musician was in their midst.

After his death, the music of Bach was seldom performed until another famous musician, Felix Mendelssohn, began to play it and introduce it to thousands of people who fell in love with the music. Today, Bach is acknowledged the world over as one of the musical geniuses of the Western world.

If only the parishioners of St. Thomas Church had given their organist a second look, they would have discovered a real treasure in their midst. Are there people in our lives right now who may be treasures in our midst, who we have refused to hear, or see, or accept?

OCTOBER 6
Where Are You Headed?

Here is a tale that can teach us something we need to learn again and again as we work our way through life. The story is about a very gifted bloodhound in England that everyone sought to use because it was such a good tracker of prey.

One day a hunter set out in search of a deer and asked the owner of the bloodhound if he could take the dog with him. The owner agreed, and the hunter and dog set out on the hunt. It wasn't long before that bloodhound caught the scent of a deer, and the hound took off chasing a full-grown male deer.

During the chase, however, a fox crossed his path, so the dog began to chase the fox. A rabbit crossed his hunting path, so he began to chase the rabbit. After chasing the rabbit for a while, a tiny field mouse crossed his path, and he chased the mouse to the corner of a farmer's barn. The bloodhound had begun the hunt chasing a prized male deer for his master but wound up barking at a tiny mouse.

What's the moral of the story? It's a rare human being who can do three or four things at the same time, moving in different directions, and do them well. How easy it is for us to get distracted by the things that are thrown at us each day. When we let that happen, we usually end up sidetracked in a place we never intended to be.

The question is simply this: If we keep living the way we are living, and doing the many things we are doing, where will we end up?

OCTOBER 7
An Inner Room

Jesus said to his disciples, "Whenever you pray, go to your inner room and shut the door and pray to your Father who is in secret; and your Father who sees in secret will reward you" (Matthew 6:6). This wonderful invitation can change your life. Once in that inner room with the door shut behind us, we are free to speak to God from our hearts. Within our inner room we can come to an awareness of God's presence.

Quite a few years ago now, when I was first learning about Zen and meditation, I used that image of going into my inner room whenever I sat down to pray. That image has been a real blessing to me. To this day I still find it very comforting to know that, at a moment's notice, I have access to an "inner room" where I can shut myself in with God.

Among Zen Buddhists there's a word that means to guide or lead a person to a heightened sense of awareness. That word is *satori* and it means "the little point." The practice of satori is a way of going into your inner room and, once there, letting your gaze fall upon something tiny in the universe. It's the kind of looking one does as they stare at a single rose or perhaps a fly on the wall. The tiny thing becomes a doorway to inner awareness, with the hope that some understanding of the universe might make itself known.

Those of us who grew up in the West have been taught that if we want to understand the world and ourselves in relation to it, we are to look at the larger picture, which is the whole universe. But in the East and among those who practice Zen, one begins to understand oneself in relation to the world by narrowing, not by widening, one's focus. In some Zen practice, narrowing the focus is like concentrating all your energy into a laser. There's more, not less, power, which can lead to a moment of heightened awareness and profound understanding.

Some Christians who practice Zen meditation focus their attention by using a short phrase from the Bible as a mantra. For example, one might whisper a four word mantra taken from the Book of Genesis, "Let there be light," as a way to come to a quiet place. By concentrating on those four simple words, a light might dawn and bring with it a new way of seeing.

Using a "little point" to illuminate the vast universe can open a doorway to the inner room Jesus spoke about where one can come to an awareness of God's presence.

October 8
Kindling Compassion

In October of 1871 a small fire started near the barn on Mrs. O'Leary's farm, which was located on the south side of Chicago. Legend has it that the fire was actually started when Mrs. O'Leary's cow kicked over a lantern. The event in itself was not very remarkable – except what started as a small fire that could have been taken care of quickly ended up becoming something much bigger.

Strong winds were blowing through Chicago that night, and before anyone could tend to the fire at O'Leary's farm, the winds had whipped that little fire into what became known as the Great Chicago Fire. By the time the fire was out, 18,000 buildings had been burned to the ground, 100,000 people were left homeless, and over 250 people died. The damage was horrific, and repair estimates soared to over $200 million. The nation was in shock at the loss of life and the property of so many. For a long time, the eyes of the country were fixed on Chicago and the immense suffering, pain, and sorrow there.

As terrible as the Great Chicago Fire was, it wasn't the worst fire that happened on the night of October 8, 1871. About 250 miles north of the Chicago fire, in the Wisconsin lumber town of Preshtigo, a forest fire of such intensity broke out that night there was no escaping it. Quickly the entire town of Preshtigo and several of the smaller towns around it were completely engulfed by flames. Nothing was left of those towns, and more than a thousand people were killed.

Not many people across the nation had ever heard of Preshtigo or the fire that destroyed it. The spectacle of the Great Chicago Fire held most folk's attention, and they could barely absorb that tragedy. They were unaware of the terrible suffering going on 250 miles to the north.

The night of October 8, 1871, saw immense suffering. So many people went to bed that night completely unaware of the horrors that would befall them before morning came. They would endure suffering in both their own wounds and pain as well as in seeing those they love wounded, in pain, and dying.

How do we respond to such intense suffering? Reaching out to others in their pain can call forth the best in us. It changes us, and shows us a side of ourselves that we may never have known existed. In a sense, it kindles a kind of fire within us that can be all-consuming in reaching out to others.

Flannery O'Connor, the insightful writer who lived with intense pain most of her life, said that pain and suffering has the ability to give you something you may not have had before you suffered: the ability to be compassionate. She said that once you take your eyes off your own pain and suffering and look outwards, everything will change for you. O'Connor wrote, "You will have found Christ when you are concerned with other people's sufferings and not your own." The beginning of compassion involves becoming aware of the suffering of others.

The winds that stirred up the flames that led to the Great Chicago Fire, as well as the fire storm that destroyed Preshtigo and the towns around it, stirred up something else as well. It stirred up an immense wave of love and compassion in the survivors and people who rushed in to heal the wounded.

In our own lives there are sure to be situations in which the people around us may be swallowed up by suffering. It will be for us to discover the small ember of compassion within us that will lead us to reach out to them.

October 9
Test Flights

A few years ago, when I was visiting one of my brothers in Florida, he and his wife took me to see a huge bird's nest. I had never seen a nest as large as this one; in fact, it turned out to be the nest of a bald eagle. That big nest made me a bit curious, so I did some research on eagles' nests.

I discovered that when a mother eagle builds her nest, she starts with some very unlikely things. At the base of the nest she arranges thorns, broken branches, sharp rocks, and a number of other items that don't seem like they belong in a nest housing helpless little birds. It seemed quite odd to me that such materials would be at the base of a nest.

As I read on, I discovered that after the mother eagle has finished the base layer, she lines the nest with a thick padding of wool, feathers, and fur from animals she has killed. This makes the nest soft and comfortable for the eggs. It is so soft and nice that by the time those baby eagles get to be flying age, the comfort of the nest and the luxury of free meals delivered right to their mouths makes them quite reluctant to leave. This is where the mother eagle's genius comes through.

Just as the baby eagles are getting used to the comforts of home, the mother eagle begins stirring up the nest. She uses her strong talons to pull up the thick carpet of fur and feathers, exposing the sharp rocks and branches and thorns underneath. As more of the bedding gets plucked up, the nest becomes more and more uncomfortable for the young eagles. Eventually, after being poked by thorns, sharp rocks, and sticks, as well as being pushed by the mother eagle, the growing eagles are prompted to leave their once comfortable home. The fledgling birds are forced to step out of the nest, fly, and move on to more mature behavior.

What is true for those baby eagles is also true of our spiritual life and development. There comes a time when our loving God will begin to stir up the comfortable nests of our lives so that our souls get exposed to thorns, sharp rocks, and sticks. This sharp discomfort, along with some strong pushing and shoving from above, will eventually force us to leave the nest and move on to a more mature spiritual life. Like those baby eagles that were once all snug and cozy in their soft nests, we will eventually be forced to step out and test our wings.

No doubt, like those fledgling eagles, we too will protest much and complain greatly about how terribly we are being treated. The truth of the matter is, however, we were not meant to lounge about in soft, comfortable nests. Rather, we are meant to soar in the heavens.

October 10
From a Tiny Seed

Scientists say that the most massive living thing on planet Earth is a tree. The particular tree they are talking about is called the General Sherman, and it is a giant sequoia found in central California's Sequoia National Park on the western slope of the Sierra Nevada Mountains. This tree is about 274.9 feet tall and has a girth of 102.6 feet near its base. It is estimated to weigh 2,756 tons. One more thing: it is approximately 2,200 years old. That is one big, old tree!

The most amazing thing about that massive tree is that its seeds, which I would expect to be big, are really quite small. They're described as being about the size of an oat flake, and according to the Guinness Book of World Records, they weigh only 1/6,000 of an ounce!

How interesting that the largest living thing on earth has its origins in a seed so tiny, so seemingly insignificant, that it weighs next to nothing. If you had never seen the massive sequoia, you might assume that the tiny sequoia seed would never amount to very much. The truth is, however, that something really big developed out of something incredibly small.

One of the fundamental teachings of Jesus was that the kingdom of God has its origins in the littlest of things. He often described it as like yeast hidden in dough or as another tiny seed, the mustard seed. It's the little things that lead to great things. It's that small drink of water we offer to a thirsty person, or the brief amount of time it takes to visit someone in prison or in a nursing home, or the relatively unimportant pieces of clothing we give to the homeless that can lead us directly into God's kingdom of love.

Little seeds of caring, little bits of encouragement offered to someone who is down on their luck, even a little smile that can change a stranger's dark day into something better; all of these things are the tiny seeds that build up the kingdom of God.

In your life right now, can you see a situation or two that may be calling for you to plant a few of those tiny seeds Jesus often taught his disciples to plant? Perhaps God is calling you to plant a tiny seed of love that will produce a giant sequoia of love for someone in your life today.

October 11
Something Greater

There are a lot of interesting stories that come out of ancient Greece. One of those stories concerns an artist who lived about 2,000 years ago, whose name was Timanthes. He became a very talented and able young artist under the direction of his art teacher, who had told him that one day he would produce great works of art.

Timanthes studied hard and worked at his craft until one day he produced a masterpiece of a painting. Crowds gather to see it and were amazed at how he had captured light and color and true beauty. Everyone said it was an exquisite work of art.

Unfortunately, Timanthes became so enraptured with his own painting that he spent days gazing at it. One morning, when he arose and walked over to look at and admire his work, he was shocked to find it blotted out with paint. Enraged that someone would do such a thing to his art, Timanthes ran to his teacher to tell him the horrible news.

To his surprise, his teacher admitted that he had destroyed the painting. "Why would you do such a terrible thing to me?" screamed Timanthes.

"I did it for your own good," his teacher replied. "That painting was retarding your progress. Start again, and see if you can do better. In fact, I dare you to do better."

For weeks Timanthes brooded and seethed with anger. In the end, though, he took his teacher's advice and produced a painting called *The Sacrifice of Iphigenia*, which is regarded as one of the finest paintings of antiquity.

Timanthes' teacher was able to see that his student had much more to give if only he could be set free, to move beyond himself. Isn't it amazing that any one of us can be held back by our own inability to see beyond what we've done, both good and bad? One of the greatest gifts anyone can give us is a push that moves us beyond what we have done to become something even greater.

OCTOBER 12
Out in the Cold

A couple of winters ago a big snowstorm struck the Midwest as well as the East Coast. The storm was massive and intense, causing most cities to declare emergencies. Schools were closed down along with government offices, banks, and businesses. Almost everything came to a standstill.

In the midst of this there a phrase that was used in almost all news reports and announcements made by the local authorities. Each report or announcement would declare the situation an emergency, then say only essential personnel should be on the streets: everyone else, all non-essential personnel, were to remain in their homes.

The words "essential personnel" are powerful. Just who are the essential personnel in a city? Well, I suppose they include the maintenance people, road crews, ambulance drivers, fire fighters, electric and gas company workers, truck drivers, and a whole host of service people who are taken for granted when things are running smoothly. These are the people we refer to as essential personnel.

Think about that phrase and what it means to be essential personnel. If there were a major crisis in your town, would you be included in the group of essential people? If you are not sure, think about what it would be like to be non-essential. That means you would not be needed, or perhaps even wanted. Being aware of this makes us consider a very disconcerting fact: the world can go on without some of us. Maybe nobody would even notice if we are gone, or even care. It's kind of scary, isn't it?

The good news is that in God's world, things are different than in our cities. In God's world we are all essential personnel. In God's world, everybody counts; everyone is needed, loved and included. There is a special place for each one of us in God's heart. No one is left out.

One of the greatest sources of pain for so many people in our world today is the sense that, in some way, those who should love them have abandoned them. They feel rejected, rebuffed, and forgotten. They feel left behind. These are the people who describe themselves as living on the fringes of the world. They are non-essential, not valued or wanted.

During winter a few years ago, I was serving food in a soup kitchen when a homeless man who had just come in from the cold said to the people in line, "Do any of you have friends or relatives out there in the cold? You better go get 'em and bring them here or they ain't gonna survive!"

That may be the best image anyone could paint of what can happen to people when they are made to feel non-essential and left out in the cold. Is there anyone like that in your life right now who needs to be brought in from the cold?

October 13
How Would You Answer?

Shortly after Pope Francis was elected, several news correspondents began to ask for interviews. In one of those first interviews, the Pope was asked this question, "If you were to sum up for the world just who is this new Pope Francis, what would you say?" Without hesitation Pope Francis replied, "I would say that I am a sinner. That's exactly who I am. I am a sinner, loved by God."

As I heard Pope Francis' response to the reporter's question I began to think of other well-known followers of Jesus who were humble enough to admit they were weak and in need of God's love. It was in admitting their weakness that they came to know God most deeply.

One of those folks was a great yet humble woman by the name of Corrie Ten Boom, a Christian who preached God's love through her witness of the suffering she and her family endured in a Nazi concentration camp. When the war was over she traveled all over the world preaching about the power of forgiveness. That forgiveness began when she came to know God wanted her to admit her own need for forgiveness. It was only then that she was compelled to forgive those who had done so much evil against her and her family. Her witness about forgiving our enemies through God's grace touched millions of lives.

At one point, Corrie Ten Boom was given an honorary degree and praised for all the good work she had done. During a press conference following the ceremony, one of the reporters asked her if it was difficult to remain humble while hearing so much acclaim.

She replied immediately, "I have never forgotten just who I am. Young man, when Jesus Christ rode into Jerusalem on Palm Sunday on the back of a donkey, and everyone was waving palm branches and throwing garments in the road and singing praises, do you think that for one moment it ever entered the head of the donkey that any of this was for him?" She continued, "If I can be the donkey on which Jesus Christ rides in his glory, I give him all the praise and all of the glory."

Corrie Ten Boom never forgot who she was. Like Pope Francis, she knew first and foremost that she was a woman who had been loved and forgiven by Jesus. Having been forgiven, from that day on, she knew she had to be an instrument of forgiveness and peace.

If a news correspondent were to ask you to sum up just who you are, as that reporter asked Pope Francis, how would you answer?

October 14
Pray for Clemency

In March of 1863, as a divided nation was on the edge of collapse, President Abraham Lincoln signed a proclamation establishing a national day of prayer and fasting. The words of that proclamation were quite profound and are just as fitting for our own time as they were for his. I have

Fr. Mark Burger

printed the words and put them in my Bible so that from time to time, I can read and consider them. Here is an excerpt from that proclamation.

"We have been the recipients of the choicest bounties of Heaven. We have been preserved, the many years, in peace and prosperity. We have grown in numbers, wealth and power, as no other nation has ever grown. But we have forgotten God. We have forgotten the gracious hand that preserved us in peace and multiplied and enriched and strengthened us; and we have vainly imagined, in the deceitfulness of our hearts that all these blessings were produced by some superior wisdom and virtue of our own. Intoxicated with unbroken success, we have become too self-sufficient to feel the necessity of redeeming and preserving grace, too proud to pray to God that made us It behooves us, then to humble ourselves before the offended Power, to confess our national sins, and to pray for clemency and forgiveness."

Those words never fail to affect me. They almost always lead me to a deeper prayer, to ask God, as Lincoln suggests, for clemency and forgiveness. Why not take these words to your own prayer?

October 15
Inner Peace and Calmness

I was having lunch with a friend this past week. As we were enjoying our meal, we looked out a nearby window and saw that the wind was kicking up. Trees began to bend to the wind and debris began swirling around on the ground. "My, look at that wind," my friend said. "A storm is surely coming."

She was certainly right, because within minutes there was a bright flash of lightening, a very loud clap of thunder, and with that, the skies opened up and a torrent of rain fell. The storm grew more and more intense as the lightning flashed and thunder boomed. I said, "I really love storms! They remind me that God is still in charge."

My friend smiled at me and said she hated storms, and had always been terrified by them. I replied that in the midst of this rather serious storm she looked very calm, cool, and at ease.

"Oh, looks can be so deceiving!" she laughed. "I learned a way to be calm during a storm from my mom when I was a young girl. She told me to remember one important sentence, and repeat it over and over during the storm. She told me if I did that, I would eventually be calm. In fact, when the wind started up a few minutes ago, I started saying that sentence over and over again in my mind."

"What sentence did she teach you?" I asked.

"Sometimes the Lord Jesus calms the storm, but most times he lets the storm go on and spends his time calming his child," she replied.

"Does that work?" I asked.

"It actually does!" she said. "It has seldom failed to bring me a sense of peace and an inner calmness. My good old mom knew what she was talking about."

I think my friend was right: her mom did know what she was talking about. If you find yourself in some kind of storm, be it weather-related or an inner storm, repeating those words my friend's mother taught her may bring you peace and inner calmness, too.

OCTOBER 16
God Abides

"And they urged him, saying, 'Abide with us: for it is toward evening, and the day is now far spent.' And he went in to abide with them" (Luke 24:29). Those words from the Gospel of Luke became vitally important to a friend of mine as he tried to cope with a cancer diagnosis he had received. His oncologist told him tests indicated that his cancer was in an advanced state, and things were pretty far along.

He asked his doctor, "Am I done for? Is there anything we can do to turn this thing around? What happens next?"

His doctor said something rather profound: "Well, we have some pretty strong and effective medications we can use, and there is something even more powerful than all of that, which is certainly available to you. Don't forget that God himself is here with us and he will remain with you all the time."

My friend said those kind words from his doctor were so helpful to him. He said that, in the middle of the night, after he had had his appointment with the oncologist, he woke up in a panic, terrified and not knowing how he would handle what was happening to him. He said he picked up his Bible and just opened it as he prayed, "God help me, I need you! Tell me what to do!"

Just as he finished speaking those words, his eyes fell on the part of Luke's Gospel that tells of the two disciples walking along the road to Emmaus, frightened because Jesus had been crucified. While they were still very confused and afraid, Jesus came along. He walked with them and talked with them, although they had no idea at the time it was Jesus. When they came to Emmaus, Jesus continued walking, and it was then the disciples said those famous words to him: "'Abide with us: for it is toward evening, and the day is now far spent.' And he went in to abide with them."

My friend realized those words were meant especially for him. As he looked at his health, he knew the cancer had spread and that, as far as his life was concerned, "the day is now far spent." He needed to feel God with him. He picked up his Bible, knelt down next to his bed, and spoke these words out loud: "Lord, abide with me for it seems that my life is almost over, and it is now far spent. Please stay with me!"

Perhaps you are in a place similar to my friend. Perhaps you too need to feel God in your life. There is no time like the present to speak the very same words my friend spoke, the same words those two disciples of Jesus spoke over two thousand years ago.

My friend has had some very difficult battles with cancer and is still fighting the disease. He tells everyone who will listen that he knows whatever happens to him, whatever he faces, he is not alone: God abides with him.

October 17
Garbage Trucks

A businessman tells of how his life was changed for the better by a taxi ride in New York City. He said it was on one of those very hectic days when nothing was going right and the whole day seemed headed for disaster.

At one point, he needed to be at a meeting across town, so he hopped into a cab and headed for the meeting. He said, "It wasn't long into that taxi ride, driving in the right lane, when suddenly a black car jumped out of a parking space right in front of us. The taxi driver slammed on his brakes, skidded, and missed the other car by just inches! Then the driver of the other car turned completely sideways and started yelling at us. The taxi driver just smiled and waved at the guy, being really friendly. So I asked, 'Why did you just do that? This guy almost ruined your car and sent us to the hospital!'"

The businessman then said that his driver explained his philosophy of the road for driving a taxi in heavy traffic every day. He said that, the way he sees life, many people are like garbage trucks. They run around full of garbage, full of frustration, full of anger, and full of disappointment, full of bitterness and foul emotions. As their garbage piles up, they need a place to dump it and sometimes they'll dump it on you.

The taxi driver said he had learned to not take it personally, but rather just to smile, wave, wish them well, and move on. He said he never takes their garbage and spreads it to other people at work, home, or on the streets. He concluded by saying, "The bottom line is that good people just do not let garbage trucks take over their day. Life isn't meant to be lived in anger and bitterness."

How do you handle the garbage trucks that drive through your day?

October 18
The Two Kinds of Reality

Most people strive to be in control of their lives. And while we like to believe we are in control, in reality we know we certainly are not. Our American tradition teaches that if we work hard enough, make sure we concentrate, and put enough time into something we can, as it is commonly expressed, pull ourselves up by our own bootstraps. We like to think of ourselves as self-sufficient and capable of just about anything we put our minds to.

In thinking about this I've had some interesting discoveries, and came across something I read back in seminary days. It was an insight from an Episcopal priest who gave a retreat I attended, and although I wrote down what he said, I failed to write down the priest's name. Here's what he said: "Let's face it, there are two kinds of reality in this world of ours. There are the things you have to work for, and there are the things you have to wait for."

I have found that to be so very true. As much as we want things to be a certain way, we can only do so much on our own to make it happen. The one thing that proves more than anything else we are not in control is the fact that sometimes we simply have to wait for things to work themselves out. For example, you cannot rush the process of grief. We cannot just will ourselves to feel better or to simply get over it. It just doesn't work that way. When you have surgery, you cannot recover any faster than it takes nature and your body to do so. You can fidget all you want and push yourself all you want but real recuperation, real healing, takes the time it takes. It cannot be rushed.

There was something else the Episcopal priest told us. He said that as future priests, we were preparing to be healers. He told us that the most important thing any healer needs to know is, all true healing comes from God and not from us. We can be instruments of God's healing power, but it is God's power, not ours. And I remember one other thing he taught us: all wounds are healed by degrees, just as much or as little as each day will bear.

Are you looking for healing right now? Are there people in your life who desperately need things to change? Are there things you have been working hard to achieve only to find that you simply cannot get there? Perhaps what you are so diligently working at achieving is something over which you are powerless.

There are many things that require us to do the one thing we hate most: to wait. Perhaps you are being asked to wait for God to do what God does best, and that is healing.

OCTOBER 19
A Funny Bridge

One of the duties of being the vice president of the United States is to preside over the U. S. Senate. The vice president keeps order during debates and can vote to break a tie if necessary.

On one occasion when Vice President Calvin Coolidge was presiding over the Senate, the debate grew so intense that one senator angrily told another to go "straight to hell." This behavior did not sit well with the members of the Senate, and there was a bit of a commotion.

Finally, the offended senator complained to Coolidge as presiding officer. Coolidge, wanting to do his best, looked up from the book he had been leafing through while listening to the debate. "I've been looking through the rule book," he said. "You don't have to go, if you don't want to."

It is said that the remark broke the tension in the room, and eventually things calmed down enough for the Senate to complete its work that day.

Isn't it amazing how often a little bit of humor can save the day just when disagreements, differences, and emotions seem to be headed out of control? The ability to laugh, especially at ourselves, is a wonderful gift. Sometimes we take ourselves too seriously, and thereby lose our perspective on life. Have you even taken yourself so seriously that you ended up feeling isolated from family, loved ones, and colleagues? It's a common human experience.

I think Calvin Coolidge knew a bit about human nature, and he knew exactly how to break the tension that day in the Senate. By adding a touch of humor to the day's debate, he built a bridge that those bickering senators could cross over and be friends again.

Is there a situation in your life right now that calls for a funny bridge?

OCTOBER 20
Take Note

One of my favorite places to visit is a cemetery. To some folks that may sound strange, but I have always found cemeteries to be quiet, peaceful places. I enjoy walking through them, reading the gravestones, praying for the dead, and thinking about what their lives must have been like. For me a walk through a cemetery gives me a good sense of how short our time here on earth really is, and it reminds me to truly savor the time I have with those I love.

Whenever I take a walk in one of our local cemeteries I think of the verse that is carved on a grave marker in a county cemetery in England. It reads:

> Pause my friend, as you walk by as you are now, so once was I As I am now so you will be Prepare my friend, to follow me.

Those words never fail to help me keep things in perspective. Time is precious and I want to make very good use of it. Our tendency is to think we have all the time in the world, and so we rather easily put off important things, thinking we will get to them someday. The people in those graves I visit probably did the very same thing until the day they realized their time was running out.

The prophetic author of that verse carved into the gravestone in an English cemetery has rightly warned us that time marches on, and we need to take note of it.

October 21
Are You?

Are you an honest person? How honest are you? I was asked those two questions by a couple of kids from our school. They said they were doing a report on telling the truth, and their questions got me thinking.

There's a story about a pastor who was walking down the street when he came upon a group of kids surrounding a dog. Concerned that the kids might be hurting the dog, he went over to investigate and asked, "Hey guys, what's going on?"

One the kids replied, "This dog is just a stray we found. We all want to take him home, but only one of us can. So we've decided that the one who can tell the biggest lie gets to keep the dog."

Now, of course the pastor was shocked. "You kids shouldn't be having a lie-telling contest!" He then launched into a ten-minute sermon about the evils of lying. "Don't you kids know that lying breaks the eighth commandment, Do not bear false witness? Why, when I was your age, I never told a single lie."

The kids began to look at their feet, and there was dead silence for about a minute. Just when the pastor began to think he'd gotten through to them, the smallest kid gave a deep sigh and said, "All right, give him the dog."

Honesty and integrity are supposed to be the hallmarks of the followers of Jesus. When Michelangelo painted the magnificent frescoes on the ceiling of the Sistine chapel, lying on his back for endless hours to finish every detail with great care, a friend asked him why he took such pains with work that would be viewed from such a considerable distance. His friend asked, why didn't he do some quick sketch, paint it, and be done? "After all," the friend said, "Who will notice whether it's perfect or not?"

Michelangelo looked at his friend for quite a while and finally whispered, "I will. Even if I could lie to the world, I could never lie to myself."

Are you an honest person? How honest are you?

October 22
Echo

Consider this little scenario: A young, inexperienced second lieutenant at Fort Bragg discovered that he didn't have the right change to buy a soft drink from a vending machine. At that very moment a young private was passing by, so he called him over and asked, "Do you have change for a dollar?"

The private said cheerfully, "I'm pretty sure I do, but let me take a look."

The lieutenant, remembering that he was a lieutenant in the army and he was talking with a private, drew himself up stiffly and said, "Soldier, that is no way to address a superior officer. We'll start all over again, only this time, show me the respect I deserve. Do you have change for a dollar?"

The private came to attention, saluted smartly, looked the lieutenant straight in the eye, and said, "No, sir!"

How much respect do you think that private had for the second lieutenant? I would imagine whatever amount of respect he had at the beginning of the exchange was certainly much less at the conclusion of their transaction.

I had a priest-mentor when I was in seminary who would tell me that if I expected to earn respect from others, I always had to be the first to show respect. He also taught that if you expect to be treated kindly, be kind. If you want to be understood, strive to understand. If you want to be loved, work at being loving. He would always finish up by mentioning that old cliché – what goes around, comes around.

I guess it's like an echo: What you send out will eventually come back to you.

October 23
His Good Friend

One of the most important questions we could ever ask ourselves is simply this: What am I becoming?

Back in the fourth century, there was a Roman soldier by the name of Martin who sought to answer that very question. He had trained in the Roman army and that was his life. Yet something was happening inside him that he didn't completely understand. It was as if he was being led to be something more than he was, but he couldn't put his finger on just what it was.

One thing kept coming to his attention. He had heard about the followers of Jesus Christ, and he was curious about the life they led and the teachings of their master. The more Martin investigated, the more intrigued he was by the apparent happiness of those who followed the Christian way of life. The more he learned about the group, the more something stirred within him.

After years of trying to understand the teachings of Jesus, Martin was on patrol when he met a nearly naked man standing in the middle of the road on a very cold winter's day. Martin felt sorry for the man, who was shivering in the damp coldness. He thought he might give the man some money, but realized it would do him little good out there in the bitter cold. So Martin took off his soldier's cloak, drew his sword, cut the cloak in two, and gave half the coat to the beggar. Martin wished the man well and continued on his way.

That night Martin dreamed he saw Heaven. There were thousands of angels there, and also a man he immediately knew was Jesus. As he looked at Jesus, Martin noticed he was wearing a torn military cloak. One of the angels present asked, "Master, why do you wear that battered cloak?" Jesus replied, "My good friend Martin gave it to me."

Martin's disciple and biographer Sulpicius Severus states that as a consequence of this vision Martin, "flew to be baptized so as to belong to Jesus." Today that Roman soldier turned Christian is known as Saint Martin of Tours. From the day of his baptism, Martin spent his life trying to lead others to his good friend, Jesus. For Martin of Tours, his friendship with Jesus defined who he was.

The dream in which Martin heard Jesus refer to him as a "good friend" helped Martin of Tours determine just who and what he was to become – Jesus' good friend.

What are you becoming?

October 24
Fighting the Good Fight

One of my favorite verses in the New Testament comes from Saint Paul, from a time when he felt his work, his life, and his suffering might be coming to an end. He realized that he was just about spent and weary from his travels to preach the gospel. Paul wrote to his friend Timothy and said, "For I am already being poured out as a libation, and the time of my departure has come; I have fought the good fight, I have finished the race, I have kept the faith" (2 Timothy 4:6-7).

Have you ever felt worthless or useless, finished, spent, or washed up? Most of us have experienced failure, loss, or feelings of depression. It's part of the human condition, and it can take a heavy toll on us. It can also produce some remarkable works of genius.

One rather famous person dealt with depression all his life. In fact he was so depressed and low that his colleagues thought it best to keep all knives and razors out of his reach. As the man looked back on his dark times and recalled how he felt, he wrote, "I would begin to think that I am now the most miserable man living. Whether I shall ever be better, I cannot tell. I awfully forebode I shall not."

Abraham Lincoln wrote those words. He carried a heavy burden throughout his life, enduring a terrible sorrow that often seemed relentless to him. In the end, however, he was able to rise above his own personal suffering and set about healing a divided nation. His own suffering made him very much aware of the suffering around him, and filled him with the desire to set others free.

Other famous folks from history have dealt with depression as well. The composer George Frederick Handel endured much suffering throughout his life, and he would try to find solace in his music, although he felt like a failure as a musician. His most famous work, *The Messiah*, was written during one of the worst times of his life, after he had suffered a devastating stroke. During this time, he experienced a particularly deep night of gloom and despair over his failures, and the next morning, locked himself in his room. Determined to fight his way through the darkness, he dug deeply into his creative genius and, working nonstop, composed a musical score that continues to thrill and inspire music lovers to this day.

Those wonderful words of Saint Paul – "I have fought the good fight, I have finished the race, I have kept the faith" – certainly could apply to Abraham Lincoln and George Frederick Handel. They can also apply to you and me and countless others who daily fight the good fight to overcome the darkness that can threaten to overwhelm us.

God has given all of us a remarkable ability to endure, to take the very thing that may drain us and turn it into something life giving for ourselves and others.

October 25
Awake

Christopher Columbus died in the year 1506 in the city of Valladolid, Spain. To commemorate his life and great discoveries, his devoted followers built a monument to him.

One of the interesting features of that monument is a statue of a lion destroying one of the Latin words that had been part of Spain's national motto for centuries. Before Columbus made his discoveries of the New World, the Spanish people thought there were no more worlds to be discovered, that earth as they knew it was all there was. Because that was the common belief, Spain's national motto was "Ne Plus Ultra," which translates as, "No More Beyond." They truly believed there was nothing more to be discovered. With the voyages of Columbus, all that changed!

So right there, in the midst of that great monument to Columbus, is a statue of a lion tearing the Latin word "Ne," or "No," out of the national motto. The new motto would then be "Plus Ultra," or "More Beyond." Christopher Columbus had shown the Spaniards – indeed, the whole world – that there is always "more beyond."

We all need to be reminded from time to time that there's more to life than what we can see or even imagine. God has so much goodness to give us that we can never really take it all in. Sometimes the daily grind of living can make us numb to the deeper, richer aspects of life. There is so much more than we know right around us, if only we take the time to pay attention.

A wise man once said that he prayed to wake up and be aware there is always more to know, more to experience, and more to become. Perhaps this would be a good prayer for us today: "O Lord, wake me up and make me more aware!"

October 26
When Tears Speak for Us

When she heard through one of her servants that a local woman had just lost her baby to illness, Queen Victoria did an extraordinary thing. The Queen, who was famous for the depth of her grief at the loss of her husband, was unsettled by the news of the baby's death and felt moved to express her sympathy.

Queen Victoria called for her driver to take her to the woman's home so she could visit. After she left, the neighbors gathered around the mother and asked what the queen had said. "Nothing," replied the grieving mother. "She simply put her hands on mine, and tears began to roll down the queen's face. Then we silently wept together. She didn't have to say anything; her tears spoke for us both."

If you have ever been afraid to visit with someone who has lost a loved one, thinking you might not know exactly what to say, don't be. Perhaps Queen Victoria's example can teach you that in times of grief, what we say is not as important as what we simply do. Sometimes it's our simple presence, or our tears or another simple gesture, which will speak what needs to be spoken.

October 27
The Shape We Are In

In the mail the other day I received a thank you note from some friends of mine. It was a wonderfully thoughtful note, and one of the things I liked most about it was the quotation on the front of the card. It was a quote from Eleanor Roosevelt: "One's philosophy is not best expressed in words. It is expressed in the choices one makes. In the long run, we shape our lives and we shape ourselves. The process never ends until we die. And the choices we make are ultimately our responsibility."

I propped that card up on my desk so I could see it and think about it as I moved through my day. That card has been a blessing because it got me thinking. I became aware of the fact that I make so many choices each day that I am probably numb to most of them, and therefore may not be thinking enough about the implications each choice has for the future.

The last thing I had to do the day I received that thank you note was attend a prayer group. Before we began our prayers, I shared the Eleanor Roosevelt quote with the group. They loved it and began to discuss it at length. One woman said she had a bookmark in her Bible with a saying on it about the choices we make, and it had given her much to think about. The quotation was: "The hardest choice we have to make in life is which bridges to cross and which ones to burn."

What kind of shape are you in as a result of the choices you have made?

October 28
Just Be Good

A student once asked me a simple question, "What can I do to be a truly happy person?" I shared with him what I had learned during my time in the desert: When you slow down enough you start to realize that we all spend too much time chasing things in the hope of being happy. The Desert Fathers would tell their disciples that the first and most important thing they needed to do was simply go about being a good person. They told the story of a wise old cat that observed a kitten running after its tail.

"Why are you chasing after your tail so?" asked the old wise cat.

The kitten stopped and replied, "I have learned that the best thing for a cat is happiness. I have been assured that happiness is in my tail. Therefore, I am chasing it, and when I catch it, I shall have happiness."

The wise old cat replied, "I too have been assured that happiness is in my tail. But I have noticed that whenever I go about running after it, it keeps running away from me. And when I just go about my business of being a good and wholesome cat, my tail seems to come after me wherever I go. You will never find happiness by running and chasing after it. You must simply go about being good and wholesome and it will surely find you."

October 29
How Good?

A young man had just been hired to work at a local bank. He was very excited, as this was his first job and he was eager to do well at it. He was a very good worker and it wasn't long before his fellow workers got to like him very much.

One day his boss called him into his office and told him, "If Mr. Jones calls for me, just tell him I'm out."

The young man replied, "Oh, are you planning to go somewhere?"

"No, I just don't want to speak to him, so tell him I'm out."

The young man left his boss's office confused and scratching his head. The novice worker didn't know what to do because he just couldn't tell someone his boss was out if he wasn't. So he went back to his boss.

"Let me make sure I understand: Are you telling me you want me to lie for you?"

The boss flew into a rage and began to scream at him. He was so outraged that he said, "Give me one good reason why I shouldn't fire you on the spot!"

The trembling young worker thought about it for a minute or two, then stood up straight and said, with as much courage as he could muster: "You shouldn't fire me. You should be happy, because if I won't lie for you, isn't it safe to assume that I won't lie *to* you? My father always told me that a good man always tells the truth and will lie for no one. I want to be a good man."

How good are you?

Fr. Mark Burger

October 30
Under the Influence

Some college students went out and got drunk. When they got back to the dorm, one of their buddies was so intoxicated that he passed out. His friends decided to play a prank on him so they spread Limburger cheese on his upper lip and left him there passed out. When he woke up the young man sniffed, looked around, and said, "This room stinks!" He then walked into the hall and said, "This hall smells awful!" Leaving the dormitory he exclaimed, "The whole damn world stinks!"

As funny as that little prank is, it can serve as a parable for us. How often do our friends influence us? That passed-out college student's perception of the world was so cleverly influenced by his friends that he thought the whole world smelled foul! It isn't too much of a reach for us to realize that our own close friends can surely influence how we experience the world, too.

There is an important moral to this story and it is simply this: One of the most important decisions we make in life is who our friends are. Think of your friends. How are they influencing you today? What kind of influence do you have on them?

October 31
Fading

Sitting in a doctor's office waiting to see the doctor, I became aware of a good number of fellow patients who looked quite sick. I was just there for my usual check-up, but some of the folks looked to be seriously ill. I wondered what the sickest of them were thinking as they waited to see their doctors. Many of the sickest ones appeared to be the calmest, or perhaps the most accustomed to waiting.

As I was thinking these thoughts, the woman next to me struck up a conversation with me. She said, "As I get older and older, I feel like God is telling me to get ready to pull up stakes and head out to the next world."

"Are you seriously ill?" I asked.

"Oh, not really, but I am just getting to a point where I realize that I'm kind of fading a bit each day. Each day a little less of me is here, and each day a little more of me seems to be heading to the other side." She looked down at the floor as she said that. I was just about to respond when her name was called and she went in to see the doctor. I thought about what she had said to me, and wondered how much of me was fading into the next world.

The next day I read something from the life of Malcolm Muggeridge. He was a British journalist who spent most of his life as an agnostic, but eventually converted to Christianity when he was in his sixties. Years later, due to the influence of Mother Teresa of Calcutta, he became a Catholic. As he got older he wrote more and more about his faith, and one item from his writings reminded me of what the woman in the doctor's office had said about fading. Here's what Muggeridge wrote:

"When you're old as I am, there are all sorts of extremely pleasant things that happen to you.... the pleasantest of all is that you wake up in the night and you find that you are half in and half out of your battered old carcass. It seems quite a tossup whether you go back and resume full occupancy of your mortal body, or make off toward the bright glow you see in the sky, the lights of the city of God."

I wonder if that lady at the doctor's office has had that same experience? The truth of the matter is, however, both Malcolm Muggeridge and the older woman are on to something. They're aware of the fact that life leads somewhere. It has a purpose and a direction. They both experienced God's gentle pull to the next life. Muggeridge said the experience was a pleasant one, and that it consoled rather than alarmed him.

Do you know that your life has a purpose and a direction? Have you felt God's gentle invitation to pull up stakes and move on?

November

NOVEMBER 1
Checking In

I read a story about the Canadian man who left the snow-filled streets of Calgary for a vacation in Florida. His wife was on a business trip and was planning to meet him there the next day. When he reached his hotel, he decided to send his wife a quick email message. Unable to find the scrap of paper on which he had written her email address, he did his best to type it from memory. Unfortunately, he missed one letter in the address and his note was directed instead to an elderly preacher's wife, whose husband had passed away only the day before.

When the grieving widow read her email, she took one look at the computer, let out a scream, and fell to the floor in a dead faint. At the sound, her family rushed into the room and saw this note on the screen: Honey, just checked in. Everything prepared for your arrival tomorrow. P.S. Sure is hot down here!

I wanted to begin with that little story because the month of November is traditionally, for us Catholics, the month we set aside to honor and remember our loved ones who have "checked in" to the next world. November first is set aside as a celebration of those who are in Heaven, and thus we call that day the Feast of All Saints. The second day of the month is called All Souls Day, and it is a day set aside to pray for the dead and for those making the transition from this life to the next. It's also a good day to pray for those we know and love who may be in their last days, who need our prayerful support

If you were to take a moment or two to think about it, who are the "saints" in your family tree who have made a deep impression on you? Who among your friends, classmates, or co-workers are the people whom you hold dear as your heroes or heroines? These first days of November are a good time to remember them and honor them.

Jesus told the apostles he was going to prepare a place for us, and he would come back to take us with him so that where he is we may also be. Those are some of the most comforting words in the Bible, and it is good for us to recall them.

All Saints Day and All Souls Day are powerful celebrations of the power of prayer to help those who are "checking in" to where everything is prepared for them.

NOVEMBER 2
Thank You Notes

As we begin the month of November I am remembering something that happened just last week. A young woman, a former parishioner of mine, sent me an email asking if I would be willing to be a reference for her as she had recently applied for a new job. Before I finished reading her email, my cell phone began to ring. It was someone from the human resources department of the company with whom that young woman was interviewing.

The director of the HR department asked if I could write a letter of recommendation for my former parishioner. As we talked about what kind of information the company was seeking, I remember saying, "I think you're not looking for a letter of recommendation, but a letter that details what I appreciate about her – more like a letter of appreciation, right?"

There was a pause. The HR director cleared her throat and said, "Well, I've never heard it put that way before, but I guess that's exactly what we are asking." There was another pause, then she added, "I guess that's how people with your calling see these sorts of things."

I laughed and said, "I suppose we do think of it in that way. I guess letters of recommendation really are letters of appreciation. I'm hoping all of you doing the interview will see what I have seen and come to appreciate about my former parishioner. She truly is a remarkable person."

The HR lady thanked me and we concluded our conversation. As I went about my day I began to think about just what I would write in that letter of appreciation. The more I thought about it, the more I began to realize that I was on to something bigger than just a letter.

I came up with an idea that this month of November could be seen as a Month of Appreciation. After all, we Catholics celebrate two beautiful feasts in the first two days of this month – All Souls Day and All Saints Day. Both of those feasts are meant to make us mindful of the people we know and love who have died and gone ahead of us. We could set aside these days to recall just what we appreciate about our relatives and friends who have died, and for whom we may still be grieving. Then I thought about what I would write to some of my deceased family members or friends if I were to write them a thank you note or a letter of appreciation.

In addition to those two great November feasts, there's also another great celebration, Thanksgiving, to consider. Wouldn't it be a great idea to take a few minutes this month as Thanksgiving Day approaches, to write out a few thank you notes to the people we truly love and appreciate? Imagine what it would be like for the members of our families if they unexpectedly received a little note of thanks from us as a way of celebrating Thanksgiving?

I finished my letter of appreciation for my former parishioner, and dutifully sent it off to the HR department. Now I am going to get started on some notes of appreciation for the people who have blessed my life. It may take some time, but I'm sure it will be time well spent.

In this wonderful month of November, how about trying to write a few thank you notes to some of the folks who continue each day to bless your life? I'll bet if you take the time to do this little simple gesture of affection you will never regret it.

November 3
Have You Missed It?

There's a story about a young man who was told by his parents that life is a gift from God, meant to make us ready for the good things that will come in the next life. He listened to them and laughed. "I've got my whole life ahead of me. It's silly to worry about death," he said. And so the young man dismissed what his parents had said.

A few weeks later, in the middle of the night, he woke up to find a frightening being at the end of his bed. "Who are you?" he cried.

"I am the angel of death."

"Is my time up?"

"Not yet," said the angel. "Before I come to take you, I will send my messengers to warn you that your time is near." Then the angel disappeared.

Relieved, the young man fell asleep.

The years went by, and he thought, "I've got plenty of time to make my peace with God. I've got plenty of time to get things together. There have been no messengers." And he dismissed his parents' words again.

That night he woke to find the angel of death sitting on the end of his bed again.

"W-what are you doing here?" he stammered.

"I've come for you," replied the angel.

"But you can't. I mean, I'm not ready."

"Well, I've kept my part of the bargain. I sent my messengers."

"What messengers?"

"How could you miss them? I sent you little reminders all of the time. Messengers like your grey hair, your wrinkles, your failing eyesight, and even your failing memory. Each of these messengers was sent to you to remind you that life is very short. And now, your time is up."

The angel continued, "What have you done with your life? Have you used it well? Has your love of God and others deepened over the years? Although your physical eyesight may have grown weaker, has your spiritual insight grown stronger over the years? Though your body has grown weaker, has your soul gathered strength from the blessings God has poured into your life?"

Then the angel asked a very scary question: "Have you been paying attention, or has your life come to a close and you only now realize that you have missed most of it?"

Have you noticed the "little messengers" that have come your way, meant to remind you life is very short? Are you paying attention to what God is doing in your life, or have you missed it?

NOVEMBER 4
A Wind-born Blessing

In the year 2737 B.C., a Chinese emperor by the name of Shen Nung discovered something he considered extraordinary. The emperor was resting comfortably under a tree as his servant was boiling some water. A breeze began to stir, and some leaves from the tree fell into the pot of boiling water. As the pot continued to boil the leaves colored the water and gave it a captivating aroma.

Intrigued by the aroma, the emperor drank some of the newly flavored water and was overwhelmed with the taste of it. From that day on he has been credited with discovering tea. He is said to have commented that it was as if heaven had dropped this gift down to him so his life might be made more pleasant, and daily problems washed away in a pleasing aroma and wonderful taste. The emperor felt that a breeze from above had blown him a true blessing.

Has God ever given you a gift that has made your life more pleasant, and washed away the grit and grime of daily problems? Have you found the "tea" that enriches and blesses your life? Why not take some time today to see if God has sent a gift-laden breeze your way to bless your daily life?

NOVEMBER 5
A Voice on the Other Side of the Door

Do you ever spend any time thinking about Heaven? I guess most of us think about it from time to time, especially if we are attending a funeral or know someone who is near death. I bring this up because for Catholics, November is a month set aside to remember and pray for the dead.

Accordingly, I was thinking about this the other day as I was going through a series of folders that I found in the back of one of my desk drawers. The folders contained some of my notes and papers from a Bible study that I had attended a few years ago with some friends. I enjoyed reading over some of the notes, and in the process I came across the following story.

A minister related the story of a dying man who asked his Christian doctor to tell him about the place to which he was going. As the doctor fumbled for a reply, he heard a scratching at the door, and he had his answer.

"Do you hear that?" he asked his patient. "It's my dog. I left him downstairs, but he has grown impatient, and has come up because he hears my voice. He has no notion what is inside this door, but he knows I am here. Isn't it the same with you? You don't know what lies beyond the door, but you know that your Master is there."

When was the last time you thought about the end of your life and what comes after that? Have you spent time considering your eternal future? What do you think Heaven will be like?

NOVEMBER 6
Living Up to Our Name

When I was in seminary we were required to study Greek. As part of our studies we would be given historical pieces to translate from Greek into English. One bit of translation I still remember is an ancient account of Alexander the Great.

According to the story, one day a very unkempt and rude soldier was brought before Alexander for disobeying orders, fighting, and drunkenness. He could be sentenced to death for any one of those offenses, but Alexander decided to let the man plead his own case. When the soldier had finished speaking, the all-powerful leader asked him, "Soldier, what is your name?"

The soldier is said to have swallowed hard, then replied, "My name is Alexander, sir." Staring the man in the eye, Alexander the Great commanded, "Change your name, soldier, or change your ways. You cannot act the way you have and bear my name. Change your ways, change your name, or your life is at an end!"

When this was read in class, the professor said that during the persecution of Christians in the early days of the Church, some of the Christians would quote Alexander the Great to the Christians who, out of fear, wanted to give up the practice of their faith. They would say to them, "If you would sell your soul to be safe, you must change your ways or change your name because you cannot be called Christian and live they way of cowardice. Change your ways or change your name."

The professor would then say, "If you were to examine the way you live, could you be challenged as some of those weak first Christians were, to 'Change your ways or change your name'?" It made us students think more about what it meant to call oneself a Christian. It's not just a philosophy, or a kind of club or fraternity, or even just a religion: it's a personal relationship of faithfulness. The name implies a commitment.

Finishing the translation revealed that Alexander the Great did pardon that soldier. Further, it was said that the soldier did, in fact, change his ways and even lived up to his name.

In the same way, Jesus pardons us when we go astray, and we, like that soldier, ought to strive to do our best to live up to the name "Christian."

November 7
Declaring Your Freedom

On July 4, 1776, a printer named John Dunlap of Philadelphia printed an estimated 200 copies of the brand new Declaration of Independence. He began to distribute them as quickly as he could so the whole world might know that freedom was born in the United States of America. Those who received copies of the Declaration treasured them. Today, however, it is believed that only twenty-four copies of Mr. Dunlap's first printing of the Declaration still exist.

In the summer of 1989, a flea market enthusiast from Philadelphia bought a painting of a farm scene for the princely sum of four dollars. When he brought the painting home, his wife hated it. The painting was quite old and very dirty. In the end the man and his wife decided to trash the painting, but keep the frame.

When the couple removed the frame they found a folded-up piece of paper hidden behind the painting. Opening the paper they discovered a copy of the Declaration of Independence – which turned out to be one of Mr. Dunlap's original copies. The couple's friends urged them to have the document authenticated and appraised. In 2000, Sotheby's auctioned that copy of the Declaration and it sold for $8.14 million.

That document is quite valuable, yet no document is as valuable as freedom itself. What price would you put on your freedom? It is so precious to us, yet we often take it for granted. When I was in seminary we studied the concept of freedom in one of my philosophy courses. I will never forget the definition of freedom that our professor gave us. He said, "True freedom is not the ability to do whatever you wish to do. True freedom is the ability to choose to do the right thing."

If that is the true definition of freedom, how free are you? Do you feel that you are free enough to do the right thing even if the people around you ridicule you, put you down, or even attack you for your choice? Do you feel free enough to be the person God is calling you to be? If not, can you truly say that you are free? If yes, just how much is that freedom worth? I think it is worth a lot more than $8.14 million, don't you?

NOVEMBER 8
When in Doubt

Every day on his way to work, a man passed by a jewelry store. He would always slow down a bit as he passed the store and set his watch by the big clock in the window.

One day the jeweler just happened to be standing in his doorway. He greeted the man in a friendly way and said, "I see you set your watch by my clock. What kind of work do you do that demands such correct time each day?"

"I'm the watchman at the plant down the street," said the man. "I have to know the exact time because one of my jobs is to blow the five o'clock whistle for the end of the shift."

The jeweler was startled. "You are kidding me, aren't you? Tell me that you really aren't doing that!"

"I sure am. Every day I walk by here, get the correct time from your clock, and then I know exactly when to blow the whistle."

"Oh no, I don't believe it," the jeweler blurted out. "Every day I set my clock by your five o'clock whistle!"

The jeweler in the story had discovered the truth of an old saying I learned from a priest who was an advisor to me when I was in seminary.

Whenever I came to him with some difficult decision, doubts, or a problem to work out, he would say, "Mark, there will always be doubt and uncertainty in your life, so you had better get used to it." Then he would quote something his father had said to him years earlier: "A man with one watch knows what time it is. A man with two watches is never quite sure."

Sometimes in life we become aware that not everything is as clear as it once was. Life experience has a way of making us see things differently. In his later years, the Methodist minister, John Wesley, made a very important observation. He said, "When I was young I was sure of everything; in a few years, having been mistaken a thousand times, I was not half so sure of most things as I was before; at present, I am hardly sure of anything but what God has revealed to me about His love."

Have you ever felt like John Wesley? Have you ever felt like that jeweler above, a bit shaken by the fact that sometimes what we had relied on has proved to be not so reliable? If you have, welcome to the human race! Doubt and uncertainty are very much a part of our common human experience. Yet even though doubt and uncertainty can be uncomfortable, almost every great discovery, every great movement forward in learning, in understanding, and in real growth has its origin in some "crack" in our view of life. Very often, doubt forces our eyes open to discover something entirely new and unexpected.

If you are feeling unsure and doubtful, don't be afraid. Remember that doubt can push us to the very edge of discovering something new.

November 9
Finding Your Diet

A naturalist observed that both the hummingbird and the vulture fly over our nation's deserts. As he studied their habits he noticed that each has a specific goal in mind as they fly over the world below. The vultures open their eyes wide and all they see is rotting meat, because that is what they are looking for. They thrive on that diet and do a great service for the world by cleaning up the carcasses that litter the ground.

Now the hummingbirds, on the other hand, ignore the smelly flesh of dead animals. Instead, they are on the lookout for the bright flowers of the desert plants. The vultures have chosen to live on what was. In a way they live on the past, and fill themselves with what is dead and gone. But hummingbirds live on what is. They seek new life. They fill themselves with freshness and sweet nectar. Each bird finds what it is looking for, and is nourished by what it finds.

If you stop to think about it, isn't that what we all do? We tend to find what we go looking for, and when it is found, it feeds us. The question that surfaces is this: What are you looking for in life and what is it feeding in you? That is a very important question.

NOVEMBER 10
God and Braided Hair

I had a conversation recently with a college student who wanted me to prove that God exists. He was telling me that his college philosophy courses had convinced him there is no God.

I said to him, "If you are convinced by your philosophy studies that there is no God, why do you need me to convince you that there is? Perhaps you are not really convinced that there is no God."

He thought a bit, then said, "Well, is there a God?"

I told him that his question reminded me of another conversation I recently had. I was talking with one of our grade school girls, who told me she and her friends were going to learn how to braid hair. "My friend's mom does hair for a living, and she is going to show us how it's done," she explained. I asked if she knew anything at all about how to braid hair, and she thought about it for a little while. Then she said, "A braid looks like it takes only two clumps of hair, but really it takes three!" (I didn't know hair came in clumps!)

"I didn't know that." I said to her.

She told me, "If you use only two clumps, I think the braid will come apart."

"Every braid I have ever seen looks to me like it has two clumps of hair," I said.

"Well you're wrong! It may look like two but it has to have three or it won't work. You gotta trust me on this," she said laughing.

"How do you know?" I asked.

"Cause girls know this kind of thing," she said.

There was a pause in our conversation. Then she spoke again. "You can't see the third clump" because it's like glue that disappears when you use it. You can't see it but you know it's there 'cause everything is still sticking together."

I thought about it for a moment and then said, "Well it's kind of like God in a person's life. You may think he is not there but by the way everything is sticking together, he must be there, right?"

She looked at me, giggled, and said, "You don't know a thing about braiding hair, do you?"

November 11
Flowing Freely

Here's an image to consider. There was a beautiful lake that was so clear and clean and cold and refreshing that animals from miles around came to drink from it. People too came to swim and to enjoy its beauty.

One year, however, after a spring of unusually heavy rains, the lake began to slowly change. It was not really apparent in the beginning, but over time it began to lose its appeal. The water that once had been clear and fresh was now covered with a green scum. The animals became ill from drinking the water. A foul odor filled the air and people who had been drawn to the lake now stayed clear of it.

Finally, someone who knew about the workings of lakes came and investigated the situation. Apparently, great piles of debris had been collecting from those heavy spring rains, and the accumulation had stopped up the dam and prevented the free flow of water. It not only stopped the flow of water into the lake, but also hindered the flow out of the lake. Work crews came and cleared the spillways, and soon the lake was fresh and clean again. The water flowed freely in and out, and the lake was once again pure.

Doesn't the same principle apply to you and me as human beings? The blessings of life flow into us from God. But we need to realize that most of those blessings are not just meant to flow in, but through us and then out again for the good of others around us, especially those in need.

Are the spillways of your love and generosity free and clear so the blessings that fill your life can flow freely to those around you?

NOVEMBER 12
What Spirit Fills Your Home?

I came across an interesting little bit of information the other day. Did you know it was the Romans who had an unwritten rule that a man must carry his new bride across the threshold of their new home before they could live there happily?

According to their custom, how one entered the door of your new home for the first time determined the future happiness of all who lived there. It was a common Roman belief that good and evil spirits gathered at the front door of every new home, and they would battle for control of it. The Romans believed that for good to prevail in the house, one must enter that house in the proper manner.

Goodness (in the form of the good spirits) could only enter the home if the first person to enter the house stepped in with the right foot first. If he did that, the good spirits were ushered in. If he entered on his left foot, evil spirits would be ushered in. This, by the way, is where we get our expression that one needs to get started "on the right foot."

Roman custom held that a bridegroom should take care to carry his new bride across the threshold because she could be so excited and in love she might forget the proper protocol and enter on her left foot, causing a disastrous life. It was the bridegroom's duty to make sure things got started on the right foot.

When I read about that custom it got me to thinking about our homes and just what kind of spirit might be reigning in them. Saint John Vianney would try to walk by every one of his parishioner's homes and bless them, "so that no vile or evil spirit may rule in them," as he put it. On visiting those homes he remarked that some of them were filled with the warm, loving presence of God, whereas others seemed to be filled with a cold, harsh, and unwelcoming critical spirit. He would quickly ask God's angels to come and set those other homes free of such vile spirits.

If you were to stop to think about it, what kind of spirit seems to reign freely in your home? Is there an atmosphere of love and caring and welcome at work in your home? Do people who visit your home feel blessed by having been there? What kind of spirit fills your home?

November 13
Fudge

I read an article the other day about a man who loved to smoke a cigarette after every meal, or whenever he wanted to sit and relax. Because his wife was a bit worried he might get cancer, she kept leaving pamphlets and magazine articles around about the dangers of smoking.

The man dutifully read every pamphlet and article his wife had left for him. One day the man told his wife he was beginning to be a bit alarmed by the strong relationship between smoking and lung cancer. She said, "Well, you're going to do something about it then, aren't you?"

He replied, "To tell you the truth, I've been thinking long and hard about it."

"So, are you finally going to stop smoking?" she asked.

"Well, I've read so many articles about smoking and lung cancer that I've decided to quit reading them; they all say about the same thing anyway."

Isn't it amazing how easily we can avoid the truth about things if it interferes with what we want to do? I remember something Mark Twain said one time: "I believe that it is vitally important to get your facts right first, and then you can distort them as much as you please!"

Many people are quite miserable and unhappy because they cannot be honest with themselves. They fall into difficulties, mostly of their own making, by not facing the whole truth about their life and situation. I see it often in the work I do with addicts and alcoholics, and with other folks as well. When I begin to work with someone in this situation, I often tell him or her of a historical figure from about 300 years ago who could serve as a model for this kind of behavior.

An English merchant marine captain by the name of Captain Fudge was famous for his lies. He told so many lies and exaggerated so many stories that even he could no longer tell what the truth really was. He even admitted he was best at deceiving himself.

His crew was so used to his lies that whenever they caught each other not telling the truth they would call each other a "fudger." By the mid 1800s, Captain Fudge was quite well known both in England and the Americas for his great big lies. Eventually it was a common thing to refer to cheating as "fudging." Merchants were often accused of "fudging their numbers or prices." Those who knew Captain Fudge said there were two things that struck them about him: first, he was fun to be with, though you could never trust a word he said; and two, it seemed he was not really a very happy fellow at all.

There is something to learn from old Captain Fudge. You will never be truly happy or truly at peace if you spend most of your life fudging the truth.

NOVEMBER 14
Have a Seat!

I was reading an account of a wedding ceremony that was held in a small Mennonite church in a little, out of the way town in Iowa. A well-known Protestant minister had been invited to perform the ceremony and preach a brief sermon for the occasion. The minister and his wife arrived at the church early so they could be there to help set up the event. As part of the preparation for the service, the minister handed the printed copy of his sermon to his wife and asked her if she would place it on the pulpit along with his Bible.

When she put the items on the pulpit she noticed there were some words that had been ornately carved in a place where the preacher could see them as he delivered his sermon. There were just seven words, but they brought a smile to her face when she read them. They were, "Stand up, speak the truth, sit down."

The minister finally performed the wedding ceremony and delivered a nice sermon, though it was a tad long. He was happy with it but wondered what others thought. So at the reception and dinner that followed the wedding he decided to fish for a compliment from his wife. He said, "So, honey, I wonder what you thought of the sermon?"

Fr. Mark Burger

She paused and asked her husband, "Did you see those carved words in the pulpit as you preached?"

"Yes, I did see them and I thought they were good."

His wife continued, "Well with those words in mind, I thought your sermon was pretty good, but you did miss a few opportunities to sit down."

"Stand up, speak the truth, and sit down": those are strong words and good advice for preachers of the Gospel. They are also truly good words for each one of us in our individual walks of life.

How valuable those words are for couples who are trying to strengthen their marriage when, in love, they speak the truth without beating a dead horse? Aren't those great words to recall for parents who are trying to guide or correct their children? How important it is to speak but not belabor the points one wants to make. Those seven words are also invaluable to every friendship, because a word spoken in truth but not overdone can bear much fruit.

In the weeks ahead as you go about the task of strengthening your relationships, consider those seven words. They could be a real bridge builder.

NOVEMBER 15
Looking

As I was praying this week before Mass, I remembered an incident from the time when I was pastor at Holy Family Church in East Price Hill. I was part of a Bible study group there, and we were studying the Gospel of Luke.

We were all gathered at the home of an elderly woman for one of the sessions, When we came to a particular verse from the chapter 19, she stopped us and said, "Can I tell you all something I know about this sentence from the Bible?" We all nodded in agreement, and she said, "First let me read this wonderful line to you: 'For the Son of Man has come to seek out and to save what was lost.'"

After she read the line, she paused for a few moments. It was apparent she was trying to compose herself because those words meant a lot to her. The woman began, "I love that line 'cause I was lost and away from God when I was a young adult. Thought I knew everything better than anybody else. I was really lost."

"Then I met this old grandma-type woman who read me this line. I wasn't impressed by it at all 'til she told me about one word in it that made all the difference for me and my life. That was the word "lost." She told me that word is important because we only lose important things. We misplace unimportant things. I might misplace my car keys, but if I can't find my diamond ring, well now, that ring is lost! When something important to us has gone missing, that thing is not misplaced. It is definitely lost."

She went on to tell us that when Jesus came and said he had come to seek and to save the lost, he was talking about someone important because only those things that are important to us can be lost. He came to save the lost because those are the folks he loves. She reminded us that each one of us is so important to him that if were turn up missing, he sees us as lost, not misplaced, and he comes looking for us.

Isn't that a wonderful way to read that one line from chapter 19 of Luke's Gospel? I don't know why it came back to me this past week in my prayer, but I'm glad it did. If you are feeling lost, take courage: if you are lost you must be important to Jesus! And if you are lost, rest assured. He is already out there looking for you.

NOVEMBER 16
From the Ground Up

The other day I was having a discussion with a friend who is a recovering heroin addict, about what it's been like as he struggles to get his life back. He had heard a fellow addict use an image at a recovery meeting once, and that image helped him describe what happened to him since he stopped using drugs. The guy at the meeting had lived and worked in Africa; here was the image he used:

"I was working in Africa as a common laborer, and the company I worked for provided three-room cabins for us to live in. One day, when I had been out working in the hot sun all day, I came home to my little cabin hoping to rest. When I came in the door I found a huge python right there on the floor, hissing at me! So I quickly ran out to my truck to get my gun."

"I crept into the house and fired a single shot right into that big snake's head. It was a deadly shot but the snake did not just slump over dead. No; it began to thrash about violently in wild spasms."

"I ran outside once again just to avoid being hit by the snake's violent outbursts. After about fifteen minutes, all was quiet in the house. When I went back inside I found that just about everything in the house had either been completely destroyed or severely damaged. The place was just a wreck. It had to be rebuilt from the ground up."

My friend said that when he had first come to stop using heroin, he thought he was done with recovery. "It was like I had shot the addiction in its head like my friend shot the snake. The problem was, however, that using the drug was only part of my problem. I had stopped using heroin, but I still had some pretty bad behaviors that were not yet done ruining and destroying my life. Until I began to address those, my life would not really be my own. Just like that python's wild spasms, so my own bad behaviors were still hurting me, as well as those around me. Shooting the snake of addiction in the head was only one step on a long road to getting my life back."

I think my friend has become truly wise as he has struggled to recover. I know I have learned a lot from him. It's a very sound spiritual principal that real change of heart is much more than just changing one behavior. Real change involves turning your whole life over to God so he can rebuild your life from the ground up.

NOVEMBER 17
Are You the One?

Karl Friedrich Gauss has been described as one of the greatest mathematicians of the nineteenth century. In every other way he was very much an ordinary schoolboy who apparently didn't stand out in his class as someone extraordinary. He just blended in as one of the guys.

One day, Gauss' entire class in the German primary school he attended was punished by their teacher for being rowdy and out of control. For their punishment, the students were assigned the problem of adding together all the numbers from 1 to 100.

The boys quieted down, scribbling numbers – all but one boy, that is. That boy looked off into space for a few moments, then wrote something down, and turned it in. He had the only right answer.

When the amazed teacher asked how he did it, the boy replied, "I thought there might be some short cut, and I found one: 100 plus 1 is 101; 99 plus 2 is 101; 98 plus 3 is 101, and, if I continued the series all the way to 51 plus 50, I have 101 occurring 50 times, which is 5,050."

When the boy's teacher heard that explanation he immediately knew this was a very special student. He spent as much time as possible tutoring him because he wanted to make sure the boy would realize how rare and brilliant a mind he actually had. Karl Friedrich Gauss became known as one of the greatest mathematicians of his age, but he probably wasn't aware of the depths of his own talents until his teacher helped him discover it.

Is there anyone in your life who, like Gauss' teacher, helped you to discover talents you never knew you had? Is there anyone in your life who may possess some extraordinary gifts or abilities, and who simply needs someone to help them see and discover them? Are you just the one?

NOVEMBER 18
A New Awareness

A few years ago, while reading an article on the retirement of Pope Benedict XVI, I remembered something from the life of a Protestant minister. At the close of a Sunday service one day, he asked everyone to be seated before they sang the final hymn. When all were comfortably seated, the pastor began to read a letter to the congregation.

In the final paragraph of his letter, the pastor announced he was leaving the parish. As the stunned congregation sat in silence, the pastor looked up and didn't know exactly what to do or say. The silence was absolute, and the only sound that could be heard was the sound of a clock ticking on the wall.

The pastor thought he had better say something more, so he cleared his throat and said, "Just remember now, the same Jesus who led me to you is now leading me to another church." There was even more silence. Finally, the choir director, who was very uncomfortable with the silence, spoke up and announced, "Let's all stand now and sing, 'What a Friend We Have in Jesus.'"

I laughed out loud when I read that story. It came to mind when Pope Benedict went into retirement because it was not something anyone had expected. I'm sure that when the Pope first announced his decision to the cardinals, they were stunned into a deep silence, like the congregation above. The Pope had come to the conclusion that the burdens of his office were just too heavy to carry any more. He announced that his strength was sapped and his energy was spent. He had become aware of the limitations his weakening health had imposed on him.

His acknowledgement of those limitations gave us all an opportunity to become aware of our own limitations. Not only that, the Pope also made us aware that we should be more sensitive to the heavy burdens those around us may be carrying. Perhaps some of the people very near to us are burdened beyond their strength but are unable to let anyone know about it.

Pope Benedict lay down the burdens he had borne and Pope Francis took them on. This courageous process might inspire us to develop a new awareness of our own burdens and limitations, and those of the people we love.

NOVEMBER 19
Don't Forget the Little Things

A young girl was sitting in a restaurant at a table by herself. As she sat there smiling and waiting patiently, a rather busy server came over to the table and asked the girl what she wanted to order. The girl, who was no more than nine or ten years old, asked, "How much does an ice cream sundae cost?"

The server snapped back, "It will be four dollars." At this, the little girl started to count out the change she was holding, making sure she had enough money. Then the little one asked, "And how much is just a bowl of plain ice cream?" The server answered, "That will be three dollars." "Okay, I'll take the plain ice cream," replied the young customer.

The server returned with the bowl of ice cream but delivered it in silence and just put it in front of the girl in a rather rude way. After the little girl had finished her ice cream and left, the server went to clean off the table. To her great surprise she found a $1.00 tip left on the table. Her tip, she realized, was the exact amount of money the little girl needed to get a sundae rather than just plain ice cream.

That little story has much to teach us. It can serve as a reminder that in each of our lives, others have made sacrifices for our well being that we may never be aware of. Even the smallest gestures of kindness may have been done for us at a greater cost to someone than we will ever know.

The only proper response to this truth is to more and more become people of gratitude. As we gather in the coming days to celebrate Thanksgiving, we will surely be grateful for the big blessings that have come our way. But let's also be aware of how richly blessed we are in the little gestures others have gone out of their way to do for us.

NOVEMBER 20
For the Storms That Are Coming

I was on vacation a few years ago on the east coast of the United States, and on one particularly lazy afternoon I visited a small museum. It was a maritime museum with lots of naval artifacts and memorabilia. One of the exhibits I remember most vividly was one that described the art of shipbuilding.

During my visit to the museum, a local man was giving an impromptu lecture on how ships were built in the eighteenth and nineteenth centuries. The speaker said the shipbuilders were a very conscientious group of craftsman who knew that the lives of the crews who sailed in the ships they built depended on the work they did. Those builders also knew the real safety of the crew depended on the ship's main mast.

In order to provide the best main mast, shipbuilders would go in search of a tall, straight tree on top of a mountain near the coast. When they found that tree, they would proceed to cut down all of the trees around it and remove any object that was protecting the tree from the harsh winds blowing in from the coast. They wanted that tree to endure the worst the sea could dish out.

As years passed and the tree continued to be abused by the harsh weather, it became stronger and stronger. Daily buffeting turned what was an average tree into a hard, sturdy trunk that could withstand gale force winds. After years of such preparation, the tree was now ready to be formed into a main mast worthy of a great ship.

As I listened to the speaker describe how the tree had been made stronger, I couldn't help but realize that God is a kind of master shipbuilder when it comes to us. Because he knows what our future may bring, God often allows us to endure some difficult and bitter "winds" in our lives that we feel might overwhelm us at any moment, yet they do not. God did not intend them to destroy us but to give us the strength we will need to weather future storms that may be just over the horizon.

If you are enduring a difficult time right now and you feel that perhaps God has forgotten you, it may very well be that God has not forgotten you. Rather, he may be preparing you for what is still to come. We need to be reminded sometimes that God sees the whole picture of our life, including our future, whereas we see only a small portion. God is truly a good shipbuilder who knows how to prepare for your future.

November 21
Change the World

Go to any post office and you'll usually find a long line of people waiting to be served by the postal workers. A customer in one of those lines at a local post office in Florida was talking with some of the people in line with her. As they made small talk, the women said she always chose to come to this branch because the postal employees there are really friendly.

The woman said she had come on this particular day to buy some stamps and mail a few letters. The folks in line with her pointed out there was no need to wait in line because there was a stamp machine in the lobby and she could put her letters in the mail box there.

"I know," she said, 'but the machine won't ask me about my arthritis or give me a warm smile and wish me a good day. I need that more than the stamps!"

There is probably more good done in the world by simple kindness than any other force or movement. Perhaps the best way to change the world for the better is to simply be kind to someone. Is there someone in your life right now who could use a simple kindness from you?

November 22
Oops!

A woman came to see me one day because she was having some difficult family problems and she wanted to find a solution. She began our conversation by saying, "Have you ever noticed how often, in our anxious desire to 'fix' a problem, we only make it worse?"

I found it interesting that she began that way because I had just read about how one "solution" to a problem led to a real disaster. In a small village in the jungles of Borneo, health workers were trying to figure out a way to deal with the spread of malaria there. They decided it would be a good idea to spray the straw huts in that small village with an insecticide in order to control the extraordinarily heavy mosquito population responsible for spreading malaria.

So in due time they thoroughly sprayed all the village huts. The lizards that normally inhabit the walls of the huts consumed large doses of the chemical and died. The village cats, in turn, ate the dying lizards; they too grew sick and died. Next, the cats' deaths resulted in an infestation of rats, which overran the village. The lizards' deaths had left the straw-consuming caterpillars free to multiply (the lizards feed on the caterpillars), and eventually those caterpillars went and gobbled up the straw thatched roofs of the village huts. The huts collapsed and the village was ruined.

The moral of the story is, I suppose, that before we impose a cure or try to fix something or someone, we had better be sure the cure isn't worse than the disease.

November 23
Christians Without Borders

I was crossing a bridge over the Ohio River the other day when traffic came to a standstill. We sat for a long time, so long in fact that people were getting out of their cars and walking to the side of the bridge to look down at the river below.

The man standing next to me began to explain that, in case I didn't know it, the border between Ohio and Kentucky ran right through the middle of the river. After he had explained this to me, he gave me a look that seemed to indicate he thought I might not be very bright. I thought I would confirm that fact, so I turned to him and said, "I don't see any dotted line running through the middle of the river." He just stared at me for a moment or two, trying to assess whether I was dangerously insane or not. Then he smiled a wary smile and headed back to his car. A woman who had been standing near us laughed out loud and said, "I think he thinks you're serious!" Then she paused and said, "You aren't being serious are you?" We laughed.

That little encounter made me think of something that had happened in Russia. A farmer owned a huge tract of farmland on the Russian-Finnish border. One day, the governments of both Russia and Finland, who were engaged in treaty negotiations to redraw the borders, contacted him and said he had to decide whether he wanted his farm to be in Finland or in Russia. The two governments were going to redraw their borders according to what he decided.

The farmer deliberated for several weeks and then finally decided that he wanted his vast farmlands to be in Finland. The treaty was completed, and the borders were drawn in a way that honored the farmer's request.

After all was said and done, Russian officials came to visit with the farmer. They wanted to know why the farmer, who had lived his whole life in Russia, now suddenly wanted to live inside Finland. The farmer answered them, "Well, you see, it's like this: all my life I have lived in Mother Russia, enduring terrible winter after terrible winter. That was fine when I was younger, but now that I am older, well, quite frankly, I don't think I could endure another Russian winter! So it's Finland for me."

That's one of those stories that either makes you laugh or groan. Why am I telling you that rather silly story? It's to illustrate something that all of us need to remember.

In the next few weeks we will be celebrating several holidays. Every year during these special days I hear people say, "Oh, I just love Thanksgiving Day," or "I just love Christmas." There's a feeling that happens at this time that is unlike any other time of the year. Yet is Thanksgiving Day the only time we can muster a genuine, universal feeling of gratitude, the only time to notice how many blessings have come our way?

Sometimes we forget that our blessings have not come from our own ingenuity or strength or super intelligence. The fact that we say we are blessed indicates there must be someone who does the blessing. We believers know from whom all blessings flow. Do we allow that sense of a loving God who freely and generously blesses us to permeate every day of our life, or do we let others push that sentiment into the borders of only one day a year? You and I know that every day is truly a day for thanksgiving.

This same thought applies to Christmas. Isn't it amazing just how generous people are at Christmas? I remember when I was pastor in the inner city, and we were surrounded every day by incredible poverty and suffering. Yet at Christmas people seemed to come out of the woodwork with offers of food and clothing and toys for needy children! Many of us who worked in that area wondered where these folks were in the middle of July or August when the food pantry ran the lowest.

I think they had created some borders into which they placed charity, such as "It's Christmas time; time to take care of the poor!" You and I both know Jesus called us to care for the poor, the suffering, the imprisoned, the hungry children not just during the holiday season, but every day, all year long.

God's love has no boundaries, no borders, no limiting lines marked on a map. God's love is as wide and high and deep as God's heart. You and I are called to be Christians without borders!

NOVEMBER 24
Finding What We Need

I had a Baptist friend who used to do something he called "Bible roulette." This is how it went: if he wanted to know what God might be thinking about something, he said he would "commence to saying a brief prayer." Then he would take the Bible and let it fall open to any page, on its own. He would then place the Bible in his lap, close his eyes tightly, and with much courage and sincerity, jab his index finger onto the open page of the Bible. Whatever verse his finger landed on he considered God's answer to his prayer!

My friend swore that God talked to him in this way. He quite sincerely tried to follow, as he put it, "in the ways of the Scriptures as he received it" from his Bible roulette practice.

Although I teased him about his prayer roulette, it became quite clear that my teasing had very little influence in convincing him that this might not be a good thing to do. He would tease me back and tell me that I was obviously not "well-versed" in spiritual things!

I remember one time when he told me that things in life were getting hard for him, so he thought he ought to "consult the Scriptures." Well, he did his usual thing and his index finger ended up on a small verse in chapter 42 of the Book of Genesis. It was a very short verse in which Jacob, the patriarch of his people, says, "Everything is against me!"

My friend grinned at me and said, "See! I told you it worked! God just told me he knows how I feel, like everything in life is against me!"

I was about to launch into an argument when he put up his hand and said, "Let's see now what it says in the chapters after this verse." He read silently for a few minutes, grinned again at me, and said, "The Bible goes on to say that God gave all the things Jacob had lost back to him, and even gave him back his son Joseph, whom he thought was dead!"

I asked my friend what that has to do with him. He replied, "It means that, while God knows right now everything in my life is against me, soon he will make it all right!" My friend just closed his Bible and said, "God is really good to me." He sighed and said it again. What could I say to that?

Although I don't recommend nor do I use the Bible the way my friend does, I did learn something from him. He truly is a person of deep faith who, like anyone, feels down and out sometimes. When he does, he tries to consult God as best he can and look for answers or comfort wherever he can find it. He obviously found some that day. In his own way, he taught me the importance of seeking God in the best way we can and to trust that God will somehow reach out to us and give us what we need.

When you begin to feel like everything is against you, how do you find comfort? Where do you seek it out?

NOVEMBER 25
The Love that Feeds Us

I've been thinking about a true story from the Second World War, about a soldier who was severely wounded. When he came out of surgery, the doctors said there was a good chance of recovery, and things looked good – that is, until the soldier wouldn't eat anything. The nurses and nuns who worked with him tried everything, but he refused all food, drinking only water and juice.

One of his buddies knew why the soldier wouldn't eat. It was because he was homesick and felt depressed and hopeless. His friend remembered that a package from home had arrived for his buddy, and quick as he could, he brought it to him in the hospital. As he sat next to his injured friend, he showed him the package, and the wounded man's eyes lit up. "Open it!" he said. As they opened the package they discovered that the wounded soldier's mother had sent him a whole chocolate cake.

The two buddies spent the whole day talking about home and eating that cake. The wounded soldier's real recovery had thus begun. With his buddy who had brought him a taste of love from home to reassure him, the soldier had hope for the future. It wasn't long before he was restored to health.

In these days of Thanksgiving that story can serve to remind us of the importance of home and the love that feeds us there. As you celebrate these special days don't forget to take a good look at the people sitting around your table, sharing food with you. Take time to consider just how much their presence and their love for you truly feeds and nourishes you. Recall also that you, like that wounded soldier's buddy, are an instrument of love and reassurance for each member of your family.

Thanksgiving is a wonderful time of the year to recall a very important truth: you are loved.

November 26
Roadblocks

People often come and ask me how they can be truly happy. There are probably as many answers to that question as there are people, simply because, as it is said, happiness is an inside job. I think what is mean by that is, true happiness cannot be imposed from the outside; it has to be brought forth from within us.

The famous pianist Arthur Rubinstein was asked what he had discovered to be the secret of finding happiness in life. He didn't think too long about

Fr. Mark Burger

it before he answered, "As long as we have what we have inside, the capacity to love, to work, to hear music, to see a flower, to look at the world as it is, nothing can stop us from being happy...but one thing you must take seriously. You must get rid of the 'ifs' of life. Many people tell you, 'I would be happy -- if I had a certain job, or if I were better looking, or if a certain person would marry me.' There isn't any such thing. You must live your life unconditionally, without the ifs."

Arthur Rubinstein was on to something there. Think about it for a moment. How often in your own life have you tied your happiness to very particular circumstances? Haven't you said at one time or another in your life that you could only be happy "if" something else were to take place? How did that work out for you? Didn't you find that your own conditions put a kind of roadblock in your journey to happiness?

Let me ask you this simple question: are you happy right now? Yes? No? If you are not happy right now there may be a reason. Perhaps even today as you read this you are living your life with a few "ifs" blocking your way. What would happen if you dropped those "ifs"?

November 27
Da Vinci's View

Do your life and your work ever feel like they are getting to you? A few months ago I told a good friend that I was feeling overwhelmed by life. He listened to me as I listed all of the various things that were weighing me down, and he said a few encouraging things. Then rather abruptly he changed the subject and began speaking about something else. I thought it strange that he said nothing else about my apparent fatigue, but I just let it go.

A few days later when I went to the mailbox, I discovered that the friend I had thought had not understood me actually understood very well. In the mail I discovered a card from him with a picture of Da Vinci's *Mona Lisa* on the front. Inside the card my friend had written a short note: "Mark, as I was listening to you the other day I was trying to think of something profound to say to you. I couldn't, so I changed the subject and talked about something else. Today I found this card and this quotation from Leonardo Da Vinci. Although I couldn't find the words, Da Vinci did. I hope they help!"

Beautifully printed on the inside of the card, was this quotation:

"Every now and then go away, have a little relaxation, for when you come back to your work your judgment will be surer, since to remain constantly at work will cause you to lose power of judgment.... Go some distance away because then the work appears smaller, and more of it can be taken in at a glance, and lack of harmony or proportion is more readily seen."

If you have gotten to a point in your life where everything seems out of focus or maybe even a bit out of control, perhaps Leonardo Da Vinci can be your guide as to some steps you can take to get a different view, a better perspective that can help you make some sense out of things. Da Vinci certainly helped me.

NOVEMBER 28
Which Is It?

A ship was wrecked off the New England coast some years ago, and many people were being lost. The situation grew desperate. Everyone on the shore who had a boat tried to make their way out to help those floating in the waters. Finally, members of the Coast Guard arrived. They began to take control of the situation and organize a rescue effort.

There was a young member of the Coast Guard crew for whom this was his first rescue mission. As he saw the terrible scene and the number of dead bodies floating in the sea among the other survivors, he realized the danger and said, "We can't go out. We'll never get back."

The grizzled old captain replied, "Get control of your fear. This is about those in danger out there. We have to go out. We don't have to come back. These people need your courage, not your fear. These folks need us and we can help. Let's get to it!"

When the people around you are in a crisis, do you offer them your courage or your fear?

November 29
A More Profound Experience

While reading a book about the American Civil War I came across a quotation from General William Tecumseh Sherman. He had written a letter to his good friend and commanding officer, General Ulysses S. Grant, in which he expressed his appreciation for Grant's support over the years. In the conclusion of his letter Sherman described how he found himself daily in the thick of battle but was not too worried because, as he put it, "I knew wherever I was you thought of me, and if I got in a tight place you would come – if alive."

General Sherman was at peace in the thick of battle because he knew there was someone out there who thought of him and would immediately come to his aid if he needed him. In your own life, do you find yourself at peace in the thick of everyday battles and struggles because you know there is someone out there thinking of you? Is there someone in your life who could describe you as General Sherman described General Grant?

The love and care that binds us together is one of the greatest gifts God gives us. In this time of the year, when we become aware of our blessings, it's good for us to take a few moments to consider how our lives are certainly shored up by those who are always ready, willing, and able to be there for us. What a blessing they are to us, and we certainly must thank God for them.

When I finished reading General Sherman's letter a question arose within me, a question we could all take some time to consider: Have I ever let the people who have loved me so much and been such a support to me throughout the years know how much I love them and appreciate all that they are to me?

Perhaps a letter to them, along the lines of the letter that Sherman wrote to Grant, might be a good way to let them know. And perhaps it would also be a great way to make our celebration of Thanksgiving a more profound experience.

NOVEMBER 30
Stand in Awe

As Thanksgiving is celebrated and the holy season of Advent is upon us, many stories come to mind, some of them with a bit of a teaching for us. I've been thinking about one story in particular these days.

In order to get ready for Christmas, a young fellow and his dad went off into the woods to bring home a Christmas tree. They walked for hours in the snow, examining every tree they found. But the trees all seemed to be missing something. As the afternoon turned into evening and darkness began to fall, the temperature dropped ten degrees and the wind started howling. Still there was no tree. Finally, the son turned to his father and said, "Listen dad, I really think we'd better take the next tree we see, whether it has lights on it or not!"

I love that story. When I first heard it, I laughed, and as I went about my business through the day, a little voice inside reminded me there was a kernel of truth in that tale. It got me thinking of how often I might miss the gifts that are right under my nose, and not accept them because they do not conform to or meet my preconceived ideas of what I am out to find. I think we all do that sometimes: we can miss the goodness of the people and the world right around us because we are seeing things with blinders on.

If this time of year, with its various feasts and celebrations, has anything at all to teach us it is that we live in a charmed and beautiful world, filled with wonders yet to be discovered. We are truly blessed. It's time to take off the blinders and stand in awe.

December

DECEMBER 1
Is It Time?

Here's a story from the days when folks were going out West by wagon train to make a new life for themselves. Travel in those days was by no means easy, and travel by wagon train was even more difficult. This particular wagon train was on its way from St. Louis to Oregon. Its members were devout Christians, so the whole group made a habit of stopping for the Sabbath day. They simply took that day off to be with God, read the Bible, and rest.

The wagon train had been on the road for quite some time, and winter was approaching quickly.

Some of the people in the group began to panic for fear that they wouldn't reach their destination before the heavy snows fell. These folks began to think that taking a day off for rest once a week was not such a good idea, and they worried it was putting everyone in danger of being stranded in the middle of winter. Consequently, a rather large group of folks proposed that the group should quit their practice of stopping for the Sabbath and continue driving onward seven days a week.

This proposal triggered a lot of heated discussion, and in a very short time there was much contention in the community. Finally it was suggested that the wagon train should split into two groups: those who wanted to observe the Sabbath and those who preferred to travel on that day.

It was put to a vote, and the proposal was accepted. Both groups traveled together until the next Sabbath day, when one group continued on while the other stopped to observe the Sabbath.

Guess which group got to Oregon first? It was the group who kept the Sabbath. Why? The group who observed the Sabbath arrived in good health and condition. When the other group, the one that traveled seven days a week, eventually arrived in Oregon, most of the party and their animals were completely exhausted, discouraged, and frustrated. Many in the party were quite ill.

Both the people and the animals in the group who observed the day of rest were so restored by that one day off they could travel much more vigorously and effectively the other six days of the week. When they arrived in Oregon, they were full of enthusiasm and ready to begin their new life in the West.

There is a great lesson in this for all of us. Taking time off to be with God, to read, and to rest a bit would do wonders for all of us. When was the last time in your busy life that you purposefully took a little down time to restore yourself? Is it time for you to do so now?

December 2
Now More Than Ever

A first grade class was discussing a photo of a family. One little boy in the photo had a different hair color than the other family members. When asked why that might be, a girl in the class suggested it might be because the boy was adopted.

A boy in the class responded that he knew all about adoption because he had been adopted, and his mom and dad had explained it all to him. Another girl asked what it meant to be adopted. Her classmate who had been adopted answered, "Adoption means that you grew in your mommy's heart instead of her belly."

If you were to take that little boy's definition of adoption seriously, just who are the people in your life that you have adopted? Who are the people who matter the most to you? Do they know it? Throughout the course of our lives many people will enter our world. They come, they go, some make an impression on us, and some do not. How many people in your life have you taken to your heart?

Perhaps this time of year, when Christians prepare to celebrate the birth of Jesus Christ, the child for whom there was no room, it might be a good time to consider if we have room in our hearts for the people God might send our way. Is there someone in your life who needs your love now more than ever? Is there room in your heart?

December 3
Your Amazing Journey

When my mom was in the I.C.U. at a local hospital, I spent a good deal of time sitting by her bed as she slept and made her recovery. I spent much of that time praying or reading, but the nurses seemed very concerned that I needed something to do while my mom was asleep.

One kind nurse bought me a book of pencil mazes. Almost everyone has worked one of those mazes, where you follow the right path to find your way out. As you move your pencil through the maze you keep running into wrong turns and dead ends until you find the one path that sets you free.

Our lives can be a lot like living in a maze. As we grow and try to make our way through life we continue to take wrong turns that lead nowhere. Often we have to retrace our steps until we can find our way again. It can be very frustrating, and sometimes we think we will never find our way out. It's at those times that we can feel stuck, like a prisoner with no escape.

Jesus came to show us that, no matter how difficult the maze you live in may seem, there is always a way out. Not even death can stand in the way of your life's ultimate journey.

There is an ancient Chinese proverb that advises: "If we do not change our direction, we are likely to end up where we are headed." In this final month of the year, it may be a really good time for us to remember that the journey ahead is filled with wonders and great adventures, and we need not be afraid to take the next step in the maze of life. How do we do that?

I know a school principal who urges high school graduates to go to college, insisting that they ought to at least start college. He uses the image of a very rough road that each one of us must travel at some time in life. On some of the roads we travel, he says, we have to travel at night, in the dark. Even though it may be dark, one does not need a searchlight shining far down along the way to walk the road safely. He assures his students that all one needs is a very small light shining one step ahead. When that step is taken, the light moves up and reveals the next step. He encourages them at least to make a beginning by taking just the next step.

This Advent, be sure to take some time to consider just where you are in the maze of life. Don't be afraid to take the next step in your life's amazing journey.

December 4
Salt Water Taffy

While on a recent vacation to Virginia Beach, I went for a walk along the beach to find some quiet and do a little praying. I had arrived a few days earlier and was beginning to realize how deeply tired I was. A walk along the ocean was just what I needed.

As I walked I began to wonder why I was so tired. I never really came up with much of an answer until later that day, when some friends and I went walking among the tourist shops. In one of those shops a machine was pulling and folding a batch of salt water taffy. The metal arms of the machine continually pulled, stretched, and folded the taffy in on itself, in an effort to get some air into the candy.

As I stood watching the process, a woman came and stood next to me. After a short time she turned to me and said, "I feel just like that taffy."

"You do, really? Why?" I said.

She said, "I have six kids and a husband, and they are always pulling at me and stretching me and pushing me to my limits. Yup, I feel just like that salt water taffy!" she said, smiling.

There was the answer to my question as to why I had been feeling so tired. It dawned on me that every one of us has duties and responsibilities that pull and tug and force us to stretch beyond where we want to be stretched. It's just the way life is. Sometimes we are unaware of the toll that daily life can take on us. That's why it's so important for each of us to take some time every now and then to pull ourselves together, rest up, and recover from the toll life can take on us.

Is it time for you to turn off that "taffy machine" in your life so you can rest and recover from life's demands?

December 5
Included

I recently came across a story about some soldiers during the Second World War. I have used it every day this past week to open my heart to what God might want to teach me through this story, and it has given me some very fruitful prayer time. Here's the story:

Some soldiers serving in France wanted to bury a friend and fellow soldier who had been killed. They loved him a lot, and they wanted to make sure he was respectfully and properly buried. It so happened they found a well-kept cemetery with a low stone wall around it, a picturesque little Catholic church with a peaceful, scenic view. This was just the place to bury their friend.

But when they approached the priest he said that unless their friend was a baptized Catholic he could not be buried in the cemetery – and their friend was not a baptized Catholic. Sensing the soldiers' disappointment, the priest showed them a spot outside the walls where they could bury their friend. Reluctantly they did so, feeling as if they had let their good friend down.

The next day, before leaving town, the soldiers returned to pay their final respects to their fallen friend, but could not find the grave. "Surely we can't be mistaken. It was right here!" they said.

Confused, they approached the priest, who took them to a spot inside the cemetery walls. "Last night I couldn't sleep" said the priest. "I was troubled that your friend had to be buried outside the cemetery walls, so I got up and moved the wall."

In my prayer this week I heard God's quiet voice ask me if there were people in my life that I had "walled out." Were there also people for whom I ought to be "moving the walls?" Each day I answered those two questions, and each day I received newer and deeper insights.

Why not take some time right now to consider the "walls" of your heart. Do they need to be moved to include someone?

December 6
How Do You Serve?

Today marks the Feast of Saint Nicholas, a man known for his humility and his generosity. He had a big heart that pushed him to be very kind and considerate, especially to the poor.

There is a story told of a Jesuit and a Franciscan having lunch one day. There were two pieces of fish on the platter, one large and the other very small. The Jesuit announced that he would serve, so he began to plate the food. He took the large piece of fish and put it on his own plate, then turned and put the small piece of fish on the Franciscan's plate.

When the Franciscan noticed it, he spoke up and said, "Hey, what's the deal here? Is this how Jesuits treat others?"

The Jesuit replied, "Whatever do you mean?"

The Franciscan replied, "Well, Father, I have been trained by holy men who practice the virtues of poverty and humility and generosity. If I had served this meal, I would certainly have put the larger piece of fish on your plate, and given myself the smaller portion!"

The Jesuit thought for a moment and then responded, "Well. Isn't that just the outcome you have in front of you? So what is the problem? Do you study poverty, humility, and generosity or do you live them?"

If that Jesuit were talking to you right now, how would you answer his question? Do you study poverty, humility, and generosity or do you live them? Are you a generous person?

December 7
Can't Remember?

One of the ushers at church last Sunday pulled me aside to tell me one of his favorite stories. It's about a guy named Bob who becomes so involved in his work and other projects that he often forgets things. Sometimes he can't remember even the simplest details.

One morning his wife said, "Now Bob, remember, the movers are coming today. Here, I'm putting this note in your pocket. Don't forget."

The day passed by, and Bob came back to his house. He went in the front door and noticed that the place was completely empty. Distraught, wondering what the heck was going on, he walked out to the curb and sat down. Just then a young boy walked up to him, smiled, and sat down next to him on the curb. Bob turned and asked him, "Hey kid, do you know the people who used to live here?"

The boy replied, "Sure, Dad, that's why I'm here. Mom told me you'd forget."

I loved that story. It got me to thinking about memories and forgetfulness. One of the Desert Fathers used to teach that as we grow older, becoming confused and forgetting things is a natural process that can be both a curse and a blessing. He said that sometimes old age imposes a heavy burden on us when it befogs us, and we begin to become forgetful. Sometimes our loss of memory is so severe it can even steal people from us, and we may come to a point where we no longer recognize loved ones. This is when forgetting becomes a curse and a severe hardship.

On the other hand, that Desert Father also taught there is another side to growing older. Age can bring wisdom, the wisdom that shows us the very fine art of forgetting. He said there is a "forgetting" that is not just the result of physical decline, but rather a forgetting on purpose. He said that some graciously wise older folks have discovered new life and joy in letting go of some of the past.

These are the good folks who would make an effort to purposefully forget past hurts, slights, and those harsh or cruel words or actions from days gone by. They learn this kind of forgetting is a real blessing that brings peace and even some comfort to our troubled world.

Why not take some time today for some purposeful forgetting?

December 8
Devotions

Since the turn of the millennium there have been terrible earthquakes, hurricanes, and other natural disasters that have caused great destruction, loss of life, and much misery. Many people and nations have rushed in to the affected countries to offer help and assistance. Tragic events often trigger momentous response from ordinary people the world over who simply want to help and make a difference. This got me to thinking about how some seemingly powerless people are able to bring about tremendous change in the world.

As I thought about this, a name surfaced in my prayer, that of William Wilberforce. A member of England's Parliament in the late eighteenth and early nineteenth centuries, he was a committed Christian who wanted to make a difference. For most of his time in Parliament he was a small, lone voice against the seemingly all-powerful slave trade. Wilberforce thought it was time for England to abolish it, and in that view he faced fierce opposition and ridicule.

William Wilberforce was an amazing young man. Some would call him eccentric or even a bit odd, but he was a true statesman who wanted to expose the evil of slavery and the slave trade. He faced so much hatred and opposition that most of his colleagues wondered how he had the strength to endure the harsh treatment that came his way. When asked, Wilberforce said his secret for persevering in his fight against slavery was private time spent in what he called his "devotions." These devotions were the hours he spent out in the woods, praying and observing God's handiwork.

He told his friends that when he spent less time in God's presence, his soul began to starve and he had little strength left to carry on the fight. He believed that every time he failed in Parliament, it was because he had relied too much on his own wit and not on God's strength. He said without our devotions we all become puny little weaklings who can do nothing for the world's poor and suffering.

These past months, as I have been thinking about all those suffering from the earthquakes and natural disasters, all the love and care that has been poured into the affected regions, I am convinced there is a vast army of ordinary, good people who, like William Wilberforce, are doing their daily devotions. Where else would they get the kind of courage, strength, and love they've shown in reaching out to the afflicted?

When you find yourself facing some difficult things in your life, or when you see a great need in the world, where do you find the strength to follow through and do something about it? Are devotions a part of your life?

DECEMBER 9
Your John the Baptist

When Harry Truman was thrust into the presidency at the death of Franklin D. Roosevelt, Sam Rayburn, the Speaker of the House at the time, gave him some fatherly advice: "From here on out, you're going to have lots of people surrounding you. They'll try to put a wall around you and cut you off from any ideas but theirs. They'll tell you what a great man you are, Harry. But you and I both know you ain't."

Harry Truman and Sam Rayburn were great friends, and they kept each other's feet on the ground, as they would say. Truman said he loved that bit of advice and was grateful to have someone like Rayburn around. They often shared conversation, ideas, and drinks in an attempt to solve the world's problems. They enjoyed each other's company.

So it was a hard day when President Truman learned that Rayburn was quite ill. Truman called his friend and discovered that Sam had announced to the House of Representatives he was going home for medical tests. He wondered why Rayburn did not stay in Washington where there were excellent medical facilities, and learned the answer when he heard Rayburn tell Congressman Jim Wright, "My hometown, Bonham, is a place where people know it when you're sick, and where they care when you die."

Do you have a friend like Sam Rayburn who helps you keep your feet on the ground, who loves to share your company, with whom you can have a drink, talk things over, and solve the world's problems? Aren't those folks a real blessing? Don't they make the hard roads we often walk on a lot easier to negotiate?

As we move through the great season of Advent, take some time to consider the people in your life like Sam Rayburn, who help guide your way. Do you realize they may well be a kind of John the Baptist for you? John's ministry was to help people find their way to God. He pointed out and announced Jesus to the people around him. Is there anyone in your life who does that for you? Is there anyone who helps you keep your feet on the ground, who knows when you're sick and will care when you die? If there is, know they are a real gift from God.

In this season of gift giving, don't forget to recall the gifts you have already received – especially from the "John the Baptists" who populate your life.

DECEMBER 10
Saints in Your Life

I was having breakfast the other morning at a local restaurant, and as I was ordering, the server called me "Father." Out of the corner of my eye I noticed that when she used that title, the man at the next table looked up at me. When the server walked away, the man asked me if I was a priest. I said yes, and he got up from his table and sat down at mine. I thought to myself, "this is either going to be good or it's going to be really bad!"

The man introduced himself, then added, "I'm a Methodist minister and I've always wanted to ask a Catholic priest a particular question. When I heard the server call you 'Father,' I thought, 'Here's my chance!'"

"Alright, then," I said, "Go ahead and ask your question."

He responded, "Tell me what you Catholics think about saints. I mean, just what is a saint, and do you pray to them or worship them?"

Of all of the possible questions that someone might ask a priest, I must say that was not the one I was expecting. I was happy to tell him about how we view saints as our spiritual friends and companions, and that we don't worship them or pray to them, but rather, ask them to pray with us for help with the trials of life. I told him the saints are those members of the Church who have lived the Gospels in an extraordinary way. "These are our Church family heroes," I said.

The minister looked at me for a few moments and said, "That's the kind of thing I'd hope you would say." He grew quiet.

I finally broke the silence and said, "What would be the most important thing that the Wesley brothers have to teach us Christians?" (John and Charles Wesley were part of the founding of the Methodist Church.) My Methodist friend smiled at me and said, "You are a sly one! You are going to try to show me that Charles and John Wesley were "saints," aren't you?"

"Exactly, that's it!" I said. "Why don't you go ahead and tell me what you, as a Methodist minister, think was the most important thing John Wesley said." He thought for a minute, and replied, "Well, it's said that when John Wesley was on his deathbed he looked around at those gathered around him and said, 'The best of all is, God is with us.'"

The minister went on, "The Wesleys actually lived those words – 'God is with us'—by trying to be with people when they were in their greatest need. An example is when Charles had himself locked in a cell with five condemned prisoners who were scheduled to be executed the next morning. He stayed with those men all night, and the men said that it felt as if Jesus himself was with them. They were executed, but they had come to know the peace of Jesus through the loving presence of Charles Wesley."

"The way you look back at those two brothers and all of the good they did, that is the way we see the saints." I said.

We had a great breakfast after that. It got me to thinking about some of the saintly people I have met through the years. I've met quite a few "saints" in my day. How about you? If you were to look back, who are the John and Charles Wesley's in your life? Who have been the saintly people in your life, and what have they taught you?

December 11
Winter Gloves

It was so cold the other morning and the wind chill so bad that I broke down and decided to wear gloves when I went out. It's quite rare for me to wear gloves when it's cold; I have never liked doing so because they seem more of a nuisance than a help to me.

Fully protected by my gloves, I got into the car, and as I drove down the street I noticed a sign in the front yard of a local Baptist Church. Here's what it said: "If you take off your right hand glove in very cold weather, you will probably find that your key will be in your left hand pocket!"

That's exactly what always seems to happen to me when I wear gloves! It is as if my gloves are out to annoy and frustrate me. That sign made my day. It captured perfectly how my winter gloves always seem to get in my way and end up controlling my mood. I know it's silly, but it's true. Winter gloves seem to have it in for me.

Are there "winter gloves" in your life that get to you? These are the seemingly unimportant things in your life that take on a life of their own and end up being a preoccupation. Are there little things that annoy and frustrate you? What do you do with those things? How do they control you? Do they steal your peace of mind or destroy your perfectly good day?

It's a very common experience.

So what are we to do when the little frustrations of life come along? Well, there are two quotes from the Bible that I have found helpful. The first is, "A cheerful heart is good medicine" (Proverbs 17:22). A good sense of humor is God's antidote for anger and frustration. I have always found a good laugh at myself cures a lot of life's petty irritations.

The second quote is, "You reap whatever you sow" (Galatians 6:7b). There are many things in life that frustrate us, yet for the most part, we bring them on ourselves by our choices. In my own case, for example, my attitude about gloves is what sets me up for frustration.

So, again I ask, what are the "winter gloves" in your life?

December 12
Masterpiece

James Whistler, the well-known American artist, wrote about an incident that taught him a lesson. He had ordered a set of blank canvases that were to be shipped to him for his use in his studio. As it turned out, the canvases got lost in the mail, and so Mr. Whistler contacted his local postmaster to report the matter. The government official was very kind, and began to write down all of the pertinent information about the situation. At one point the postmaster asked Whistler, "Are these canvases of any great value?" Whistler's reply was "Well no, not yet."

When James Whistler reflected back on that conversation he had an insight. He said that, just as a blank canvas can have limitless value if it allows an artist to create a masterpiece on it, we too have limitless value when we allow the masterpiece God has created in us to come forth. His continued reflection on the value of those canvases brought another insight: Each day is like a blank canvas that God puts into our hands to do with as we wish.

Those are great insights. Why not take a moment and think about the masterpiece you can create with the new day opening up right in front of you?

December 13
Chores

Do you dread doing your chores around the house or running errands or just doing those jobs that daily life requires? As you go about doing your daily chores, here is something to think about.

When an elderly gentleman was asked how he maintained such a positive, generous attitude through all the ups and downs of life, he did not hesitate in answering. He said that he first learned about the importance of attitude when he was just a boy.

One day, when he had just turned twelve, his mother sent him to pick a quart of raspberries. This did not make him happy at all, but reluctantly, he dragged himself to the fields where the berries grew. He thought his afternoon was ruined for sure.

Then, in a burst of insight, a thought hit him. He would surprise his mother and pick two quarts of raspberries instead of one! With that thought, everything changed.

Rather than drudgery, his work now became a challenge, and he rushed to complete it. He said he enjoyed picking those raspberries so much that, seventy years later, the incident is still fresh in his mind. The chore hadn't changed, although his attitude had. It was then he realized that attitude is everything.

December 14
What Service Is All About

Recently I spent some time with a young man from my parish who had just joined the U.S. Marines. He had not yet reported for duty, but only talked with a local recruiter who had filled his head with images of the great things he was about to do for his country.

The young man was so full of enthusiasm for his future in the Marines that it was almost contagious. "You know that this will not be easy?" I asked him.

He was a bit taken aback by my question, then replied, "I'm ready; I know I can do it. My dad did it, and if he could do it, I'm sure I can too. You can do anything for those you love," he said.

As I listened to him gush about how great it will be for him to be a Marine, I began to think about all those men and women who, from the very beginning of our nation, have been filled with the same youthful idealism and enthusiasm. I thought of one of my favorite American heroes, George Washington, who was also full of enthusiasm for serving the nation. Being a bit older when he took up leadership, however, he had a lot more insight into what the future might hold.

On July 3, 1776, the day before the signing of the Declaration of Independence, Washington wrote a letter to his wife, anticipating the hardships soon to occur. Here in part are his words: "In a few days, you will see a Declaration setting forth the causes which have impelled us to this mighty revolution and the reasons which will justify it in the sight of God. I am fully aware of the toil and blood and treasure that it will cost to maintain this declaration and support and defend these states; yes, through all the gloom, I can see the rays of ravishing light and glory."

No less than the young, soon-to-be-Marine I spent time with recently, George Washington was full of enthusiasm for his nation. He was also well aware of just what it might cost, and still, he was fully committed. In the midst of the gloom that would surely come with war, he could still see light and glory.

Are you fully aware of what your commitment to your loved ones might cost you? I'm sure you are, and I'm equally sure that – like that young man headed off to serve his country and like George Washington in his day – you too are fully ready to pay the price for those you love. Love is what service is all about.

December 15
The Gospel Again, for the First Time

I just received an early and unexpected Christmas gift. Here's how it all came about. I was coming out of the grocery store and was met by a beautiful young woman in a Salvation Army uniform, smiling at me as she rang a small bell.

Fully expecting that she was going to ask me for a donation, I began to reach for my wallet when she put her hand on my wrist. "You don't need to give me any money, sir," she said.

"Isn't that why you're standing here ringing that bell?" I asked.

"No, that's not what I was going to ask you," she said.

"Well, if you're not going to ask me for money, what were you going to ask me?"

Smiling again at me, she said, "Sir, I was just going to ask you one simple question, and then I had hoped we could have a conversation."

"Ask away!" I said.

There was a brief pause as she cleared her throat, then she asked, "How is it with your soul?"

I replied, "I can't remember a time when anyone ever asked me how things were with my soul! In fact, I think you asking me that question just improved my soul a whole heck of a lot!"

My reply seemed to make her day. "Sir, would you let me tell you a little about Jesus Christ?" she asked.

I told her that I would love for her to tell me about Jesus. Once I agreed, she launched into a fifteen-minute description of how God so loved the world that he sent Jesus. She was overjoyed that I was listening to her tell the story.

Before I could reply, one of my parishioners recognized me and called out, "Hey, Father Mark!"

The young Salvation Army worker looked a bit shocked, then asked if I was a priest. When I said that I was, she said, "I hope I didn't offend you!"

I said, "In no way am I offended. I loved listening to you; it was like hearing the Gospel for the first time all over again! You began by asking me how it is with my soul. After being with you, I'm sure that my soul is in much better shape."

When was the last time someone told you the Gospel of Jesus' love again, for the first time?

December 16
A More Beautiful Place

I was speaking recently with an old man who loves to grow things, especially tomatoes. He says that the neighborhood kids think he's a crazy old man because they've seen him talking to his tomato plants. "I don't care if they laugh," he says. "Let 'em laugh. I always have the best tomatoes in the whole county!"

The old man continued talking about his plants and the kind of care he gives them. "If people treated each other half as kindly as I treat my tomatoes, why, the world would be a very beautiful place! You see, I make sure they have the water they need, I pinch off the extra leaves so as not to drain off precious energy, and yes, I talk to them to encourage them. And I say, why not?"

"Every living creature needs help to overcome the obstacles that stand in the way of their growth. When I spend time in my garden among the tomatoes, I come away knowing just what to do when I'm among my family and friends. I know that they, like my beautiful tomatoes, need a bit of encouragement to get through life. I try to do my part for the tomatoes and the people that the good Lord just happened to entrust to my garden in life."

"I don't know what kind of garden God put you in charge of, but I know one thing for sure – if you tend it well, the world will always turn out to be a far more beautiful place. We all have a role in making God's world a beautiful place."

Have you made the world that God has given to your care a more beautiful place?

December 17
Lifting Your Spyglass

There's a story told about one of England's most famous naval heroes, Lord Horatio Nelson, who was legendary for his decision-making ability. In

1801, he was second in command of a fleet. During a certain battle, Nelson was told that the admiral had sent up signal flags ordering Nelson to retreat. Nelson turned toward the signal flags, lifted his spyglass to his previously blinded eye, and then said he couldn't see any such order. He then led his men in an attack that completely defeated the enemy. Nelson had been insubordinate, but he won a great victory.

There is a rather famous saying that is said to have come from Nelson's exploits that day, to "turn a blind eye" to something. It simply means we choose to not see something we don't want to see. Have you ever raised a spyglass to your "blind eye" and thereby "turned a blind eye" to something? Have you ever purposefully chosen not to mention or notice one of your children's mistakes or faults? If you have, then you have turned a blind eye to those failings. Of course, this can be good or bad, depending on what you are choosing to not see. Love determines which it is.

Are there situations in your life that call for you to lift a spyglass to your blind eye? Are there situations that demand you not turn a blind eye to them? Of course, it is love that will determine what you choose to do.

December 18
Those Who Serve

During the American Revolution, a man in civilian clothes rode past a group of soldiers struggling to make repairs to a small fortification. There was a lot of work that needed to be done before nightfall, and there were too few men doing the work. In the group, the civilian noticed there was a man barking out orders to the soldiers but not pitching in to help.

The civilian got off his horse and quickly jumped in among the soldiers, lending them a hand. As he worked, the man barking orders started to scream at him and ordered him to work even harder. Finally, as the work was done and the soldiers and the civilian began to straighten up and get a drink of water, the civilian turned to the "barker" and asked him why he hadn't stopped to help with the work.

The man looked sternly at the civilian and stood up straight to assert his authority. Then he spoke with great dignity, "Sir, I am a corporal!" The civilian apologized, passed some water to the exhausted soldiers, turned to the corporal and said, "Corporal, next time you have a job like this and not enough men to do it, go to your commander-in-chief, and I will come and help you again. The work is for all of us to do." With that, General George Washington got back on his horse and rode off.

Have you ever known anyone like the corporal above? Have you ever known anyone like Washington? Jesus tells us that what's in one's heart determines how they treat others. We are called to be those who serve. What's in your heart?

DECEMBER 19
Look Again

I've been thinking of an old story that has often been told and retold, especially in the Eastern Orthodox Church. According to the story, there was a devout abbot from a monastery who decided it was time for him to take a prolonged spiritual retreat. He wanted to be out in nature during his retreat, so he planned to spend it in a small cabin located on an island in the middle of a large lake near the monastery.

The abbot informed his fellow monks that he would use his retreat time to go deeper in prayer and grow closer to God. He would be away for about six months, and would remain on the island with no other person seeing him or hearing from him in all that time.

While the abbot was away, two monks were standing near the shore of the lake, soaking up some sunshine. As they stood there conversing, they could see a figure in the distance moving toward them, although they could not make out who it was. As the figure moved closer, it turned out to be the abbot, walking on water, and coming rather quickly toward shore.

The abbot came near them, waved, passed by the two monks, and continued on to the monastery. Finally, one of the monks turned to the other and said, "All these months in prayer and our abbot is still as pinch-fisted and stingy as ever. After all, the ferry only costs 25 cents!"

As funny as it is, monks often use the story to make the point of reminding us of how easily we can miss the significance of something that is right in front of us, simply because we think we know all there is to know about someone. Because we have lived with someone for a long time, or have known friends for quite a while, we often assume we know all about them. Yet there may be much more to them than we know.

Every so often it is good for us to take a new look at those we love. Sometimes because we are so familiar with them, we may miss the goodness and the miracles God is working in and through them. We may only notice their foibles or little faults, and miss the extraordinary things they are doing.

Just think of each of your family members: aren't they really a marvel? Perhaps today is a good day for all of us to take another look at those we love and notice what a gift they are to us.

December 20
The Whole Nine Yards

Have you ever heard the expression "the whole nine yards?" I've heard it used but never stopped to consider where the term originated.

According to an elderly veteran of World War II with whom I had breakfast one day, the term comes from fighter pilots. The pilots had machine guns mounted on their planes, and the ammunition for those guns came on 27-foot-long belts. If a pilot used up the entire belt of ammunition firing at one target during a combat mission, the pilot would report that he gave the target "the whole nine yards." Since then, the term has come to mean giving your all to someone or something.

After that war veteran explained it to me, it occurred to me that the expression could be a great way to describe how committed we are to something or to someone. Ask yourself, for example, are you giving your job or your spouse or family "the whole nine yards" of your attention, enthusiasm, or love? When you think of your relationship with God, does God get the whole nine yards of your life?

December 21
Because of Jesus

Recently I came across the story of General George Pickett's baby. During the last days of the Civil War, the Confederates were locking horns with the Union soldiers outside of Richmond. It was the cruelest time of the whole war.

One night, the Confederate camp was lit with bonfires. The Union guards discovered that the Southern troops were celebrating the birth of General Pickett's son, word of whose arrival had just reached the army. General Ulysses S. Grant, who had seen so much death during the conflict, was moved by the event. He ordered the Union lines to help the Confederates celebrate the birth of Pickett's baby by lighting up the scene with additional bonfires.

The next day Grant's officers sent a graceful letter through the lines under a flag of truce, communicating their congratulations to General Pickett on the birth of his son. Grant is said to have remarked that, in the face of such a terrible thing as war, every new life must be welcomed with great joy because of the hope that comes with each newborn child.

In just a few days we will be celebrating the arrival of another child, God's own Son. With the birth of that child, true hope came for each of us. As you gather with your family and friends in these next few days, why not take a few moments to consider how each person born into your family has brought hope and joy to you. At the same time, recall too just how much hope and joy is possible in your life because of Jesus.

DECEMBER 22
The Best Gift This Christmas

There's a story about Abraham Lincoln before he became president, when he was practicing law. In court during one of his cases, he was asked a question. Lincoln did not answer right away but remained silent in an apparent attempt to collect his thoughts, and his opponent pressed him to give an immediate response.

At this, Lincoln paused even longer, and then is said to have replied, "Better to remain silent and be thought a fool than to speak out and remove all doubt." I am sure that Lincoln eventually responded to his opponent's inquiries, but not until he truly ready to do so. He would not be rushed or pushed into saying something he did not mean to say. This may well be one of the things that made him a good lawyer.

I've been thinking about Lincoln's slow and steady response this week while meditating on a particular line of Scripture that I have been using as a kind of mantra. It's from Psalm 141:3, which reads, "O Lord, guard the door of my mouth." The Desert Fathers would often advise using that verse from Scripture as a way to keep us from turning our words into weapons that might wound or harm someone.

As I considered Lincoln's words, which I'm sure made everyone in the courtroom laugh, I wonder if Lincoln knew that verse of Scripture. Maybe he even had prayed that a "guard" be at the door of his mouth. I'll bet he probably did, and that may well be why he developed ways to keep himself from giving too quick a response.

I've been asking God to put a guard at the door of my mouth so that I might not be too quick with what I think or say. After all, I'm pretty sure it's much better to get people laughing than hurting. I would like to recommend that little verse of Scripture to you as well, as you continue your spiritual practices during this holiday season.

Keeping a guard at the door of our mouths may well be the best gift we could ever give our families or friends this Christmas. Using that quotation has helped me keep the door of my mouth from flying open and causing all kinds of verbal mayhem! Maybe it can help you as well.

December 23
Safely Home

One of the first American astronauts gave a lecture in which he described what it was like to be in a rather small space capsule, speeding along in the vastness of space. He said that his first thoughts were about how snug and secure he felt in this tiny environment. It felt comfortable because he knew that everything he needed to stay alive in the coldness and darkness of space was contained in the tiny capsule in which he was riding.

At that point in the lecture, the astronaut paused for what seemed a very long time. Then he looked around at his audience and said, "All at once, as I gazed out the small window of the space capsule at the vast universe that went on as far as I could see, I came to a realization that scared me to death. It began to dawn on me that this space capsule on which I was so earnestly relying was built according to a system of giving contracts to the lowest bidder. It dawned on me that finding my way back home was completely in the hands of some unknown, lowest bidder! That thought made me very much aware of the importance of choosing well just where I ought to be placing my trust."

After I read about that astronaut's talk, I began to examine just how I choose to live my life and in whom I place my trust. The season of Advent is coming to an end, a time that reminds us of John the Baptist, who pointed his disciples in the direction of Jesus and told them to trust in him. Why not take a few minutes to consider just where you have been placing your trust? Is it in something better than what some "lowest bidder" might offer?

Jesus came to show us how to put our whole lives in God's hands and to trust that he will lead us safely home.

DECEMBER 24
Heavenly Peace

How about a little Christmas story on this Christmas Eve? A man suffered from a devastating stroke that affected his legs, one arm, and most of his speech. The poor fellow was frustrated because he was unable to communicate well with other people, and he was especially sad that he could not speak with his wife. As a result, his life was filled with loneliness and quite a bit of anger.

One day his parish priest came to visit him. The pastor found it difficult to communicate with the man and felt rather awkward. He was tempted to ignore the man and simply talk to his wife, but he decided to try asking him simple questions, much as people do when talking to a baby. This did not work either, and the priest began to feel he had done little to bring comfort to his parishioner, and that he had failed him as a pastor.

As the pastor was getting ready to leave, he remembered reading that some stroke victims can sing even though they cannot talk. Realizing he had nothing to lose and everything to gain, the pastor began singing these words, "Silent night, holy night, all is calm, all is bright."

Instantly, in what seemed like a miracle, the man who suffered the stroke, the man who had such difficulty communicating with anyone, began singing. There was no stuttering, no breakdown in forming words. He just sang the words, "Round yon virgin, mother and child. Holy infant, so tender and mild." As the man reached for his pastor's hand to hold, his wife joined in the singing, "Sleep in heavenly peace, sleep in heavenly peace." With those words, suddenly, there was "heavenly peace," and God was born once again.

If your life is difficult at this time, perhaps that stroke victim has a gift to give you. If you are frustrated by the things that have stolen your joy or peace, maybe it's a good time to begin singing.

December 25
Artists Who Work in Living Flesh and Blood

A couple of months ago, I went to the Cincinnati Art Museum. It turned out to be a very good experience not only because of the good art there, but also because of a conversation I had with a woman as we were looking at a painting by Vincent Van Gogh.

The woman had overheard me asking a docent where I would find works by Van Gogh. As the docent led me to some of Van Gogh's paintings, the woman followed us. When I had been looking at the paintings for about ten minutes, she approached me and asked, "Do you like Van Gogh?" When I said that I did, she asked several more questions in rapid succession: "Do you know much about him? Do you know that he was a wonderfully compassionate, caring man who is much misunderstood, and was abused and rejected by almost everybody in his time? Are you able to see his pain and suffering in the beauty of his art?"

When she finally paused to take a breath, I looked at her and said, "I knew some of that, but not all of it. And, I'll bet you're about to tell me more about him, aren't you?" She was unfazed by my answer and indeed, launched into telling me more.

The women said, "Vincent Van Gogh was a good soul who was consumed by a zeal for helping humanity. Human suffering compelled this very religious man to reach out to others, to be there for those whom no one else would ever reach out to. Did you know that he gave up art for a while so he could go off to work with poor miners in the Belgian coalfields? Well, he did. He even convinced a missionary society to send him there."

"He gave away everything he had to help the coal miners. He reached out and sat for hours listening to people, encouraging them and seeking to let them know that God loved them. The missionary society made fun of him and revoked his authority to represent them. He stayed with those folks in the fields, however. Do you know what he said? He said, 'We artists work in marble and clay and many colors, but I also want to work in living flesh and blood, as did Jesus, the greatest of all artists.'"

At the end of her little speech, the woman turned to me and said, "So what do you have to say to that?"

"Wow!" I replied. "You said all of that in almost one complete breath!" I thanked her for telling me about Van Gogh.

The woman then asked, "Do you go to church?" and invited me to come to her church on the following Sunday. I told her was kind of busy on Sundays, but that I really appreciated being invited into her "church family."

On this Christmas Day, when you are with your own family as well as with your church family, take some time to notice what today is about. It is about God himself working in living flesh and blood by choosing to be one with us.

Today marks the day when you and I and God and all of humanity becomes family – God's work of art.

DECEMBER 26
Believing Is Seeing

I know it's the day after Christmas, but I would like to ask you to think about one of the apostles, who has nothing to do with the Christmas story. He has, however, something important to teach us that might help us see Christmas in a new way.

Many people feel closer to God at Christmas time than at any other time during the year because they see something happen in people that makes them seem nicer or more generous. Then again, there are people who find it hard to believe in people's goodness, even at Christmas. This is where the apostle Thomas comes in.

Thomas refused to believe that Jesus was truly raised until he could put his fingers in the nail marks and his hand into Jesus' side. Jesus gave him the opportunity to do just that, and true to his word, Thomas did believe. Then Jesus told him, "Have you believed because you have seen me? Blessed are those who have not seen and yet have come to believe" (John 20:29).

Do you believe? Have you seen God at work in your life? Many people long to see God but have not been able to find him.

I am reminded of a story about a man who wanted to see and hear God. He went out to a hilltop and yelled and pleaded with God: "Speak to me!"

Nothing happened. A bird sang. That's all he heard. The man sighed. Disappointed, he again begged God to speak to him. All he heard was the sound of children playing in the distance.

The man sighed again. "Please God, touch me!" he cried, and the wind blew across his cheek. Discouraged at not having his plea answered, the man prayed: "God, why don't you show yourself to me!"

Just then a butterfly flew across his path. The man sighed once again and disappointed, headed for home. When he did get home, convinced that God had forsaken him, he didn't notice his daughter running out to greet him, because he felt abandoned by God.

Have you ever felt like that man? Have you ever seen God? Many folks, like the apostle Thomas, would say, "seeing is believing." Jesus would say it another way: "Believing is seeing."

DECEMBER 27
A Light For Them

I had breakfast with an elderly woman the other day, and she was just full of stories. She told stories about her life, about the lives of some of her schoolmates and friends, and some stories about her relatives as well.

As we continued to talk, I asked her if she had a favorite story that she likes to tell. She said her favorite story to tell her grandkids and great-grandkid comes from the First World War. She loves to tell them that story when they seem lost or confused and in need of advice. I asked her to tell me the story, too.

A British soldier in the First World War had lost his will to fight, and he deserted. Trying to reach the coast for a boat to England that night, he soon got lost and ended up wandering in the pitch-black night. He was terrified, and began to lose hope of ever finding his way back.

In the darkness, he came across what he thought was a signpost. He began to climb the post to see if he could read the sign at the top. As he reached the top of the pole, he struck a match and found himself looking squarely into the face of Jesus Christ. He realized that, rather than running into a signpost, he had climbed a roadside crucifix.

Startled, he let go of the post and fell on his back. Looking up into the black sky he heard a voice inside his head say, "If you hold on to me, you will stop running and you will find your way out of the darkness." He knew right then and there that he could not abandon his fellow soldiers. He had to go back. In so doing he found himself no longer in such a dark place, and he was able to live as a man of courage.

I love that story! The woman who shared it with me told me it had gotten her through many hard times. "You be sure to tell that story to some of your people!" she said. "I'm sure every one of them could use it when they hit those terrible dark days that can come to any one of us." I promised her that I would, and I have shared it many times with those who feel lost or in darkness. It has been a light for them as well, I'm sure.

December 28
What God Will Make of Us

We are quickly heading to the end of the year, and a new year is just a few days away. Whenever I get to this time of the year I begin to think about how time is such a mystery to us.

At various points in our life we see time in different ways. When we are young and in school, for example, we think time just slowly edges on like a great glacier. At other times, when perhaps we are busy raising a family or building a career, it seems that time speeds by so fast it makes us almost dizzy. In any case, we just don't seem to be happy with how time works itself out.

This reminds me of a story that is often told about President James Garfield. Before he was President of the United States, he served as the president of Hiram College in Ohio. Well, it was when he was heading Hiram

College that a father asked him if the course of study could be simplified so his son might be able to go through school faster and be done with it.

James Garfield pondered for a moment, cleared his throat, and said "Certainly, but it all depends on what you want to make of your boy. When God wants to make an oak tree, he takes a hundred years. When he wants to make a squash he requires only two months. So, what is it you want to make of your son?"

We live in an age that doesn't want to wait for anything. We love things to be given to us as fast as possible. The truth of the matter is, however, that God does things according to his time and his purpose. When God is at work in us, things cannot be rushed, expedited, or fast tracked. It doesn't really matter whether time seems to be passing too slowly or too quickly. God's time comes to us in God's good time, and he knows what he is going to make of each of us.

DECEMBER 29
A Hole in the Bucket

At some point in their career, every boss has faced the problem of how to teach their workers the importance of time. Here is a case in point.

A new employee had been caught coming in late for work three times in the four weeks since he was hired. On the fourth time the foreman decided he had had enough of this, so he thought it was time to read the new guy the riot act.

"Look here," he snapped, "don't you know what time we start work around here?"

"No, sir," said the new employee, "you're all always working when I get here."

Obviously that new employee was not aware of the importance of time. That employee has much to learn, not just about his employment but about his personal life as well. Carl Sandburg said, "Time is the coin of your life. You spend it. Do not allow others to spend it for you."

When was the last time you examined how you are using your time? As one of our most precious possessions it really is important that we make sure we use it well. After all, time is in limited supply even though we may think we have all the time in the world.

It's been said that more time is wasted not in hours but in minutes. Think about a bucket of water with a small hole in the bottom. That bucket gets just as empty as a bucket that is deliberately kicked over. In either case, the water is lost. Whether we waste a few minutes at a time or hours at a time, time wasted is time forever lost.

How are you using the precious gift of time that has been entrusted to you?

DECEMBER 30
When at Sea

Some boys were playing on a beach with a large beach ball. By accident the ball was thrown too high and, driven by the wind, landed in the water. No thought was given to it for a few minutes until one of the boys noticed it was going farther and farther from shore.

One of the boys decided to retrieve the ball. After entering the water he realized that it was farther from shore than he had thought. Grabbing hold of the ball proved more difficult than he had expected, for it was riding high on the waves. Each time he sought to grip it, the ball slipped out of his hands and he was drifting toward the open sea.

About this time he noticed that he was quite a distance from shore, and realized, too, that he was getting tired. All of the sudden fear gripped him as he realized that he could really drown. Because his fear caused him to start shaking, he knew he was in trouble and had to do something quickly. Without even being aware of doing so, he began to talk out loud to God, calling on the Almighty to protect him. Even though his prayer seemed to have come out of nowhere, it brought him reassurance that God would help him, and his fear was replaced by confidence.

Suddenly the thought occurred to him that he should swim around the ball so that each attempt to grab it would push it in toward the shore. The plan worked. In a matter of minutes he was able to step on shore with the retrieved ball. The experience taught him that every one of us has the choice in every situation: succumb to fear or have faith, to drift towards disaster or toward home.

December 31
All The World has Changed

In 1845, Elizabeth Barrett, one of the greatest English poets who ever lived, met a man who changed her life forever. His name was Robert Browning, and he was a poet as well.

The two poets fell in love and in 1846, they married. They described their relationship as the greatest gift they had ever received. Robert Browning used to call his wife "my little Portuguese" because of her dark complexion. He said that his world would light up when he saw her across the room.

One evening after supper, Elizabeth rose from the table, walked over to her husband, and put her arms around him as she placed some papers in his pocket. On those papers she had written something for him. She called it, "Sonnets From the Portuguese".

Most scholars consider Elizabeth Barrett Browning's poems to her husband the finest love poems ever written. For Elizabeth these poems were a written record of the love the two shared. One of Robert's most beloved lines in the poems she had written was this: "The face of all the world has changed/ Since I first heard the footsteps of your soul."

Isn't that a beautiful thing for someone to say? When I read those lines I began to think of all of the people I know who have changed my life simply by walking into it. I found there were so many people who have truly changed the face of the world for me that I just simply had to offer prayers of thanksgiving to God for such rich blessings.

As one year ends and a new one begins, it's a great time for each of us to notice how many wonderful people have graced us and our lives by the gift of their presence. Just take a few moments to consider how your life has been blessed since you first heard the "footsteps of the soul" of each member of your family, or each of your friends. If you take some time with this you will certainly begin this new year with a boatload of gratitude for the many blessings received and those yet to come.

Made in the USA
Las Vegas, NV
30 October 2022